What Experts and Influencers in Birth, Wellness, and Motherhood Are Saying About Tara Menzies

"Tara has such a gift for sharing the Word in a way that illuminates God's love, mercy, grace, goodness, and faithfulness for us through all seasons of motherhood. The Christian Hypnobirthing classes and app have been such a blessing to countless clients (and myself, too!) in discovering how to connect to God uniquely through pregnancy, birth, and postpartum. Wherever you are in your parenthood journey, Christian Hypnobirthing will encourage your heart and align your mind with truth, helping you experience parenthood in the peace and joy we were designed for."

– Jeanna McNeil, Birth Doula & Childbirth Educator,
By Design Birth Doula Services, @bydesignbirthdoula

"Combining physiology, neuroscience, psychology, and faith, Tara Menzies provides tools and resources to help expecting mothers understand their choices and have the best birth possible."

– Dr Stuart Fischbein, Obstetrician,
Co-Author of Fearless Pregnancy, and Co-Host of
The Birthing Instincts Podcast, @birthinginstincts

"I always love attending births where my clients are playing tracks from the Christian Hypnobirthing App. Listening to them during labour really helps them to focus their mind, whilst at the same time, reminding them of the blessing that God is bestowing on them, giving them a sense of courage and peace."

– Sallyann Beresford, Author of *The Art of Giving Birth*, @theultimatebirthpartner

"Christian Hypnobirthing was such a powerful tool for me throughout my pregnancy. It really helped prepare my mind, body, and spirit for the faith-filled home birth of my dreams! Talking with Tara before my birth allowed me to work through any fears and reservations I had. She is such a positive, encouraging person!"

– Alexandra Bartee, Content Creator, @plantifulalex

"The Christian Hypnobirthing app and course have been so incredibly helpful in bringing me peace and comfort throughout my pregnancy. Tara's ability to mix hypnobirthing with scripture and prayer is everything I've needed."

– Emilie Berkman, Founder of The Peaceful Mother, @the.peaceful.mother

"Anything that Tara touches embodies Proverbs 16:24: "Gracious words are like a honeycomb, sweetness to the soul and health to the body." Her work has brought me & my family comfort in not only childbearing seasons but also times when things just feel heavy. Her scripture tracks have carried us through those moments when you don't even feel like you have the words to pray or mental clarity to pull open scripture. I'm so honored & blessed to have found her and her encouraging and empowering content!"

– Maddie Baines, Wellness Advocate and Birth Photographer, @waterednwell

"Tara and her work are world-class. Not only is she a beautiful human but she's created something so amazing that I never hesitate when I have a Christian client to unequivocally recommend Christian Hypnobirthing. And have seen incredible results!"

– Blyss Young, LM, CPM, Midwife and Co-Host of *The Birthing Instincts Podcast*, @birthingblyss

"Tara Menzies' Christian Hypnobirthing is something I've recommended to anyone who is looking to invite more peace into their pregnancy, birth and postpartum experience. It kept my nervous system calm and centered during a very chaotic time in the world to be giving birth and I'm so grateful it was created. We are fearfully and wonderfully made beings that carry life that God has breathed — He will carry you through it all. What a gift and reminder of God's word through this app to empower and support your sacred journey. Christian Hypnobirthing speaks life over birth rather than the constant fear that's usually pushed. Step into that power!"

– Steph Jolly, Content Creator, @stephsjolly

"Tara's work is such a gift. During a very difficult pregnancy with my first child, the Christian Hypnobirthing tools were a godsend. Connecting with my body, with God, and with my unborn child, it made such a difference."

– Carlie Palmer-Webb, MS, The Christian Sex Educator, @thechristiansexeducator

"Tara's Christian Hypnobirthing truly transformed my birth experience. After one birth center and two hospital births, I knew I wanted my 4th to be at home. Tara's work helped me see the glory in birth and truly helped me have the calm and redemptive homebirth that I prayed for."

– Elizabeth Lucenti, Homemaker, @thehomemadefam

"I absolutely LOVED the Christian hypnobirthing app. I used the audio affirmations every single night as my husband did a perennial massage (to prepare for labor and hopefully reduce tearing). These affirmations spoke truth into my mentality of birth! That I was created for this! That my body knows how to birth my baby! That I am safe! I would breathe as I listened to these affirmations. The recordings are SO calming and wonderful. I will be absolutely using it for every single labor prep! 10/10 recommend."

– Natalie Zima, Registered Holistic Nutritionist, @nataliezimaa

"This was my first birth, and I was a little anxious beforehand, but Tara Menzies' Christian Hypnobirthing course gave me so much peace of mind for my home, unmedicated delivery. She was incredibly kind and genuine, and her blend of faith and relaxation techniques made me feel confident and prepared, which I'm forever grateful for because I had an amazing labor and delivery."

– Jessica Cromartie, Lifestyle Influencer and Entrepreneur, @heygorjess

"As a mama of two, I was able to have not just one, but TWO incredible, spirit-filled home births, and I owe a lot of the mental prep and spiritual support I used leading up to and through labor, to Tara Menzies' Christian Hypnobirthing. I truly believe that our mindset and thoughts are powerful, especially in labor, and I would highly recommend her resources for any expecting mama."

– Sarah Grace Meckelberg, MS, RD, Hormone Dietitian, @sarahgracemeck

"Beyond grateful for the heartfelt work of Tara Menzies and Christian Hypnobirthing. As a mother of four and a home-based Certified Nurse Midwife, I have found the faith-filled resources she provides for families to be a wonderful wealth of information for pregnancy, labor, birth and postpartum. Professionally, I am grateful for the Healing after Miscarriage support that has helped me to help countless families navigate loss."

– Nancy Pol, MSN, APRN, CNM, Founder and Certified Nurse Midwife Emergence Midwifery and Wellness, @emergence_midwifery

"I downloaded the Christian Hypnobirthing app during my second pregnancy and it felt like the missing piece to the puzzle and truly helped me to remain grounded and rooted in my faith in Christ for strength. I also used it during my third pregnancy along with the course, which was so thorough and amazing. I connected with Tara and she is so genuine, calm, uplifting, and knowledgeable, and always willing to help however she can!"

– Erin Stanczyk, Co-Founder of EatMoveRest, @erinstanczyk

"As a Christian Doula, it's amazing to have access to Tara's Christian Hypnobirthing resources. My clients are always so reassured and grateful to hear about her app and course. With all the tracks that are framed in scripture and in prayer, it really helps them prepare for birth."

– Rev Helena Whitwell, Doula and Deacon in the Church of England, @doula_helena

FAITH-FILLED CHILDBIRTH

A Christian Approach to Hypnobirthing

TARA MENZIES

Faith-Filled Childbirth

A Christian Approach to Hypnobirthing

Tara Menzies

Copyright © 2025 Tara Menzies. All Rights Reserved. No portion of this book may be reproduced, stored in a retrieval system, or transmitted in any form or by any means—electronic, mechanical, photocopy, recording, scanning, or other—except for brief quotations in critical reviews or articles without the prior permission of the author.

Published by Game Changer Publishing

Paperback ISBN: 978-1-965653-35-7

Hardcover ISBN: 978-1-965653-36-4

Digital ISBN: 978-1-965653-37-1

Disclaimer:

This publication contains the opinions and ideas of its author and is intended to provide helpful and informative material on the subjects addressed. The information contained in this book is not a substitute for the advice or presence of a qualified medical practitioner, midwife, or obstetrician during birth, any part of pregnancy, labor, or postpartum. It does not represent, in fact, or otherwise, an alternative to appropriate medical care or professional medical advice in any way, shape, or form. The reader should consult their medical care provider before adopting any of the suggestions in this book or drawing inferences from it. The author and publisher disclaim any responsibility for liability arising directly or indirectly from the use of this material by any individual.

www.ChristianHypnobirthing.com

Contents

Foreword *By Midwife Lindsey Meehleis, LM, CPM*	xiii
Introduction	xvii
1. From Fear to Faith	1
2. The Power of Words	13
3. Your Faith-Filled Toolbox	41
4. Where Should I Give Birth?	99
5. Who's Looking After You?	117
6. Informed and Empowered	153
7. Birth	189
8. Postpartum	203
9. Conclusion	221
10. Extra Resources	227
Thank You	241
Acknowledgments	243
References	245

Dedication

For Will, Charlie, and Sam.
Each day with you is a blessing.
Thank you for being my family.

Foreword

By Midwife Lindsey Meehleis, LM, CPM

For over two decades, I have had the privilege of walking alongside countless strong women and their families as they journey through the sacred experience of childbirth. Each birth—whether it's the first or the fifth, a natural home birth or a cesarean—is a divine reminder of the everyday miracles that weave the fabric of this life. Birth invites us to reach deep within, confront our shadows, and discover our strength. Like running a marathon, there are moments when you question your body's ability to continue. At mile 18, doubts creep in: "Can I do this? Will my body make it? There's no way I can finish!" But then, through surrender and trust, you push through. You remember that the only way out is through—and you just do it. Birth is no different. You cannot have light without darkness, nor can you realize your strength without facing the possibility of your weakness. This is where the beauty lies. Every time a woman gives birth, she uncovers within herself the tools she'll need to parent that particular child—tools that will serve her through the teen years and beyond. This is just one of the many sacred gifts birth offers.

If birth has taught me anything, it's that it has deepened my spiritual connection to God more profoundly than any scripture I've read or any church service I've attended. Every time I witness the miracle of birth, I feel Heaven and Earth converge in a way that words cannot capture. It is a gift I hold in deep reverence, and it guides me in all I do. Preparing for each birth, anchoring myself in prayer has become one of my most cherished rituals. Whether navigating Southern California traffic or sitting in the stillness of night, I speak directly to God —praying for protection and expressing gratitude for the miracle about to unfold. As I step through the doors of a home where a new soul will soon arrive, the most important tool I carry with me is faith. Faith in our Creator, faith in the body's innate wisdom, and faith in the sacred timing of all things—birth, life, and, ultimately, death.

As a midwife, I feel it's my duty to honor the care provided by our ancestors throughout time. I call this "womb to tomb" care— Midwives were always the original Family Physician, walking with families through all of life's transitions, including death. It is with this deep faith that I approach my role, and it is this same faith that Tara Menzies so beautifully brings to the world through her work. We accept that birth is as safe as life itself. There is inherent risk in everything we do. While our culture often encourages us to let others hold that risk for us, birth is one of life's moments we must face head-on. Hospitals may urge you to hand over your risk to them, but we encourage the opposite. Rather than being passive in life, we must look it in the eyes, trust our God-given intuition, and make decisions that are right for us, our babies, and our families. This is no time for victimhood. You wouldn't turn your back on the ocean, and I hope you wouldn't avoid it out of fear. Instead, you learn the rhythm of the waves, observe the tides, and navigate the dangers. Birth is much the same. In creating *Christian Hypnobirthing* and now *Faith-Filled Childbirth*, Tara offers women a profound invitation to lean into their faith —not just in the birthing room, but in every aspect of life. She reminds us that childbirth is not merely a physical journey but a spiritual one, where trusting in God's design for our bodies is essential to everything we do.

Over the years, I have witnessed firsthand how surrendering to faith—allowing God's will to flow through each contraction, each breath, and each moment—transforms the birth experience. As John 16:21 says, "When a woman is in travail, she has sorrow because her hour has come; but when she is delivered of the child, she no longer remembers the anguish, for joy that a child is born into the world." This scripture, which I've held close during countless births, reminds us that we don't need to understand the "how" of birth; we simply need to trust the One who created it. On the other side of surrender lies ecstatic joy.

Tara's work serves as a bridge, reconnecting women to their faith and their bodies, helping them embody the essence of miracles. Through her compassionate guidance, she shows women how faith can be their greatest tool, not just in birth, but in navigating the complexities of mothering, being a devoted wife, and facing life's challenges. The strength you find in birth is the strength you carry throughout life.

Faith-Filled Childbirth is more than a book; it is an offering to every woman seeking spiritual empowerment as she steps into one of life's most sacred gifts. Tara's wisdom, rooted in scripture and grounded in the belief that we are divinely designed to bring life forth, is truly a blessing to this world.

It is my deep honor to write these words in celebration of the profound impact Tara's work has had on me and so many others. Her words have filled the birth rooms I've been privileged to enter. My hope is that this book will inspire you to trust more deeply in the miracles that await, to find beauty in your strength, and to lean fully into the faith that will be your greatest gift.

With faith, love, and overflowing gratitude,

Lindsey Meehleis
Traditional Midwife
@lindseymeehleis

Introduction

After a difficult start to our parenthood journey, including three consecutive miscarriages, when I fell pregnant with our rainbow baby, Charlie, I found myself feeling almost constantly anxious and worried. My sister-in-law told me about something called *hypnobirthing*, which she said had helped her with anxiety during her pregnancies. At first, I didn't like the sound of it. *Hypno* sounded pretty strange, and as a Christian, I didn't want to do anything that went against my faith. After looking into it, I became more relaxed when I found out it had nothing to do with a man on stage waving a pocket watch in front of someone's face or any kind of mind control, and was simply a relaxation practice for birth using positive words and imagery, combined with antenatal education. There were times, though, when I was listening to some of the relaxation tracks, that I would find myself having to change certain words, like *the universe* or *inner goddess*, to make them fit with my personal beliefs, so I decided to google "Christian Hypnobirthing" and was disappointed to find that it didn't exist.

A little later in my pregnancy, I came across a Christian book, which, while helpful in some ways, was quite discouraging of natural birthing methods and instead suggested that just by having enough faith, birth could be pain-free. Unfortunately, because of this, I stopped using hypnobirthing techniques to prepare for my birth and decided that I would just have faith, like the book said. One of the major downsides to the idea of a pain-free birth being the result of having enough faith is that if you are experiencing pain, you start blaming yourself. It puts the responsibility solely on the mother and doesn't take into account the environment she's in, how supported she feels by those around her, whether she's able to labor in an upright position, the position of the baby, and the many other factors that massively impact the level of comfort a woman feels during childbirth.

When I went into labor with my son, we set off for the birth center. Unfortunately, when we arrived, they told us it was full and sent us to the labor ward. I was given a midwife who kept telling me I would need drugs and ended up insisting I get hooked up to an IV, have constant monitoring, and also convinced me to have my waters broken. The process was a far cry from what I had envisioned, and I felt deeply shocked by the level of pain I was in. I thought it must have been because of a lack of faith, or that God had abandoned me, or that I was doing something wrong. I had no awareness of the massive impact that intervention, the hospital environment, and fear have on how our body works during labor and how we experience pain.

I had really wanted to give birth unmedicated, but it had become so painful, and with being strapped to the monitor and having the IV in my arm, unable to move around, and all the midwife's negativity, I felt exhausted, disheartened, and like it was impossible. Thankfully, my husband was an absolutely incredible support; he had been doing light touch massage on me for hours, and when I felt I couldn't go on, he reminded me of our prayers in the lead-up to birth and that I could do it. Just after that, I had one of the most spiritual experiences of my life. It was a profound moment, and one I don't really know how to describe. It was like time and space disappeared, and it was

Introduction

just me and God for a moment. I was able to see that God had never abandoned me, that he had been with me the whole time, but that there were many other things going on that were making the birth experience so much more difficult than it was designed to be.

Suddenly, I got this renewed strength, and I started praying, filled with this knowledge that I could do it. Not long after, I started getting the urge to push, and the midwife kept telling me not to, and that I wasn't anywhere near ready. I reached down and shouted, "I can feel his head!" The midwife then went running out of the room to get help. I got down on my knees, leaned against the bed, and in about ten minutes, our beautiful boy was born, weighing in at a hefty 9lb 8oz—an absolute miracle.

Despite feeling very grateful to have a beautiful baby boy, in the days and weeks that followed Charlie's birth, I spent a lot of time reflecting on what happened and couldn't help feeling that it was so much more difficult than I believed it could have been. While it was overall a positive outcome, there was a lingering feeling of trauma. I remember thinking that it would have been such a different experience if I'd had relaxation tools and breathing techniques that could have helped me stay calm and positive, reminding me to draw near to God, and if I'd been educated on the different routine procedures so I could have made informed decisions instead of feeling coerced into things I didn't fully understand. I really felt that Christian mothers deserved to have tools like those provided in hypnobirthing, but which aligned with their beliefs, and would help them feel God's strength, love, and support throughout birth.

This idea of a faith-based hypnobirthing app just kept coming into my mind, so I decided to look into the process of creating an app. After googling it and finding that it cost, on average, $40,000 to make an app, I gave up hope that it was possible. We had no savings as we'd just put all our money into the deposit to buy our two-bedroom apartment. I didn't know anyone in the tech industry, and I had no coding experience myself, so it just felt totally unrealistic.

A few days later, I was listening to the Bible while breastfeeding

Introduction

Charlie, and Matthew 19:26 was read, where Jesus says, "With man this is impossible, but with God all things are possible." Even though I'd probably heard it many times before, it just really stuck out, as if I was hearing it for the first time. I was so surprised that I stopped the recording and skipped back to listen to it again. It was totally mind-blowing to me, and it still is. It is such a radical and mind-expanding thing to say. *With God all things are possible.*

I felt encouraged that God wanted me to create this app, even though I didn't have the money, the contacts, or the tech skills. I believed there must be a way. It took many months of researching, writing, and working out how to use app-building software, mostly done while our son was napping, or during the night. One baby step at a time, God made a way for it, and the Christian Hypnobirthing App was released on App Store and Google Play over Easter in 2018. It was only getting a few downloads a week as we didn't have any budget for marketing, but step by step, through word of mouth, it started to grow.

When I found out I was pregnant with our son Samuel, just two months after releasing the app, it felt like a wonderful opportunity to be able to test it out on myself. I would listen to it every night while going to sleep. It was amazing how much more peaceful I felt, with so much more trust, and virtually none of the anxiety I'd experienced in Charlie's pregnancy. It felt like there was something about the combination of the beautiful, encouraging scriptures reminding me of God's love for us, combined with the breathing and visualization exercises helping me to regulate my nervous system, that felt special and different from any of the traditional hypnobirthing tracks I'd listened to in my first pregnancy.

When I started having contractions with Samuel, instead of rushing off to the hospital, I put the tracks on and drifted in and out of sleep. This happened a couple of nights in a row (prodromal labor), and instead of getting annoyed, I tried to see it as my body being able to do its important work while I was still able to rest. Even if the contractions were too strong to sleep through, I'd just keep the tracks playing while lying on my left side, breathing, and relaxing, drifting between consciousness and sleep. Then, by morning, they would disappear.

On the third night, I was resting while listening to the tracks, and I felt that the contractions were growing in intensity, and coming more frequently every three or four minutes. So we decided to go to the birth center. We picked a different birth center this time that was less likely to be full, but surprise, when we got there, it was full again! This time, instead of letting that send me into a downward spiral, my husband and I both literally laughed and said, "Of course it is." They sent us to the labor ward, and my husband and I cracked jokes and laughed, other than when I had to focus on breathing through the contractions.

The midwives who examined me weren't convinced I was in active labor and were going to send us home, as I was only two centimeters dilated. Thankfully, they ended up letting us stay in a waiting room and said they'd transfer me into a labor room once I was in active labor. I turned the lights off in the room, turned on the Christian Hypnobirthing tracks, and just sat there praying and breathing while my husband had a little nap. After about an hour, I felt the need to get on all fours and was instinctively doing these cat/cow-type movements. I said to my husband I had to go to the bathroom, and from the noises I was making, my husband called the midwife. She came in with a wheelchair to take me to a labor room, but I was already giving birth in the waiting room! They recorded it as 12 minutes of active labor and eight minutes of pushing. He was born en caul, which means my waters never broke and he was born in his amniotic sac. This is really rare and happens in less than one in 80,000 births (although interestingly, a lot of our app users have reported having en caul births, and I've since heard theories that it's more common in undisturbed births).

It was such a surreal experience, as it was so much more comfortable and enjoyable than Charlie's birth. Even though the pressure in those final minutes was big and very intense, it never felt unmanage-

Introduction

able. Because of the practice I had done with the tracks and being able to labor undisturbed in that room, completely relaxed as I listened to them, I was able to follow my God-given birthing instincts, and my body was able to work as it was miraculously designed to, optimizing my oxytocin and endorphin levels, and helping labor to be as efficient and comfortable as possible. A total night and day experience compared to my first birth.

The wonderful thing is, this wasn't just a fluke. It wasn't lucky. Having a positive, faith-filled birth has now been experienced by tens of thousands of women who have used our Christian Hypnobirthing app and course to prepare for birth. Because when you are educated about how our bodies work during birth, have the knowledge to make informed decisions, and actively train your mind and body to embrace birth (instead of fighting it), you give yourself the best chance of experiencing a far more joyful, empowering, and spiritual experience than what most of us have been taught to believe is possible.

I wanted to write this book because while the relaxation practice done with the app is incredibly important, childbirth education is equally important, and unfortunately, the brief birth classes at most hospitals often fall short in preparing women for a truly positive birth experience. So, I have laid out this book in much the same way as our online Faith-Filled Childbirth Course is laid out in the hopes of making faith-filled childbirth education more accessible and affordable for as many parents as possible.

In this book, you can expect to find out how miraculously the body has been designed to work in labor, the effect of fear vs faith on the physiological birth process, the pros and cons of where you choose to give birth and who you choose as your care provider, exercises and tools to help you feel as relaxed and confident as possible throughout your birth, as well as information on routine procedures, pain relief choices and more, to help you make informed decisions about what's best for you and your baby. What you will not find in this book are recommendations for you personally. While I am a qualified hypnobirthing teacher accredited by the Royal College of

Introduction

Midwives, I am not a doctor or a midwife, and I am not medically qualified. The information in this book is general and should not be taken as medical advice, so please be sure to talk to your medical care provider for personalized advice on your pregnancy, birth, and postpartum.

I'd like to note that while I share scriptures, my own personal experiences with faith, and tools to help you feel connected to God, my view is that faith is deeply personal. It may be that some of the tools or stories in this book don't resonate with your faith specifically, and that's okay. It's estimated that there are around 30,000 different denominations of Christianity worldwide, so there are bound to be some differing views. My belief is that there is far more that unites us than divides us, and my focus is on helping you achieve a faith-filled birth experience–as defined by you. So please feel free to take whatever is helpful for you and leave the rest.

There may be things in the book that ignite a strong emotional response in you. Whether this response is negative or positive, it's great to try not to judge it, but just bring awareness to your feelings. Strong emotional reactions can be wonderful messengers to help us look deeper into why we feel the way we do.

I also just want to clarify that despite my personal birth experiences being unmedicated, this is not a natural birthing book. There is a time and a place for medication and surgery, and we can be incredibly grateful that those options exist when necessary. In the different chapters of this book, medical interventions and options will be discussed. Please read those chapters, even if they're not what you're planning, because knowing your options will help you make informed and empowered decisions. I also suggest letting go of superstitions like "if I think or talk about (*insert fear here*), then it will happen." What I've noticed is actually the opposite of that. If there's a fear that you're struggling to let go of, often, one of the best things you can do is learn more about it and talk about it with your care provider. Typically, once you've spoken about it, found out the facts, and maybe even created an action plan, you're then able to fully let go of that fear and put your focus back onto creating the pregnancy, birth, and postpartum experience that you really want.

Whether you're planning a water birth at home, a cesarean in the hospital, or anything in between, this book has tools to help you feel informed, relaxed, and empowered throughout, and my hope and prayer is that it will help you to draw near to God throughout this precious time, and have a positive, faith-filled birth experience.

> To help you get set up for the best birth possible, we recommend combining the education in this book with regular relaxation practice using the Christian Hypnobirthing app. Creating an account gives you free access to our Positive Affirmations track, our private online community, and our "12 Scriptures for a Faith-Filled Birth" printable. You can also try all of the tracks free for a week when you subscribe. Cancel any time in that first week, and you won't be charged.
>
> **The Christian Hypnobirthing App**
> **SCAN THE QR CODE:**

1

From Fear to Faith
UNDERSTANDING OUR MIRACULOUS
DESIGN FOR BIRTH

"I praise you because I am fearfully and wonderfully made."
— Psalm 139:14

*I*f you're like most people, throughout your life, you've probably seen hundreds of images and scenes of painful, terrifying births. It honestly amazes me how many movies and TV shows depict birth in such an awful way. If you speak to most people about birth, it is automatically assumed that birth is a terrible and difficult experience that women have to endure/survive. Want to know what's so deeply tragic about this? One of the biggest causes of pain during childbirth is *fear*. So, we have a society that perpetuates the narrative that birth is painful and terrible, which causes women to fear birth, which makes their birth experiences more painful. And while this may seem like news to you, what's so disappointing is that the understanding of fear's impact on the body during birth is not a new concept. It has been widely discussed and researched for some years, but that doesn't make for great television.

Renowned obstetrician Dr. Grantley Dick-Read spoke extensively about what he called the fear-tension-pain cycle.[1] The idea is that when we feel fearful, our muscles tense up (including the muscles of the uterus), and they are no longer able to move and work with the ease that they were designed to. This tension and restriction cause pain, which leads to more fear, which leads to more tension, and more pain, and this is what leads to the excruciating pain that most people associate with birth.

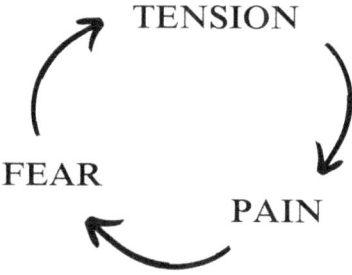

In his book *Childbirth Without Fear* (first published in 1942), Dr. Dick-Read describes being called out to attend a home birth in one of the poorest areas in London, and his surprise when he tried to give the mother chloroform during labor, but she refused it. Later as he was about to leave, he asked her why she'd refused the pain relief, and she answered, *"It didn't hurt. It wasn't meant to, was it, doctor?"* After witnessing so many painful births working in the hospital, this chance encounter, seeing a mother give birth unmedicated at home with no pain, prompted him to start looking into how this could have been possible, eventually leading to his theory that fear causes pain in childbirth. While Dr. Dick-Read's theory still holds true, we've since gained a far greater understanding of how the nervous system and different hormones impact the body during labor, so I'd like to dive a little deeper into the science behind *why* fear causes pain in childbirth.

You've probably heard of the *fight-or-flight* or *stress response*. It is an automatic physiological response to a stressful or frightening event. When we go into fight or flight, the sympathetic nervous system is activated, which triggers an acute stress response, preparing the body to fight or flee. In this state, the blood rushes to the arms and legs to give them the extra oxygen they need to fight or make an escape. On the flip side, our parasympathetic nervous system (also referred to as *rest and digest*, or *feed and breed*) relaxes our body and helps run processes like digestion, waste removal, and reproduction.

When we are in the rest and digest state during labor, the uterus has all the blood and oxygen it needs to work as efficiently as possible. Whereas when we are feeling afraid, the blood rushes away from the uterus to the arms and legs, as our autonomic nervous system will always favor saving our lives over giving birth. So, basically, if during labor a mother is feeling relaxed and remains in the parasympathetic nervous system, this helps her produce peak levels of oxytocin (the hormone responsible for contractions), helps keep that lovely blood and oxygen in the uterus (allowing the uterus to work as efficiently as possible), and helps increase endorphins (our body's natural pain relief). But if a mother becomes fearful or stressed and her sympathetic nervous system is activated, blood and oxygen rush to the limbs to help her get away from the threat (even if it's just in her mind), meaning the uterus is now unable to work efficiently, muscle movement in the uterus becomes more and more painful, and may even stall completely.

Below is one of my favorite exercises to try to demonstrate to you how this works:

HAND SQUEEZY EXERCISE

Set a timer for one minute (about the length of a contraction during active labor) and begin squeezing your fingers into your palms, making a fist and then releasing them. Continue squeezing and releasing your hands, but stretch one arm up above your head, and keep your hand as high up as you can while resting the other on your thigh in front of you. Continue to vigorously squeeze each hand into a fist, then immediately release your fingers straight, then tighten back into a fist again. Do this for one minute.

What did you notice? I always find this exercise surprisingly hard. By the end of a minute, the fingers of my hand that's in the air are aching, and the pain seems to be going down my arm. Interestingly, the hand resting on my knee feels fine. It still feels like it's been working, but without that really painful feeling. This is because as the blood moves down your arm, away from your hand, the muscles of the hand that's in the air have less blood and oxygen to do the job they're trying to do than the one that's in your lap.

The uterus is basically a bag of muscles with an inner layer of horizontal, ring-shaped muscles and an outer layer of vertical muscles. The ring-shaped muscles are packed tightly at the bottom, keeping your baby secure throughout pregnancy, but during the first stage of labor (or the *up stage* as we say in hypnobirthing), those vertical muscles make a wavelike motion, pulling the ring-shaped muscles *up* and out of the way of your baby, and building the fundus (at the top of the uterus), which will then work to push your baby *down* during the second (or *down*) stage of labor and out into your arms. Isn't God's design incredible?

As those vertical muscles contract, it creates a wavelike sensation, which is one of the reasons why in hypnobirthing we often refer to contractions as *surges* or *waves* as it more accurately describes the feeling you experience, and it also just sounds a bit nicer. I try not to get too hung up on this, though, as many medical professionals that you come into contact with are likely to call them contractions, so for that reason, I use the word interchangeably.

Understanding how the uterus is working in labor can make such a massive difference to your birth experience. So, in an effort to illustrate it more fully, I'm going to share a quote from midwife Carla Hartley:[2]

"The purpose of labor contractions and retractions is to BUILD the fundus, which will, when it is ready, EJECT the baby, like a piston. Without a nice thick fundus, there is no power to get baby out... the cervix does not dilate out... it dilates UP as a result of the effort to pull muscles up into the uterus to push muscles up to the fundus... the cervical dilation is secondary to that. The cervix is pulled up as a result of the building of the fundus. Assigning a number to cervical dilation is of little consequence, and we make a huge mistake by interpreting progress or predicting time of birth to that number. Any experienced midwife or OB can tell you that the cervix can be manipulated and that a woman whose cervix is at 7 could have the baby in a few minutes or a few hours. What is important is to keep her well supported for the purpose of the appropriate chemistry, to keep her well hydrated and nourished for muscle strength, and to believe in her. We should not be measuring, poking, or interpreting her labor. We should be supporting her so that her physiology and that of her baby are unhindered, so they can finish what they started."

In the picture that follows, on the left, the cervix is still long and thick. Whereas on the right, the combination of the outer layer of vertical muscles of the uterus working to pull upwards and the weight of the baby's head pressing down has helped the cervix to efface (thin) and dilate (open). Once the cervix is fully dilated (10cm), the inner layer of horizontal ring-shaped muscles that have gathered at the top of the uterus (fundus) now begin to push the baby downwards.

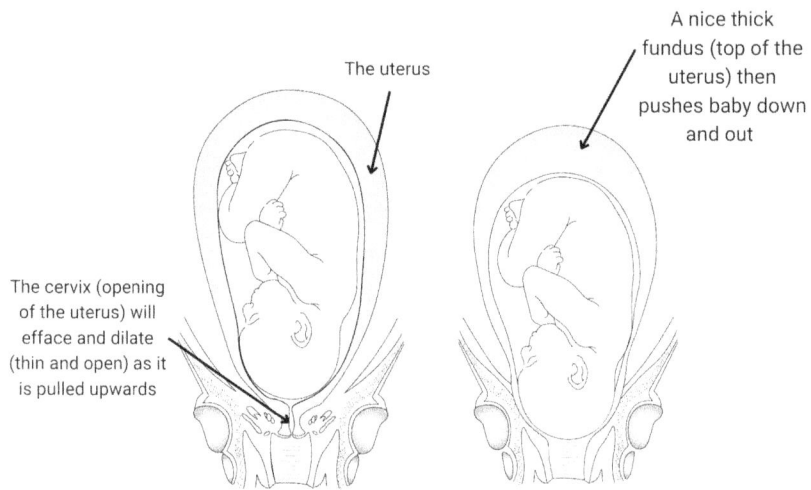

Being able to visualize what's happening in your body when you begin to feel those wavelike sensations can help you to stay relaxed and calm. If you understand what's happening, you can feel a deep sense of peace, knowing that your body is working as it's been miraculously designed to.

TENSE FINGER EXERCISE

For a moment, tense all your fingers on one hand as much as you can, and while tensing them, use the other hand to try to move your tense fingers. Then shake that hand out and use the other hand to move your fingers when they are loose. Notice how much more difficult it is to move them when they are tense.

If you are tensing during surges, then the muscles of the uterus are unable to move as easily, making the process of building the fundus and thinning and opening the cervix take longer.

So, if we think logically about it, when we are fearful, and bracing every time we have a contraction, we have the combined effects of tension stopping the muscles of the uterus from moving as they should, making progress slower and more difficult, as well as your uterus having to work with less blood and oxygen, making contractions more painful. To summarize, tense muscles are not able to work as well, so staying relaxed is absolutely key.

Sometimes, plans change or stressors come up, and how we respond to the stressor in those moments will have a much bigger impact than the stressor itself. In these situations, it's great to know that there's something called the challenge response, which is actually the idea that if we see something as a challenge (and something we can overcome), it can even have a positive effect. Whereas if we see something as a threat, it is much more likely to send us into that fight-or-flight response.

An example of the challenge response is the difference between my two birth stories. In my first birth, when I was told the birth center was full, I went into a fight-or-flight response, and as a result, labor became excruciatingly painful. Whereas, when the exact same thing happened in my second birth (the birth center was full), I felt an internal sense of, "Okay, no worries. I'm going to stay in my relaxed, faith-filled state, no matter what challenges come at me." I was then very quickly able to get back into a relaxed state, as it is considerably easier to move from a challenge response back into the parasympathetic nervous system than it is to come back from a fully-fledged stress response.

So, if and when challenges arise (in birth or in life), it can be really helpful to remember that small amounts of stress can even be good for us, and to try to frame things in a way that helps us develop strength and resilience. Yes, things can happen in the outside world that are beyond our control, but we get to control our inner world and choose how we respond. We can choose to keep praising God through the storm, and what's amazing is that often, when we do, it is so much easier to navigate. No matter what challenges we face, he will carry us through.

The hormonal dance that goes on during labor is complex, but one of the most important hormones (that I've already mentioned a few times) is oxytocin, so I'm going to explain in a little more detail what it is. Oxytocin (often referred to as the "love hormone") is produced in the hypothalamus and then released into the bloodstream by the pituitary gland. The main function of oxytocin is to facilitate childbirth as it is responsible for labor contractions, but it is also responsible for our letdown reflex (during breastfeeding), bonding, orgasm, promoting positive emotions like trust and happiness, and can even help reduce anxiety and depression.[96] Oxytocin production is increased via a positive feedback loop, meaning that oxytocin causes an action that then stimulates more of its own release. There are lots of things we can do to naturally support and increase oxytocin production, like relaxation, worship, movement, and massage, which I will be discussing in detail in the Faith-Filled Toolbox chapter.

Another important hormone to mention is beta-endorphin (one of the endorphins released naturally during stress or pain), which has an even stronger pain-relieving effect on the body than morphine.[97] During labor, beta-endorphins help to relieve discomfort and contribute to the trance-like feeling that many women experience when they labor unmedicated, which can help mothers move instinctively to support their baby's journey through the birth canal. Beta-endorphins also contribute to the oxytocin positive feedback loop because as the sensations of labor become stronger, the body increases beta-endorphin levels to make the laboring mother feel more comfortable, which also increases oxytocin, which increases contractions, causing the body to release more beta-endorphins, further increasing comfort. With this in mind, is it possible to see how, if we do our best to train our mind and body to relax and trust God throughout birth, we can avoid getting into that *fear-tension-pain cycle* and are able to get into a *trust-relaxation-oxytocin cycle* instead?

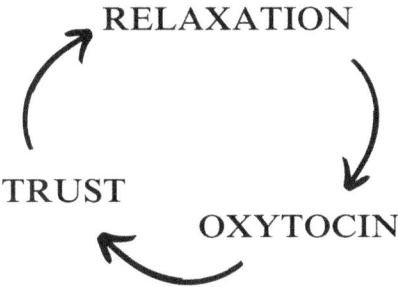

So, the more you're able to trust that God is with you no matter what kind of birth you have, the more deeply you're able to relax, the more oxytocin and endorphins increase, helping your body work as efficiently and comfortably as possible, which helps you to trust even more, which helps you feel even more confident and relaxed. And as the surges strengthen and become more powerful, instead of tensing or fighting them, you surrender and relax deeper, allowing the uterus all the blood and oxygen it needs to work beautifully and efficiently to birth your baby, just as it's been miraculously designed to do. What a different cycle that would be! And *this* is what we will be working to achieve throughout the chapters of this book.

– BIRTH STORY –

ELISE'S UNEXPECTED UNASSISTED BIRTH

I had planned to have an unmedicated labor with my firstborn son at a birthing center, but when my labor stretched over 40 hours with back labor and loss of sleep and energy, I was desperately ready to go to a hospital and get an epidural. I made peace with this and found the beauty in his birth story, and two years later was not planning to try again with my daughter. However, because of all the COVID restrictions, I was highly motivated not to end up at a hospital this time around, but nervous about the pain and how long things took with little progress last time.

I found Christian Hypnobirthing and immediately fell in love with the tracks and listened every night while stretching or in the shower from week 30 of pregnancy on! I could feel the positive affirmations sinking into my spirit, and every time I would doubt that I could do this, I would remind myself of the scriptures and affirmations I was listening to on the app!

At 38 weeks and 6 days, I was feeling the signs of what I thought could be early labor, but was doing my best to ignore them because I thought things could potentially take days to progress. I went for a long walk in the morning while listening to the app and easing my mind of any tensions and fears. I went about my day playing with my toddler, resting when he napped and even went to my family's home for our usual Sunday night dinner. All the while I was feeling cramps that I was convinced were just Braxton Hicks and an overall uncomfortable feeling.

By the time we got home (around 9 p.m.) I was feeling stronger cramps and I began to get ready for bed while my husband put my toddler to bed. We watched two movies to distract and to pass some time. All the while the contractions were coming strong but were only around 30 seconds in length, way too short to be the real thing… I thought!

By this point, it was 1:00 a.m. and my husband said, "Well, it's almost morning and we can reevaluate and call the midwife in the morning!" But this was when things picked up in intensity and I suddenly threw up what I had eaten for dinner and my body began involuntary shaking (what I didn't realize in the moment was most likely transition). I tried to lay back down in bed but was no longer coping well. My husband suggested I get up and move around to change positioning. I moved to the bathroom and with the next contraction landed on my hands and knees on the bathroom floor. I was starting to get concerned and discouraged with how powerful they were and thinking I had so much longer to go. I asked my husband to get my phone and play the Christian Hypnobirthing app, and with the subsequent contractions, I felt my body start to push baby girl down.

Without me trying or doing anything at all, my body was doing exactly what it was designed by God to do! By this point, I was feeling so much pressure and looked down to see her amniotic sac and I asked my husband to confirm. We both realized that this was really happening right here in our own home with no time to call the midwife and no time to call my parents to come pick up my son sleeping in the other room! I remember we shared a look of "Okay, we can do this," and I continued to pray Philippians 4:13, "I can do all things through Christ who strengthens me" out loud like I had been on and off throughout the labor.

My husband helped me move into the shower and before the water even hit my back, I was hit with another wave and the ring of fire feeling (which was very intense but also very short for me). My husband encouraged me in these last two pushes and that the baby's head was almost out. I kept saying "Jesus, Jesus" out loud because that's all I could think of in the moment, and from the top of my lungs I yelled at him to sing to me! My husband sang out "Jesus, Jesus" with me, and with the last wave I was crumpled on top of him, and he reached down to catch our baby girl! I dropped to my knees in the most glorious relief and held our precious little girl for the first time.

I didn't hear her cry right away, and then my husband gently peeled back the last bit of amniotic sac that was covering her face, and she immediately let out a big cry! Thank you, Jesus! At this point, we called the midwife, who arrived within 30 minutes to make sure both baby and I were just fine! I had already delivered the placenta and was tucked in bed cuddling the sweetest little girl! My midwife assisted us in the clean-up and weighing of the baby and quietly left my husband and me to rest in our own bed!

This experience was so powerful, so spiritual, intimate, and so much calmer and more relaxed than I had ever imagined possible. It was the birth of my dreams that I had been praying for! A redemptive birth that was fast and focused on God and his strength, instead of surrounded by fear. I am grateful for the privacy of having this birth in my own home with just my husband and I and God there to guide us! Something I did not feel confident to plan for!

I am so grateful to have found Christian Hypnobirthing as I believe it really helped me bridge the gap between the kind of birth I wanted and had read about and how to achieve that for myself! I am forever grateful to have this birth story! I look forward to telling my daughter one day and to have this beautiful faith-filled experience that I will never forget!

2

The Power of Words

"The tongue has the power of life and death."
— Proverbs 18:21

What is hypnobirthing? Different programs have different definitions. In a very basic sense, it is antenatal education combined with relaxation exercises that are practiced in the lead-up to and during birth, but one of my favorite definitions was what I was told when I was doing my hypnobirthing teacher training. I asked the instructor, "What is hypnobirthing?" and she said quite simply, "Hypnobirthing is words." When we change the words we use around birth from negative to positive, or as I like to say, from fear-based to faith-based, this impacts how we feel, which impacts our body and our birth experience.

We cannot underestimate the power of the words we listen to and the words we say to ourselves. Take a moment to think about a time in your life when someone said something that hurt you. Maybe it was just a few words, but it impacted you. They might have even said, "I was only joking," afterward, but the damage was already done.

Now think about a time someone said something that uplifted you, that gave you hope, and was *life*-giving. Maybe their encouragement even led you to make a decision that changed the course of your life? Words are so important. Jesus said, "Heaven and earth will pass away, but my words will never pass away" (Matthew 24:35). How powerful is that?

When we bring this awareness to language, we can start to see how it impacts the body. So, if someone asks a woman in labor, "On a scale of one to ten, how much *pain* are you in?" her mind begins actively looking for pain, which can actually heighten those sensations and increase tension in the body, leading to more pain. If instead we were to ask, "How *comfortable* are you?" this can help her feel relaxed and safe, which can potentially increase the hormones that increase comfort. It is common in hypnobirthing to refer to the sensations of birth as *powerful* or *intense* instead of *painful* because pain is usually an alert from the body that something is wrong. But the sensations of a healthy, normal labor are not wrong; they are good. Yes, it can feel intense and powerful as our uterine muscles work hard to bring our baby into the world (just as we can feel the intensity of our muscles contracting when we do a rigorous workout at the gym), but that doesn't mean that we can't handle that intensity. I love the birth affirmation: "My surges cannot be stronger than me because they *are me*."

The words we use around birth impact how we feel and how our body will react to labor. As I mentioned in the first chapter, the reason in hypnobirthing that we often refer to contractions as surges, waves, or rushes is because it more accurately describes the sensation of our uterine muscles pulling up in a wavelike motion during the first stage of labor or pushing down in the second stage. It's great to understand that all we have to do during these waves is relax, focus on our breathing (the breathing exercises on the Christian Hypnobirthing app are particularly helpful), and move as we feel to move, and then we get this beautiful rest period for a few minutes where we can return to total relaxation. Taking the fear out, and knowing that all we have to do is ride the waves, allows our mind and body to embrace the sensations instead of fighting against them.

There are lots of different ways we could describe contractions. In midwife Ina May Gaskin's *Guide to Childbirth,* she often refers to them as *rushes* and describes the feeling as "an interesting sensation which requires all of your attention." Part of embracing them is being able to describe them in a way that doesn't cause fear. I was interested to know how our Christian Hypnobirthing mamas would describe the sensation of contractions and what helped them to surrender and relax into them instead of fighting them, so I asked our followers on Instagram. The question was in two parts and only allowed a limited number of characters to answer.

Question: How Would You Describe Contractions? What Helped You Embrace Them?

Answers:

- "Surges rising up to a peak and then subsiding. Each wave brings baby closer."
- "Intense and just leaning into them as opposed to fighting them."
- "Tight squeezing of my abdomen, intense pressure in lady bits."
- "What helped was honestly letting it happen."
- "Intense pressure! Focusing on relaxation – I used Christian Hypnobirthing!"
- "A focus of your entire body, mind, and soul on one thing – and then relaxing!"
- "Riding a wave."
- "Intense sensations. I reminded myself that God designed our bodies to do this."
- "Power surges, warm and intense. My body was doing what it was made to do."

- "Viewing them like a wave."
- "Waves are only at their peak for a moment before falling."
- "Tightening in my pelvis; I would breathe through them and go head to toe and relax one part by one."
- "Your breathing track helped me prepare for contractions!"
- "Back labor contractions were intense and strong."
- "Letting energy out with moans helped!"
- "I visualized a wave crashing on the seashore to help me through contractions."
- "I called them waves, visually saw them as waves with my eyes closed."
- "A wave of tightness that increases in strength. A comb, breathing, and the hypnobirthing tracks."
- "Slow, deep breathing."
- "Focusing on the other parts of my body and my senses! My arms feel the wind. Etc."
- "Big waves of intensity – breathe in for 4, low *moooaannn* out for 7."
- "Intense pressure in my lower belly. I didn't think I was in labor because I expected sharp pain."
- "My husband helped me – breath work too!"
- "Waves of intensity. I embraced them best by breathing along with your soundtrack and visualizing baby coming down!"
- "A tightening that peaks, and then subsides."
- "I visualized ocean waves every time and had your soundtrack on! I made sure I wasn't tense and took very deep breaths. Fully surrendered."
- "Strong and intense."
- "Curiously observing them?"
- "Acknowledged but not fearful or tense, just breathe."
- "The real thing won't slow down. Strong cramping that comes in waves. Embrace by low moans and hip pressure."
- "Knowing that each one got me closer to my baby."

- "I embraced them by being reminded to breathe through them."
- "Contractions felt like a squeeze from a strong man, one that you know you'll be released from."
- "Intense, powerful, focused."
- "Deep breathing, low moans, swaying."
- "Intense tightening – takes your breath away. Uncomfortable but not necessarily "painful.""
- "I stayed in the zone, focused, and breathed through! They were never overwhelming!"
- "Thanks to relaxation and breathing, it felt like stronger cramps than during my periods."
- "An incredible tightening that overpowers all your senses."
- "My body working to its maximum, like doing a sprint on each wave. Lots of visualization."

One of the things hypnobirthing tends to emphasize is a focus on what you *want* instead of what you *don't want*. My friend, who is a teacher, said she noticed that if the students were running in the hall and she yelled, "*DON'T* RUN," they'd keep running, but if she said, "Walk please," they would slow down and start walking. Another everyday life example could be if I wanted my husband to pick up some milk when he was at the shop. Instead of saying, "*Don't* forget the milk," I'd say, "Please *remember* the milk." Have you ever been driving and seen a pothole and thought to yourself, *I don't want to drive into that pothole!* and then driven straight into it? Next time, try focusing on the smooth part of the road where you *want* to drive and just see if it makes a difference.

Over the years, some of our app and course members have shared that they've experienced pain-free births, which is obviously amazing, and I'm always excited to hear that, but I actually tend not to use that term a lot because, to me, the focus of the words *pain*-free is still on *pain*. The same goes for "I want a birth that's free from fear," as the focus is still on *not* experiencing fear instead of what you *do* want to experience. So, that's why I say *faith-filled birth* because, for me, that means the focus is on what I want to experience. I want to have a birth that is full of God's love. I want to feel relaxed and confident. I want to feel the presence of the Holy Spirit with me throughout. There's a lot more to birth than just not wanting to experience pain, and sometimes, if we become very attached to a certain idea (like having a pain-free birth, or even wanting birth to go exactly as we've planned), then it can mean we feel like a failure if that's not what we achieve. Not only that, but sometimes some discomfort can actually be good for us, and if we automatically see any discomfort as a bad thing, we may miss its purpose.

Doula and Childbirth educator Claire Fagin captured this so perfectly when she shared:

"The discomfort of pregnancy prepares us for the discomfort of birth, and the discomfort of birth prepares us for the discomfort of motherhood. As a society, we are so uncomfortable with being uncomfortable. We desperately try to bypass discomfort, and we measure our success by how well we are able to do so. I see this happening in both medicated and unmedicated birth spheres. Whether you plan to medicate OR meditate yourself into a pain free birth, we are making the avoidance of pain the goal. By making the avoidance of pain the goal, we are missing the point. Pregnancy requires us to stretch. Birth requires us to shatter. Postpartum requires us to sort through the pieces and rebuild. It is uncomfortable for a reason. This discomfort is where the growth happens - it's part of the perfect design. When we think we can't be any more pregnant, our babies decide to wait a few more weeks. And we continue on. When we think we can't handle another contraction, another contraction comes anyway. And we breathe through it. When we think we can't be any more tired, our babies call out for us. And we answer their call. When we think we have reached capacity, our capacity expands. As you move through pregnancy, dream about birth and prepare for postpartum, plan for discomfort. The discomfort is where the transformation takes place. The pain is where we meet our truest selves. Let it crack you open."[95]

Faith-Filled Childbirth

What I teach is never about disconnecting from the sensations of birth, but overcoming fear, and experiencing God's love and connection throughout. This gives our body the best chance of working as it's been miraculously designed to, while also being able to accept the path that God has for our baby's birth, even if it involves discomfort. While you may not hear this sort of thing in other hypnobirthing programs I feel it's very important to share, as I've heard far too many women say they felt like a failure if they experienced pain or their birth didn't go according to plan... But as Midwife Mary Cronk said, "Women do not fail; their bodies do not go wrong. Some births, in some circumstances, sometimes need some help." The word *failure* again is a very powerful word, and it's used far too much in the birth world, such as in these examples: *failure* to progress, *failed* home birth, *failed* induction, or phrases like she had an *incompetent cervix*. Someone needs to give the medical world a lesson on the power of words!

Please remember this: a woman cannot fail in birth. Have women been failed by the system or their care providers? Yes. But a woman never fails in birth, no matter what kind of birth she has. She has grown a human being from scratch, which is a monumental feat and totally miraculous. Researchers at Duke University studying the limits of human endurance determined that the physical intensity of pregnancy is similar to running a 40-week marathon.[86] Professor Herman Pontzer, who co-authored the study, said, "Pregnancy is the most energetically expensive activity the human body can maintain for nine months." No matter how your baby is born, please know that there is no failure. What you've done is absolutely miraculous.

We may not be able to change the words others say to us, but we can change what we say to ourselves. We can choose to focus on words that will empower and encourage us. We can choose to focus on what we *want*, not what we don't want.

EXERCISE: SEVEN LEVELS OF WHY

Take a minute to write down a few words that describe the kind of birth you would love to have and make them words that excite you! Empowering? Joyful? Relaxed? Faith-Filled? Fun? Whatever resonates with you personally. Then ask yourself, *Why is it important for me to have a (your answer) birth?* Write down your answer and then ask, *Why is it important for me to (your answer)?* Keep asking and answering until you've asked yourself *"why"* seven times.

> **For example:**
> "I want to have a blissful, fun, empowering birth."
>
> **Why is it important for you to have a blissful, fun, empowering birth?**
> Because I want to give my baby the best start in life.
>
> **Why is it important for you to give your baby the best start in life?**
> Because I want them to be happy and healthy.
>
> *Continue this until you've gone seven levels deep.*

By uncovering our true "why," we can get a new level of determination to achieve the kind of birth we truly desire, which can become the driving force that helps us to accomplish it. It may also uncover other things that you weren't expecting. Maybe some fears or negative beliefs that you can address. Regardless of what comes out as you ask yourself why, try not to judge yourself, but use it as a tool to help you know if there are any areas which you feel may need to be worked on and why having the kind of birth you're dreaming of is important to you, which will give you the resolve to do everything in your power to achieve it.

The language we use is constantly influencing how we feel about birth, whether we will fear it or whether we will embrace it, and that will, in turn, affect how our body works in labor (as discussed in the first chapter). The really interesting thing about this is we've had course members who have shared that not only has this knowledge impacted their births, but bringing awareness to their language has changed many aspects of their lives, including their relationships with their spouse, their children, and how they feel about themselves. We had a course member who said changing her language and using the relaxation techniques had helped her profoundly with her IBS symptoms, and I also received this message just yesterday from a mother dealing with charley horse muscle spasms:

"I just wanted to reach out and say thank you for making this app. I paid for the classes and have been using the hypnobirthing meditations each night. I have a horrible Charley Horse in my calves when I'm pregnant, and in the past, they would last three to four minutes long, and be excruciatingly painful. This pregnancy, when I've gotten the muscle cramps, I've remembered the meditations, and it's absolutely amazing. Where before I was afraid and tense and in pain with the Charley horses for minutes at a time, now I breathe and meditate and they last maybe a few seconds because I'm so relaxed and focused. It's been great practice for feeling surges during labor and I can only imagine how much it'll help me in a few weeks when I give birth to my third baby. You guys have helped me face my fears and turn them into resting in God's strength instead. It has made a huge difference. Thank you, thank you, THANK YOU."

We cannot underestimate the impact of the words we say and listen to on our body and soul; far beyond just pregnancy and birth, they impact all areas and aspects of our lives. I even do this with period cramps now, telling myself, "This sensation is *good*; my body is working as it was miraculously designed to." I usually notice an immediate improvement as my body relaxes.

> *"Your own soul is nourished when you are kind,*
> *but you destroy yourself when you are cruel."*
> – Proverbs 11:17

Many of us have an inner voice that can be pretty cruel at times, particularly toward ourselves, and often, that voice has been shaped by hurtful things that were said to us as small children. Whether the people who said those hurtful things were doing it out of love or not, the result is that we can find ourselves still living from a place of shame, guilt, or fear.

While there's a lot that I'm grateful for in my childhood, it was also a common occurrence to be threatened with hell, or being struck down by God for disobedience. The damage from this meant that I was so anxious I lived in an almost constant state of fight or flight, and wanted nothing to do with God or Christianity during my mid-twenties. It amazes me how many churches are still using this kind of language today with small children, with no regard for how powerful and frightening the imagery of a word like *hell* can be. It was a journey of healing to come to know God as a Father who loves me, not one who wants to cause me harm.

One of my favorite scriptures is, "As a mother comforts her child, so will I comfort you" (Isaiah 66:13). It helps me not only to see how much God loves us but also serves as a beautiful example of how I want to parent my own children. I'm certainly not a perfect parent, and have made a lot of mistakes, but I do my best to remember that Jesus said, "Know the tree by its fruit" (Matthew 7:15), and Paul went on to describe the fruit of the Spirit as love, joy, peace, forbearance, kindness, goodness, faithfulness, gentleness and self-control (Galatians 5:22).

I can understand that many parents who use fear to control their children are doing so because they want to protect them. But the truth is, harsh punishments and threats will usually lead a child to feel anxious and unsafe around their parents, and instead of actually changing a negative behavior, they are just more likely to hide it. It breaks the safety and trust in the parent-child relationship, meaning that as the child grows older, they are unlikely to come to their parents when they have problems. Alternatively, when we approach parenting and discipline from a place of gentleness, forbearance, kindness, and self-control, we are far more likely to help our children to know that they are safe with us, that they can come to us with any problem, and be met with open, loving arms. While this may feel more challenging for us in the short term, the impact is lifelong.

Sometimes, as a parent, staying calm can feel incredibly challenging, particularly if a lot of noise or yelling is triggering for us. It helps me to remember: "The LORD is gracious and compassionate, slow to anger and rich in love. The LORD is good to all; he has compassion on all he has made" (Psalm 145:8). Amazingly, this description of God is repeated nine times throughout the Old Testament, which is more than any other verse in the Bible. Not only that, but when it is first written (in Exodus 34:6), it is how God describes himself when he appears to Moses on Mt. Sinai. Given how often it is repeated, and that it is originally a revelation from God about himself, then surely if we are looking for a fundamental verse to understand God's nature, this is it. *Gracious, compassionate, slow to anger, and rich in love.* And as a parent, I try to use it as a powerful reminder that if I can *slow* myself down, and come from a calm and grounded place of love, I'm going to be more compassionate toward myself, my husband, my children, and everyone around me. So even if the modeling we had growing up wasn't as kind or patient as we would have liked, we can always look to God's example of love, compassion, and patience for guidance and help in our parenting journey. We can accept that we will make mistakes, but keep doing our best each day, and remember that God knows our hearts, he sees our struggles, and he is with us every step of the way, helping us and guiding us.

Knowing the power of words can also help us to be much more aware of the words we speak over ourselves and our children. I remember years ago being at a friend's house and his mother calling him a "stupid boy" in a kind of joking way. I asked him about it, and he said she always called him a stupid boy, but that it was just a joke and, if anything, it was an affectionate term. While he did his best to brush it off, I couldn't help feeling like there was some sadness there as he talked about it. There's almost no doubt that during the times in his life when he made mistakes, there would have been a voice in his head telling him that he was stupid, instead of reminding him that everyone makes mistakes, and all he had to do was keep trying. While we may not be able to change the things that were said to us as children, we can choose to stop the cycle. That doesn't have to be our story anymore. And we can start speaking words of life and encouragement over ourselves, our spouse, and our children.

If you have a deeply fearful or mean inner voice that has been shaped by things that were said to you as a child, trying to change the way you speak to yourself might feel difficult at first, but just bringing awareness to what that inner voice is saying can be a wonderful place to start. This is particularly important as you embark on the journey of motherhood because, as mothers, we can be so incredibly hard on ourselves.

So, for example, your inner voice might say, "I can't believe I forgot diapers! Everyone in this baby group is so much more organized than me. I'm such a bad mom. What's wrong with me?"

You could just start by noticing what you're saying to yourself. Once you notice, then those thoughts become separate from you. Once the thoughts are separate from you, you're in a position to question if the thoughts are really true. Which could go something like this:

- **Is this thought that *I'm a bad mom for forgetting diapers* really true?**
  - No, it's not. Yes, I forgot the diapers today, but I'm sure I'm not the first mother to forget diapers, and I won't be the last! They might have some spare diapers at the baby group, and if not, I can always nip out and buy some.
- **How does it make me feel when I repeatedly think, *I'm a bad mom*?**
  - It makes me feel like a failure. Like I want to give up. Like I should just stay home and not leave the house.
- **How would I feel if the opposite was true? What if I flipped it around and I knew that *I'm a good mom*?**
  - I'd feel confident. Even if things are difficult at times or I make a mistake, I know that I'm the best mom for my baby, and I'm doing the best I can in the circumstances of this moment. I'd feel happier and lighter.

Changing your thoughts doesn't have to be this formal and structured. The more you practice just becoming aware of negative thoughts, the process of questioning them and changing them becomes easier.

EXERCISE: OVERCOMING A NEGATIVE INNER VOICE

If you'd like to try this exercise, think of an unhelpful negative thought or limiting belief you have about yourself that you think a lot. Then ask these questions:

1. Is this thought really true? Could this be a misinterpretation? Or an exaggeration? Do I have all the possible information?

2. How does it make me feel when I think this thought?
3. How would I feel if the opposite was true? What would life be like?

Next time you have that negative thought, try flipping it on its head and saying the opposite to yourself ("I'm a good mom"). Write that positive version of the thought on a Post-it note and put it on your fridge, or save it as your lock screen on your phone.

BE YOUR BEST FRIEND

Another helpful way to change your inner voice is to think of what you'd say to your best friend. If your friend was struggling with something, would you berate them, tell them that they'll never achieve it, and should just give up? I'm guessing not. You'd probably offer words of kindness and support. And you can do the same for yourself.

Often preparing for birth is compared to preparing for a marathon, and guess what one of the most important things most top athletes learn to master is? Self-talk. Self-talk and visualization have been proven to be two of the most powerful tools in improving performance.[3] MRI evidence has suggested that certain neural pathways can be increased when people practice self-affirmation. And learning to adapt and direct our self-talk isn't just supported by science. 2 Corinthians 10:5 says, "Take captive every thought to make it obedient to Christ." This leads to another great question to ask ourselves when our self-talk becomes negative: Is this thought in line with what Jesus teaches us? Is this thought coming from a place of love, compassion, and kindness? Does this thought reflect God's love for me?

If you're not sure what to say to yourself that will help you feel more positive and confident about birth, this is where listening regularly to the tracks on the Christian Hypnobirthing app can really help. Often, I've had mothers tell me that right before their baby was born, in a moment of anxiety where they weren't sure if they could do it, an affirmation or scripture from the app came to mind, and helped them find that extra strength they needed. It can also be really helpful if your birth partner listens to the tracks too. Sometimes, all it takes is a gentle touch on the back, and a birth partner saying, "You're safe," or "I'm here," or "You're doing amazing," for a mother to fully relax and release.

ANIMALS DON'T TELL SCARY BIRTH STORIES

Another observation about the power of words and the stories we tell is that we don't see the same level of intervention and difficulty during birth in the animal kingdom. Animals do not have a culture of fear of birth. The bunnies at work don't say to the pregnant bunny, "Just you wait. You'll be begging for the epidural!" And because they are unable to pass down horrible stories, they go into birth with no fear, simply following their God-given birthing instincts, and as a result, most mammals in the wild give birth to their young with little to no issues.

Anyone who's had a pregnant cat will know that you can prepare a lovely bed for your cat to give birth in, but on the actual day of labor, they're nowhere to be seen. Eventually, you'll find them under a bed or hiding in a box surrounded by all their kittens. Cats instinctively know to seek out a dark, private place to give birth because that's where they feel safe, and can fully relax, which optimizes their hormones for birth.

I grew up on a cattle farm, and would often help if there was a cow having any difficulty in labor. Of the cows that had already given birth, almost none needed any help during birth. Of the heifers (first-time moms), normally only around 5-10 percent needed some extra support. But the majority of the time, they'd go and find somewhere quiet during the first stage of labor (the up stage), and change positions as they wanted (lie down and get up) for a few hours. Then, during the second stage (the down stage), the cow would normally lie on their side, and the calf would be born within half an hour to an hour.

I heard recently about the birth of a very high price foal to a prize-winning racehorse, and one of the main instructions to everyone on the property was that no one was to go near the laboring mare, or do anything that could possibly disturb her. After hearing about this, I decided to research further and found the following instructions from equine vet Simon Constable: "The majority of foalings proceed easily, and excessive interference may cause problems. If possible, the mare should be observed quietly from a distance, so that any problems are seen quickly, but without disturbing the natural foaling process."[4] I think it's so important to note here the level of respect for the physiology of birth. This is not blindly trusting birth—if they notice that things are not going as they should, then they are close by to swiftly give her extra support or help if she needs it—but they are respecting the birth process, knowing that it normally works best with as little disturbance as possible.

On the whole, if most mammals are able to give birth with such low rates of intervention, why then do humans seem to have such high rates of intervention and seemingly experience far more pain? During Ina May Gaskin's time as a midwife at the Farm Midwifery Center, they had a C-section rate of less than two percent.[5] So why then do some hospitals have C-section rates as high as 70 percent? Why are there higher rates of induction than ever before? There are multiple answers to these questions. The impact of where we choose to give birth and who we choose as our care providers are incredibly important factors, and I will be addressing those choices in the coming chapters. But for the moment, the power of words, the power of our stories, and particularly the fear we pass down through generations cannot be underestimated, and if we want to improve birth experiences for women worldwide, then we need to change how we view birth. We need to change the words we use. We need to change the stories we tell. Which leads to a very important story, and a very important question that I've been asked many times over the years.

HOW CAN YOU TELL WOMEN THEY CAN HAVE FAITH-FILLED BIRTHS WHEN GOD CURSED WOMEN? ISN'T BIRTH MEANT TO BE PAINFUL?

I need to ask you to bear with me during these next paragraphs. I do not profess to be a theologian; however, I have spent a lot of time pondering this question, searching for answers, and I'm going to discuss a few different viewpoints as this is an incredibly important question to ask and talk about, particularly knowing the power that words have. So, let's take a look at that NIV version of the verse:

> *"I will make your pains in childbearing very severe;*
> *with painful labor, you will give birth to children."*
> – Genesis 3:16

Not exactly what you want to hear as a pregnant woman. So initially, my first thought on this was that if women were cursed by God to experience painful births, but then Jesus died for us, took our sin upon the cross, and set us free from sin (including the sins of Adam and Eve as well), then shouldn't that mean we are free from that curse? ("Christ redeemed us from the curse of the law." – Galatians 3:13)

Now, for some, that idea alone is enough for them to believe that birth doesn't have to be a severely painful experience, and that a confident, relaxed, faith-filled birth is possible. But there are potential issues with this point of view. Some have pointed out that God never actually cursed Eve, that he cursed the ground and the snake, but didn't actually curse Eve, and have questioned whether women are even cursed at all. Others point out that we still live in a fallen world, and there is still sin, so that verse still applies to us, even with Christ's sacrifice. Others suggest that the verse from Galatians is in reference to the law and doesn't apply to the verse in Genesis.

So, let's just put aside that initial idea for a moment, as this next one is absolutely what has impacted me the most. In the original Hebrew, the word *etseb* is used in relation to both Eve and Adam, but it has been translated differently. So, when translated into English for the woman, it was translated as *pain*, but for the man, it was translated as *toil*. Now that may not sound like a big deal, but the impact of this one word is huge.

Here is a quote from the essay "Let Us Go Up to Zion" by Ian Pravan:[6]

> *"[The word etseb] is used of emotional pain and the pain involved in work. It can also be used of a more generalized kind of pain. It is never used elsewhere in the Old Testament, however, to refer to labor pains, or birth pangs. Conversely, there is a well-established vocabulary which is routinely used for labor pain: tsarar, khebel, and khul. If we take our lead from the meaning of etseb elsewhere in the Old Testament, Genesis 3:16 refers to the agony, hardship, worry, and anxiety of the circumstances in which children are conceived, born, and raised, and in which they die. This is the same word's clear meaning when describing the man's work in the field in the very next verse (Genesis 3:17)."*

The Bible Project has a video called "Does God Punish Women with Pain in Childbirth?" where Tim Mackie (who holds a degree in theology and a PhD in Hebrew Bible and Jewish studies) talks in more depth about this verse, looking at the original Hebrew. He translates the verse as follows:[7] "I will greatly multiply your grief and your conception; in grief you will birth children" (Genesis 3:16).

Based on Tim Mackie's translation, the Hebrew word that has been translated into most English versions of the Bible as *childbirth* is actually more accurately translated as *conception*. So, you could interpret the verse as meaning that women will experience emotional difficulty and grief in the relationships in which we conceive children (i.e., our relationships with our spouse) and in birthing and raising those children. Viewing the pain Eve was cursed with as emotional to me just makes so much more sense.

As a mother of two boys, now when I look at Eve's life in reference to what God said directly to her, and think about the emotional pain and grief she endured in losing her beloved son Abel, killed by his own brother, it is almost unbearable to think about. And then when I think about that verse in regard to our own lives, even with Christ's sacrifice, and the blessing of once again experiencing love and relationship with God, we still have to navigate human relationships, which can be really difficult. And those relationships can become even more complex when we have children. How much harder does marriage feel when we have different views on parenting? How much anxiety do we go through as parents, wanting the best for our children, but not always knowing what that is? And even though carrying, giving birth to, and raising children is an incredible blessing, I'm pretty sure that most women would say it can be really hard work at times.

For me, this verse actually feels far more profound when I think about it in the context of the original Hebrew word *etseb*. I really recommend watching the video on YouTube (Does God Punish Women with Pain in Childbirth? by the Bible Project), as it goes into a lot more detail and is really fascinating to think about. You can watch it here:

> Does God Punish Women
> with Pain in Childbirth?
>
> by the Bible Project
> SCAN THE QR CODE:

The translation of that verse is an incredible example of the power of words. Because if you think about it, the way that verse has been translated has deeply impacted the lives of millions of women and babies around the world. As a woman, having the words "I will make your pains in childbearing very severe" versus "I will greatly multiply your grief and your conception" spoken over you, are two different worlds. A mother I spoke to a while ago said every one of her six births had been incredibly painful and traumatic because she was so fearful of birth as a result of that passage in Genesis. After realizing she was not cursed with physical pain in childbirth, she went on to have an incredibly peaceful and comfortable birth with her seventh baby, and it was a deeply spiritual and redemptive experience for her.

I'd like to point out here that I do not intend any disrespect toward the huge amount of work that has gone into translating the Bible. It's a blessing to have the opportunity to read the Bible for ourselves in our own language. But as Tim Mackie points out in the video, every translation of the Bible is an interpretation. The NIV committee had around twenty scholars assigned different books, and they had to vote on passages and choices where they didn't agree. Mackie says, "So I never want to undermine confidence in our English translations, but there are some times where you can see how the vote swung, and Genesis 3:16 is one of these."

I think this is such an important and valuable lesson, and it's particularly important in regard to decisions around your birth and your parenting choices. Often, we can just blindly accept what people say to us as truth, whether it be our parents, our pastor, our doctor, or our midwife, because we consider them to be authority figures and that they must know better than us. And, of course, we can truly appreciate sound advice from a loved one, or a professional in their field. But human beings are fallible. We are not God. And no matter what advice someone gives you, ultimately, we are the ones who have to live with our choices and the choices we make for our children. For me, learning to tune into what I call my God-given maternal instincts, and finding confidence in my own voice, has been an ongoing journey, but an incredibly important one.

To help illustrate, I'm going to share a story from when I didn't follow my God-given maternal instincts. When our son Samuel was about two, we noticed he had enlarged tonsils. It was during the COVID-19 lockdowns, so when I called the doctor, she said we couldn't come in but that I could just describe the symptoms. I told her that his tonsils looked big, that I thought they were uncomfortable for him, and he was snoring at night. She told me that it was fine, and that they don't remove tonsils from children that young. Symptoms hadn't improved about a month later and I called up again and was told the same thing. They still wouldn't even see him to do an assessment. A few months later, we moved from the UK to Australia; there was still no improvement with his snoring, he was waking up in the night, and had general irritability, so I booked an appointment with a specialist. The specialist couldn't believe the size of his tonsils, and said they should be removed as soon as possible. He said that they were so big they would have been causing him difficulty swallowing meat, speech delay, and potentially impacting his sleep and mood.

Over the past six months or so, I had watched my baby boy go from a happy child to a miserable one. I had been frustrated when he would spit out meat. I was exhausted from being up with him multiple times a night. I was confused as to why his speech development was delayed. And deep down, I knew something was wrong, but I didn't pursue it. I trusted that the doctor knew better than me. I bawled my eyes out when I realized the amount my beautiful boy had struggled because I didn't get a second opinion. So, I just want to encourage you, that if something doesn't feel right to you, keep praying about it. Keep seeking answers. Get a third, fourth, or fifth opinion if you need to. God has given us maternal instincts for a reason.

I believe that the gut feeling we have, that deep sense about something, is there for a reason, and is prompting us to look further. I'm not necessarily saying that it's always right, but it may be alerting us to something we need to look further into. For example, if someone has used a Bible verse in a way that doesn't sit right with me, often when I've looked the verse up, I've found that in context with the rest of the chapter, the verse meant something completely different, or that looking at the original Hebrew or Greek gave a much richer meaning that made more sense to me. "Ask and it will be given to you; seek and you will find" (Matthew 7:7). If deep down inside something doesn't feel right to you, keep asking, keep seeking.

How you interpret that verse in Genesis is totally up to you. The truth is, though, you don't actually need to know about mistranslations, or any of the other ideas I mentioned previously, to see that God's design for birth is good and full of his love for us. All you have to do is look at the physiology of birth to see that. It is such an incredibly beautiful dance that happens between the mother and baby. Many scientists now believe that it's the baby that initiates labor by releasing a protein that signals to the mother's pituitary gland that they're ready to be born.[87] So long as the mother feels relaxed and safe, oxytocin increases, and surges begin. As the muscles of the uterus work in waves drawing up to the fundus, simultaneously thinning and opening the cervix, the baby is able to move down, supported by gravity and the surges, all done without any conscious thought. Going through the birth canal, the baby's adrenaline increases, helping him clear his lungs in preparation for breathing for the first time. Endorphins (often referred to as nature's narcotic or nature's pain relief) are released in both mom and baby, making birth feel more comfortable. Oxytocin increases, warming the mother's skin in preparation to regulate the baby's temperature when he is laid on her chest. Her temperature literally changes depending on how warm or cold her baby is! The mix of oxytocin and endorphins help provide euphoria for both mom and baby at birth, and the oxytocin helps mother and baby to bond and causes mom's breasts to be filled with colostrum, which provides nourishment for baby's first feed, stabilizing his sugar levels.

The oxytocin peaks that happen during an unmedicated physiological birth and in the first hours postpartum are the highest you will ever experience in your entire life. The only thing that would come close to it is orgasm. So that gives you an idea of just how transcendent, beautiful, and wondrous birth has been designed to be. I could go on and on, but I hope that tiny snapshot will help to remind you that birth is not a punishment. Are there factors that can increase discomfort? Yes. Can it be hard work? Yes. Do we sometimes need help or intervention? Yes. But in the majority of cases, if the mother feels safe and relaxed, and is able to labor relatively undisturbed, moving instinctually to positions that feel right for her (with intervention only when necessary), then birth is able to unfold as it's been beautifully designed to, with the cocktail of birth hormones helping birth to be as comfortable, efficient, and euphoric as possible. Whether a mother feels that way, however, is deeply impacted by the words that are said to her, the words she chooses to listen to, and most importantly, the words she says to herself.

PROTECTING YOUR BIRTH MINDSET

Unfortunately, when you're pregnant, it seems like every single person has a negative birth story to tell you. I was at IKEA when I was about seven months pregnant, trying to put my flat pack furniture in my car, and the IKEA car park manager felt the need to run after me, telling me about his wife's terrible birth experience. Why he had this urge, I really don't know. It always surprises me how people feel the need to tell pregnant women awful birth stories. What's so difficult about this is that often people use very strong language and vivid imagery in their stories, and these words can have a really big impact on how we feel about birth. Given that we know how much fear impacts birth, it's really important to try to lessen the amount we expose ourselves to fear-inducing stories.

This can be hard because I would never want to disregard anyone's birth story. Obviously, it's a lived experience for them and one that has really impacted them. So, it's not about denying their story, but we still have every right to protect our birth mindset. We can show a level of understanding and empathy while also knowing that just because that was their story doesn't mean it has to be ours. So, you could say, "Sorry, I'm just going to stop you there. While I realize you've gone through something really difficult and I'm so sorry you experienced that, I'm trying my best to feel positive and excited about my upcoming birth, so if you wouldn't mind waiting until after I've given birth to share your birth story, I'd really appreciate it." Or if they refuse to listen, as one mother suggested to me, you can just put your hands over your ears and say "la la la la la" and walk out of the room...

Finding a balance between protecting our birth mindset and also accepting that sometimes birth can go in ways we didn't plan can be challenging. We don't want to be listening to things that make us fearful, but at the same time, there are cases when plans have to change, or intervention is necessary, and if that is the case we want to be able to graciously accept that help, while remaining in our calm, faith-filled state. For me, I really believe the most important part of creating a faith-filled birth mindset is knowing that no matter how birth unfolds, God is with us, and by filling our minds with his life-giving words of strength, love, and support, we help encourage our bodies to relax and work as they've been miraculously designed to, producing optimal levels of those wonderful birth hormones, while also accepting the unique path that God has for our baby's birth.

I'd love to encourage you to join our private Christian Hypnobirthing Community group on Facebook. It's a wonderful space to connect with other mamas, request prayer, read positive birth stories, and support each other. The link is in the community section of our Christian Hypnobirthing app, or you can scan this QR code with your phone:

Christian Hypnobirthing Community group on Facebook

SCAN THE QR CODE:

Faith-Filled Childbirth

– BIRTH STORY –

MYAH'S POSITIVE HOSPITAL BIRTH AS A FIRST-TIME MOM

Being a first-time mom, I didn't really have a set birth plan, because I knew that it was unrealistic to have those expectations when you never know how your labor and birth will go. I really hoped for a natural birth, though. Toward the end of pregnancy, I talked with Levi (my husband) and said I wanted to use a TENS machine during early labor (0-4cm dilated) and then the only form of medical pain relief during active labor (4-10cm dilated) was gas and air. I'd also been listening to the Christian Hypnobirthing tracks since I was 30 weeks pregnant and planned to listen to them during my labor and birth.

I went into labor at around 5 p.m. on the 16th of June (I'm pretty sure having hot Nando's chicken is what put me into labor as I'd had it an hour before I went into labor), and at this point, I was four days over my due date. Early labor lasted around 24-25 hours for me. After around 20 hours in early labor, we decided to go to the hospital at around lunchtime on the 17th of June. My contractions were three minutes apart lasting at least a minute and had been like that since around 2-3 am that day. The hospital was really busy that day, and I didn't end up getting examined until around 4 p.m. When they checked how dilated I was, they said I was only 2cm. This was really disheartening and hard to hear as I was already so tired and had not slept in over 24 hours. The midwife told us that it would be best for me to go home and continue laboring there. They gave me a script for some painkillers and sent me on my way. I decided to pick up the painkillers from the chemist on the way home, just in case labor got too intense. I took one in the car to try and see if that would ease my contractions so that when I got home I could possibly get some rest.

Once I got home, though, I started to feel really unwell and felt like I needed to poop and vomit at the same time. I sat on the toilet and then my waters broke as I vomited. We then rang the hospital and they said that I could try staying at home a little longer and possibly jump in the shower or

I could come in. I decided to jump in the shower and see if that would help ease the pain. It did not.

As soon as my water broke, my contractions started to become way more intense. Early labor was a breeze compared to this (I was still able to play Xbox, hold a conversation, and relax while in early labor). When I jumped in the shower, it didn't help at all. I was feeling very overwhelmed, and I rang my mum. She told me to get out of the shower and go back to the hospital. I really didn't want to get back in the car (contractions in the car are the worst), and I just wanted the pressure down below to go away. I cried to my mum that I wanted an epidural and that I just wanted the pain to go away.

I was feeling out of control. I was very adamant that I did not want an epidural when Levi and I were talking about pain relief, but at this point, I just wasn't coping. My mum told Levi to put a dress on me and head to the hospital. We then jumped back in the car and headed back to the hospital. Levi also reassured me that I could do this and that my body was capable of birthing our baby.

At this point, I put on my Christian Hypnobirthing tracks, and I just got in the zone and I no longer felt out of control. My mindset just switched, and I felt totally at peace. When we arrived at the hospital, Levi parked out in front of reception and asked the receptionist for a wheelchair. There was no way I was up to walking to the labor ward.

When we got to the labor ward, I felt the urge to push. I immediately requested gas and air. They then checked me and I was 10cm dilated, and I was ready to push. I was pushing for around two hours before Zion was born. For some of the two hours I was on my back on the bed as I was so exhausted and couldn't stand without feeling like my legs were going to give way. The midwives then suggested I lean over the head of the bed while on my knees; that way gravity would help speed things up. Those two hours seemed like a lifetime, but once he was born, it was such a relief. All the pressure and pain disappeared. I was listening to the Christian Hypnobirthing tracks the whole time I was pushing, and honestly, I can't even remember hearing them, it was like an out-of-body experience.

Once he was born, the first thing I asked was, "Is it a boy or a girl?" And Levi yells out "A BOY." My birth wasn't over yet, though; I still had to deliver the placenta. This happened about 15 minutes later via controlled cord traction (which is where the midwives put tension on the cord and help pull out the placenta once it has detached from the wall of the uterus).

After this had happened, the midwives then had to examine me to see if I had torn; honestly, this was probably more painful than giving birth as everything was very tender and swollen. I asked them to turn the gas and air all the way to max if they wanted to examine me. Thankfully I only had a second-degree tear (tear through skin and muscle), which didn't need stitches. In the end I had my dream birth experience, which I am so thankful to God for, as I know that lots of women don't get that.

The Christian Hypnobirthing tracks honestly played a massive role in my labor and birth. I don't think I would have had my dream labor and birth without them. I would 100% recommend them to any pregnant moms out there! I will certainly be using them with my pregnancies in the future.

3

Your Faith-Filled Toolbox

"So do not fear, for I am with you; do not be dismayed, for I am your God. I will strengthen you and help you; I will uphold you with my righteous right hand."
– Isaiah 41:10

Sometimes, people mistakenly think that unless you have a perfectly calm birth where your baby just slips out between breaths, then hypnobirthing hasn't worked. I'll let you in on a secret. Hypnobirthing (or at least the version that I teach) has little to do with the mechanics of the birth you have, and everything to do with how you *feel* in the lead-up to, during, and after birth. As soon as you begin feeling calmer and more confident, you change the hormones that your body releases, which your baby is being bathed in every day as they grow. Studies show that higher levels of the stress hormone cortisol in pregnant women have been linked to changes in infant brain development of the amygdala,[26] which is involved in a child's social and emotional development. So, by educating yourself on pregnancy, birth, and postpartum, increasing your confidence, and having tools to help you stay calm and relaxed, you are not only setting yourself up for a better birth and postpartum experience, but you're also helping your baby's healthy brain development while in the womb. Women who feel confident going into birth are more likely to have a positive experience during birth,[27] so even if birth goes differently from how we envisioned it, we can still have a positive, faith-filled experience when we're able to make decisions from a fully informed place, with tools to help us feel calm and connected to God regardless.

Because oxytocin and endorphins are the hormones that help labor to be as comfortable and efficient as possible, all the tools I suggest in this chapter are designed to help increase those hormones, as well as some other suggestions to help you feel happier and healthier throughout pregnancy and beyond. If you find it difficult to make time to practice prayer, mindfulness, breathing exercises, etc., it may be motivating to visualize your baby being bathed in all those beautiful feel-good hormones (like dopamine, serotonin, endorphins, and oxytocin) every time you practice, and to know that even just a few minutes each day can have a positive impact on both you and your baby.

PRAYER, GRATITUDE, AND WORSHIP

Different studies[25] have shown that prayer has positive effects on overall mental health, reducing anxiety and increasing feelings of connection and gratitude, and it has even been shown to increase physical healing and heart health. One benefit I really notice is how prayer helps me to come back to the present. If I don't actively pay attention to my thoughts and work to direct them, they tend to go straight to worrying about the future. Prayer is such an important tool for me each day, even if it's only for a few minutes, to bring my thoughts back to God and to his goodness, and rest in that beautiful peace. Sometimes, it's just as simple as taking a deep breath and saying, "Thank you."

Faith-Filled Childbirth

"Be still and know that I am God."
– Psalm 46:10

When I think of prayer, I often think of Psalm 46:10: "Be still and know that I am God." Interestingly, in this verse, the words "be still" are translated from the Hebrew word *rapha*. *Rapha* could also be translated as to *let go*, to *release*, or to *make yourself weak*, or in other words, to *surrender*. Often, we desperately try to control things that are beyond our control, which can cause a huge amount of stress. When we can practice letting go of things that are beyond our control, it will benefit us immensely not only during birth, but in all aspects of our life. I really recommend this verse for labor, but also in any moment where you start feeling tense or overwhelmed. If you want to, try taking a deep breath and then saying, "I let go, I release, I surrender. I trust you, Lord."

If you're not sure how to pray, The Lord's Prayer (Matthew 6:9-13) might be a helpful place to start as that's how Jesus taught us to pray, but it also doesn't have to be as formal as that. Prayer is really just a conversation with God. So, it could be as simple as sharing what's on your mind or asking for guidance. If you'd find it helpful to have a bit more of a structure when praying, you may want to try "Thank you, Sorry, Please." You start by thanking God for the things in your life that you're grateful for, saying sorry for anything you feel you need to apologize for, and then putting any requests you have to God.

One thing I like to try to do each morning when I wake up is think of something specific from the day before that I'm grateful for and thank God for that specific thing. Starting the day with thanks and praise is a wonderful way to help direct our mind to focus on what's good in life. It's easy to focus on all the things that are wrong in our life, but just as easy to focus on what's right. There are so many verses in the Bible on thanks and praise, and unsurprisingly, studies have shown that gratitude is immensely beneficial to us. Gratitude has been shown to help improve sleep, our mood, and immunity, and has even been shown to decrease depression, anxiety, the risk of disease, and difficulties with chronic pain.[28]

> *"I will give thanks to you, Lord, with all my heart;*
> *I will tell of all your wonderful deeds."*
> – Psalm 9:1

Gratitude is also an incredible tool for birth, as not only does it increase oxytocin, but physiologically, our brains can't feel fearful and grateful at the same time. Given we know that fear has such a negative impact on birth, it's great to know that gratitude is a powerful tool to combat it. If you have the Christian Hypnobirthing app, I really recommend giving our "Gratitude and Creative Visualization" track a listen, or just find moments to incorporate time for thankfulness into each day. As a family, each night at the dinner table, each of us shares at least one thing that we're grateful for from that day, which is a beautiful and fun practice to incorporate. Another wonderful way to boost oxytocin and direct your thoughts toward what you're grateful for is worship music. Leading up to labor, it's a great idea to put a playlist together of all your favorite worship songs, or songs that help you feel happy, relaxed, and connected to God. Music can also help reduce pain, distract, and pass the time, help you to relax, and if you dance or sway to it, it may even encourage baby's descent through the birth canal.

EMOTIONAL RELEASE AND THE 90-SECOND RULE

While it's true that we always have the choice to focus on things that help us feel good, there are undoubtedly times when circumstances will make us feel sad, angry, and fearful, and that is okay. There are no bad emotions. Being able to feel a full range of emotions is healthy and a normal part of life. Growing up, many of us were taught to repress our negative or less attractive emotions, which can unfortunately lead to dysfunctional ways of dealing with these feelings. As the saying goes, "What you resist–persists." So, what might have started as a few annoyances, after being pushed down, and pushed down, then becomes explosive anger, or manifests in other unhealthy ways. The good news is there are healthy ways to express how you feel. Assertive communication is neither passive nor aggressive. You share your wants and needs with confidence but also listen and respect the needs of others, with an ability to compromise. Taking deep breaths and allowing yourself time and space to process how you're feeling can help you navigate more intense emotions, and sometimes, you just need a good cry.

I really recommend speaking through fears, worries, and frustrations with your midwife or care provider, as that can help to release them. Often, when we speak out the truth that we've been holding inside, the fear loses any power it's had over us. "The truth will set you free" (John 8:31).

Emotional release can be a great tool for birth, as it is a powerful form of surrender. So, if despite all the prayer, worship, and positive affirmations, you still feel sadness, fear, or anger coming up during labor, know that it's OK to cry and speak out to God about how you're feeling, and allow yourself to feel it. My only suggestion would be to try to stick to the 90-second rule.

Brain scientist Jill Bolte Taylor describes the neurological process she calls the 90-second rule as, "When a person has a reaction to something in their environment, there's a 90-second chemical process that happens; any remaining emotional response is just the person choosing to stay in that emotional loop." Essentially, that means that when we get triggered by something, so long as we don't interfere with the emotion, that fear or anger that washes through our body only lasts for 90 seconds. During that time, all we need to do is breathe and ride the wave (much like contractions), and then it will pass. This also means that if we continue to feel angry, sad, or fearful, it's because we are feeding that loop with the same triggering thoughts.

Even when we're in very difficult situations, we have the power to choose an empowering meaning and break the loop. Holocaust survivor Viktor Frankl wrote, "When we can no longer change a situation, we are challenged to change ourselves. Everything can be taken from a human but one thing: the last of the human freedoms—to choose one's attitude in any given set of circumstances, to choose one's own way." While we cannot always choose our circumstances, we can choose our reactions to them. So, if during labor it became apparent that your birth plans had to change, or things were going differently to how you'd imagined them, or for any other reason you felt like weeping and crying out to God in anger or frustration, give yourself 90 seconds to let it out, cry, yell into a pillow, feel the feelings and breathe through them, or whatever feels right for you. But once that 90 seconds is up, put the Christian Hypnobirthing app back on or do a deep breathing exercise and do your best to find an empowering meaning in these new circumstances. This will mean your body can release the stored or blocked emotions without allowing them to pull you into the *fear-tension-pain cycle*.

Paul wrote: "But he said to me, 'My grace is sufficient for you, for my power is made perfect in weakness.'" We do not need to fear having moments of weakness, as it is often in those moments of total surrender that we finally allow God to be our strength, to be our power, and to find rest in that trust. On the other side of that release and surrender, we find strength and renewal.

ASK, AND YOU WILL RECEIVE

"Ask and it will be given to you; seek and you will find; knock and the door will be opened to you. For everyone who asks receives; the one who seeks finds; and to the one who knocks, the door will be opened."
– Matthew 7:7

As I mentioned earlier, prayer is really just a conversation with God, but sometimes we forget that conversations have two sides. It can be so helpful to ask God questions and then sit in that space and stillness, ready to receive. As you approach the really important choices about birth, I cannot emphasize enough the power of praying on your decisions. If your birth partner is happy to pray with you, then it can be a wonderful thing to do together and help you both to feel peace and clarity. I'd recommend reading this whole book or doing a childbirth educational course, as well as doing your own research before making any decisions on where to give birth or who to choose as your care provider, so you can remove any fear and approach prayer on these decisions from an informed and empowered place.

As well as asking specific questions about important decisions, it can be wonderful to ask more general questions, too. You may want to start by finding somewhere comfortable to sit or lie down, listening to some worship music, or playing the relaxation music from the app, taking some deep breaths, and inviting the Holy Spirit into the space. Then, when you feel ready, ask God whatever is on your heart. If you're not sure what to ask, here are a few suggestions:

- "Lord, is there anything you want to say to me?"
- "Is there anything you want me to know about this situation?"
- "What do you want me to do now?"
- "God, is there anything you want me to surrender or let go of?"
- "Is there anything you would like to give to me today?"

You may also want to note down what comes to you in a journal, or if you receive an encouraging word or affirmation, you could write it on a Post-it note and put it somewhere you'll see regularly.

UP BREATHING

Our breath is one of our most powerful tools for bringing us back into the parasympathetic nervous system during labor, and the wonderful thing is, you don't need to remember to pack it! Even if you forgot the fairy lights, essential oil vaporizer, and the birth pool, you always have your breath with you.

In hypnobirthing, we do a breathing exercise called *up breathing* during the *up* (or first) stage of labor. The reason it's called that is because it's done while the muscles of the uterus pull *up*. Traditionally, many hypnobirthing methods suggest breathing in through the nose for a count of four and out through the mouth for a count of seven or eight, but put simply, up breathing is just a shorter in-breath and a longer out-breath. It is the longer out-breath that helps to slow down our heart rate, telling our body that we're safe to come out of fight or flight and bringing us back into that relaxed rest and digest state. This relaxes our body, increasing oxytocin and endorphins, which help us to feel more comfortable (and even euphoric) while allowing the uterus to work as it's miraculously designed to. This breathing technique isn't specific to birth; it's also used in mindfulness practices to help with anxiety and insomnia. So, it is a great tool to have available to you for all kinds of situations.

Some mamas may find they don't like counting, or feel like the breath out is too long (particularly later in pregnancy), or would rather just breathe through their mouth instead of their nose (or vice versa). In these instances, please feel free to adjust the exercise to what feels comfortable for you. It's great to remember that it's called a *relaxation practice*, not a *relaxation perfect*. If it feels too long for you, make it a bit shorter. If you don't like breathing through your nose, breathe through your mouth. Trust what feels good for you, as that's what will help you to relax the most. If it's easier, you can just focus on taking a slightly shorter in-breath and a slightly longer out-breath. As simple as this sounds, I have used this breathing technique so many times and it is amazing. Not only was it fantastic during labor, but I've since used it during smear tests, exams, or just any time that I feel stressed. I literally started doing it at the dinner table the other day because sometimes, mealtime with little kids can be stressful! It is such a helpful tool.

To help you get it into your body, give it a quick try now. Simply breathe in for four seconds and then breathe out for seven seconds. Repeat this four more times. You've just breathed through the average time of a surge! How do you feel? It's great to keep in mind that during the first stage of labor, surges normally only last for around a minute or a little longer, and all you have to do during them is breathe. You may find the affirmation "I can do anything for 60 seconds" or the scripture "I can do all things through Christ who strengthens me" helpful to have in the back of your mind while you breathe. Then, after the surge, you get a beautiful rest period where you can totally relax again. You can also use the breathing exercise on the Christian Hypnobirthing app for guidance if you'd like.

It's great to practice up breathing regularly throughout pregnancy and life in general. Incorporating this breathing exercise into a daily relaxation practice (along with practicing prayer, visualization, and gratitude) that you do for even just a few minutes when you wake up and as you go to sleep at night can help bring you back into the parasympathetic nervous system, setting you up for a more calm and confident day, and more restful sleep at night.

DOWN BREATHING, MOOING, AND HORSE LIPS

Down breathing is the breathing exercise used in hypnobirthing during the *down* (second) stage of labor when the muscles of the uterus have gathered at the top of the uterus (the fundus) and then begin pushing your baby *down*. This is often referred to as the pushing phase, during which many women are still encouraged to "push push push" their baby out, even in cases where there's no medical indication to rush this process. Research[29] does not support this widespread practice of forced or directed pushing, which has been shown to stress the mother's cardiovascular system, reduce oxygen, and trigger changes in the baby's heart rate. There's also evidence that forced pushing has the potential to increase pressure on the baby, the umbilical cord, and the tissues of the perineum, resulting in more tears and a weaker pelvic floor, which can result in urinary incontinence. So instead of doing forced or directed pushing, *down breathing* is a way of helping support your body's self-directed pushing.

During transition (where you move from the muscles of the uterus pulling up and gathering at the top to then beginning to push your baby down), your adrenaline increases to help give your body the energy needed to push your baby out. This sudden increase in adrenaline can sometimes lead women to feel overwhelmed for a few minutes and is normally the point they say something like, "I can't do this anymore!" or "I need the epidural!" If you suddenly feel that sense of overwhelm, it's encouraging to remember that you are likely very close to meeting your baby, and hopefully, your birth partner, doula, or care provider will also remind you of that in that moment!

Upon reaching full dilation, you may get an immediate urge to push, and during contractions, you may instinctively start bearing down (this will probably feel like you need to do a really big bowel movement–sorry for the imagery, but that really is how it feels), which is a great time to start doing the down breathing. To do down breathing, you take a deep breath in fairly quickly (no counting) and as you breathe out slowly, you think about sending that breath down through your body. While this breath is still helping you to relax, as you push the air out through your lips, there's a bit more pressure to the airflow when compared to up breathing. If you put your hands on your abdomen as you practice down breathing, you will feel your muscles engage as you focus on sending the breath down. This is what people often refer to as "breathing your baby out." Once the surge ends, you go back to totally normal breathing and then begin doing it again when the next surge comes.

The great thing about doing this instead of forced pushing is that it gives you something to focus on and helps you support the work your body is already doing while also being much gentler on your baby and your perineum. During this time, your baby's head may move further into your vagina, then bob back up a bit, then move a little further, then bob back up a little again. While this may feel a little like one step forward and two steps back, what it's actually doing is gently stretching the tissues, which helps to protect the perineum, and allows your baby a gentler entrance into the world.

If you don't enjoy doing the down breathing, you may prefer to make "ooooo" or "moo" sounds. So, you'd take a fairly quick breath in, then a slow "*mooooooo*" out. Open, low moaning, or mooing sounds can feel really good during the pushing phase, or you may feel like making other noises, which can be great too. I would just suggest trying not to get too high-pitched, as high-pitched squeals or screaming may increase tension in your pelvic floor. If you start feeling that you're going in that direction and it's making you tense up, you may want to try doing horse lips, as that is a great exercise for releasing tension in the jaw, which is connected to tension in the pelvic floor. To do horse lips, simply puff your lips as you breathe out, allowing your lips to flap as the air is exhaled (which sounds a bit like a horse).

One more thing that I'd like to note about the pushing phase is that some women get to full dilation, and they don't feel the urge to push straight away. This is normal and is actually a way for your body to give you a rest before the pushing phase. Childbirth educator and activist Sheila Kitzinger called it the *rest and be thankful* phase. One mother told me recently that when she got to full dilation, her contractions just disappeared; thankfully, she had a midwife who knew about the rest and be thankful phase, and encouraged her to rest during this time. She literally just lay on the bed and slept for an hour while fully dilated. Then suddenly, her contractions came on in full force, and she pushed her baby out minutes later. If she had been giving birth with a care provider whose policy was, "You're 10 cm, so it's time to push!" she may have spent that hour pushing and straining, putting enormous stress on herself and her baby and potentially causing extra unnecessary damage to her pelvic floor. It's great to keep in mind that so long as mom and baby are both doing well and labor is progressing normally (which your care provider should continue to monitor), you can embrace the rest and be thankful phase, knowing that your body will push your baby out when it's ready.

One of the best times to practice down breathing is while you're having a bowel movement. If you practice regularly in the lead-up to birth, then it will be much easier to remember to do it when your body starts pushing in labor. To remind yourself to practice, put a Post-it note on the back of your toilet door.

VISUALIZATION

Most of us know that practicing something makes us better at it, but for a first-time mom who has never experienced birth, how are you meant to practice? This is where visualization is such a powerful tool. It allows you to rehearse birth, even when you've not actually experienced it. When we vividly imagine something, our brain struggles to distinguish between whether it's real or imagined, which impacts the way our body responds. This is one of the reasons I don't suggest watching scary movies, the news, or other stress-inducing material during pregnancy, because your brain responds to it as if it's real and starts increasing your adrenaline and cortisol levels. In fact, one of the issues we face as we prepare for birth is that we have likely already done a huge amount of rehearsing our birth in our minds, but not the kind of rehearsal that helps. For many of us, over the years of our lives, when someone has mentioned the word birth, we already have negative imagery that runs through our head on repeat, shaped by film, television, and our Aunt Mabel, who loves telling pregnant women how awful birth is.

By actively choosing to visualize the kind of birth we want, we help rewire our brains to stop firing off stress hormones the second we think about birth and instead start feeling positive and even excited about it. Does this actually work? You bet! It's used by some of the world's top athletes and performers because not only does it work, it has been shown to significantly improve performance. Birth is a mental game, so if we don't believe a positive, faith-filled birth is possible, we have already lost. We need to start with the belief and the vision, and from there, it becomes possible.

> *"For truly I tell you, if you have faith the size of a mustard seed, you will say to this mountain, 'Move from here to there,' and it will move. Nothing will be impossible for you."*
> – Matthew 17:20

World Champion Golfer Jack Nicklaus said, "I never hit a shot, not even in practice, without having a very sharp in-focus picture of it in my head." Legendary boxer Muhammad Ali famously said, "If my mind can conceive it and my heart can believe it – then I can achieve it." And what I always come back to, time and time again, is that Jesus said, "With man, this is impossible, but with God, *all* things are possible." If it were not for that scripture from Matthew 19:26, I might never have made the Christian Hypnobirthing app. Our beliefs shape our lives, and they absolutely shape our birth experiences.

One of my favorite examples in sports where visualization was key to record-breaking was in 1954 when it was considered impossible for a human to run a mile in less than four minutes. Up until that point, humans had tried so many ways to break this record, even including setting wild bulls behind athletes, yet it hadn't been possible until Roger Bannister did the impossible. As an athlete, Roger Bannister wasn't known for training the hardest or the longest, but he was known to close his eyes and visualize each step of the race. He said, "The mental approach is all-important because the strength and power of the mind are without limit. All this energy can be harnessed by the correct attitude of mind." What I find even more fascinating than his breaking the impossible four-minute mile was that within just a year of breaking it, four more athletes also managed to do it. But how could that be? In their book, *The Power of Impossible Thinking*, Yoram Wind and Colin Crook pose the following questions: "Was there a sudden growth spurt in human evolution? Was there a genetic engineering experiment that created a new race of super runners? No." What Bannister had overcome was not just physical. "What changed was the mental model. The runners of the past had been held back by a mindset that said they could not surpass the four-minute mile. When the limit was broken, the others saw that they could do something they had previously thought impossible."[30]

It's great to seek out where we have our own impossible four-minute miles. It's easy to look at positive birth videos and think, "Well, that's all well and good for them, but that isn't possible for me." I invite you to challenge that kind of thinking and adopt the idea, "If they can do it, then I probably can too." This means that instead of feeling down or jealous of others when we see them achieving things we'd like to, we can allow them to inspire us. The women in the positive birth videos that I share regularly on Instagram didn't just get lucky and have positive birth experiences by accident. Most of them listened to the tracks on the Christian Hypnobirthing app every night as they went to sleep for weeks (if not months) in the lead-up to labor, spent time vividly imagining the birth they wanted, read positive birth stories and watched positive birth videos, did an antenatal education course, ate nourishing foods, moved their bodies regularly, worked to release fears, grow their faith, and build a team that would support them in achieving the birth they wanted.

Even in situations where mamas had to have unexpected interventions, taking that time to build their faith and resilience allowed them to embrace the necessary changes and experience a faith-filled birth, regardless. It may be helpful to know that women who have been in a coma have given birth vaginally, with no intervention. They didn't need to consciously do anything. Their body just birthed their baby because that's what it's designed to do. Many of the challenges we face during birth are mental and revolve around deep-seated negative beliefs about birth, ourselves, and our bodies. Being pregnant and preparing for birth is an incredible invitation to challenge those beliefs and to remember that we have been fearfully and wonderfully made (Psalm 139:14) by a God who truly loves us. In doing so, we gain the opportunity for birth to be a transformative experience, which allows us to step into being our true, authentic selves, shining our light and allowing others to shine theirs, also. What a beautiful gift to give our children as we enter motherhood.

The track "Gratitude and Creative Visualization" in the Christian Hypnobirthing app leads you through a detailed visualization exercise, which helps you to create a vision for your version of a wonderful postpartum, birth, and pregnancy experience, but it can really be as simple as sitting for a few minutes and daydreaming about how you want your postpartum, birth and pregnancy to look, and actively seeing yourself having that experience. Feel the feelings, the excitement, the love, the joy. Get those feelings in your body. Seeing all the tiny moments and details really helps it to feel real and also makes it feel more achievable. If you see yourself breathing confidently and calmly through the surges, as they become stronger and more powerful, knowing God is with you, and every surge is good and bringing you closer to meeting your baby, you are so much more likely to actually do that on the day, because you've already rehearsed it.

In addition to creative visualization, we also have another visualization exercise on the app, based on the golden thread breath, blowing the dandelion seeds off the dandelion, and visualizing the blooming rosebud. These more traditional visualization exercises for birth are great for aiding in relaxation and can give you something to focus on, which helps to take your mind off trying to control birth and allows your body to do the work it needs to do without your mind getting in the way. It can be great to practice these visualizations at the same time as practicing your up breathing and down breathing when you wake up in the morning, take a bath, a nap, and/or as you're going to sleep at night.

ENCOURAGING SCRIPTURES

Scripture can be a wonderful source of strength and encouragement throughout pregnancy, birth, and postpartum. I listened to the Christian Hypnobirthing tracks almost every night for about three months in the lead-up to my labor with my second son, so by the time I gave birth, I had many of the scriptures memorized. Just reading back over these scriptures now brings up such emotion in me, as they really have been such a source of strength and comfort over the years. Having my favorite verses to hand has helped me to keep trusting in God's plans, even when they've looked different from what I'd envisioned.

Below are the verses from our "Encouraging Scriptures" track on the Christian Hypnobirthing app. Feel free to make a note of your favorites and write them out or add your own. Alternatively, we also have a free printable download called "12 Scriptures for a Faith-Filled Childbirth" that is automatically emailed to you when you create an account in the Christian Hypnobirthing app if you'd like to print that out. Writing them out on Post-it notes or cards and putting them up around the house can be a beautiful visual reminder of God's love for you and that he is with you throughout this amazing journey.

- Matthew 19:26 - "Jesus looked at them and said, 'With man this is impossible, but with God all things are possible.'"
- Psalm 23:1-4 - "The Lord is my shepherd; I shall not want. He makes me lie down in green pastures. He leads me beside still waters. He restores my soul. He leads me in paths of righteousness for his name's sake. Even though I walk through the valley of the shadow of death, I will fear no evil, for you are with me."
- Mark 11:24-25 - "Therefore I tell you, whatever you ask for in prayer, believe that you have received it, and it will be yours. And when you stand praying, if you hold anything against anyone, forgive them, so that your Father in heaven may forgive you your sins."
- Psalm 61:2 - "When my heart is faint, lead me to the rock that is higher than I."
- Proverbs 29:25 - "Fear of man will prove to be a snare, but whoever trusts in the Lord is kept safe."
- Psalm 16:8-9 - "I have set the Lord always before me; because he is at my right hand, I shall not be shaken. Therefore, my heart is glad, and my whole being rejoices; my flesh also dwells secure."
- Joshua 1:9 - "Be strong and courageous. Do not be frightened, and do not be dismayed, for the Lord your God is with you wherever you go."
- Psalm 46:1-3 - "God is our refuge and strength, a very present help in trouble. Therefore, we will not fear though the earth gives way, though the mountains be moved into

the heart of the sea, though its waters roar and foam, though the mountains tremble at its swelling."
- James 4:8 - "Draw near to God and he will draw near to you."
- Psalm 55:22 - "Cast your burden on the Lord, and he will sustain you; he will never permit the righteous to be moved."
- Isaiah 40:11 - "He tends his flock like a shepherd: He gathers the lambs in his arms and carries them close to his heart, he gently leads those that have young."
- Psalm 30:5 - "Weeping may endure for a night, but joy cometh in the morning."
- Isaiah 46:3-4 - "Listen to me, descendants of Jacob, all you who remain in Israel. I have cared for you since you were born. Yes, I carried you before you were born. I will be your God throughout your lifetime – until your hair is white with age. I made you, and I will care for you. I will carry you along and save you."
- Psalm 56:3 - "When I am afraid, I put my trust in you."
- Numbers 6:24-26 - "The Lord bless you and keep you, the Lord make his face shine on you, and be gracious to you; the Lord turn his face toward you and give you peace."
- Isaiah 26:3 - "You keep him in perfect peace whose mind is stayed on you, because he trusts in you."
- Psalm 121:1-3 - "I lift up my eyes to the mountains—where does my help come from? My help comes from the Lord, the Maker of heaven and earth. He will not let your foot slip—he who watches over you will not slumber."
- Psalm 71:6 - "Yes, you have been with me from birth; from my mother's womb, you have cared for me. No wonder I am always praising you!"
- Isaiah 41:10 - "Do not fear, for I am with you; do not be dismayed, for I am your God. I will strengthen you and help you; I will uphold you with my righteous right hand."

- Psalm 127:3-4 - "Children are a gift from the Lord; they are a reward from him. Children born to a young man are like arrows in a warrior's hands."
- Psalm 91:1-16 - "He who dwells in the shelter of the Most High will abide in the shadow of the Almighty. I will say to the Lord, 'My refuge and my fortress, my God, in whom I trust.' For he will deliver you from the snare of the fowler and from the deadly pestilence. He will cover you with his pinions, and under his wings, you will find refuge; his faithfulness is a shield and buckler. You will not fear the terror of the night, nor the arrow that flies by day, nor the pestilence that stalks in darkness, nor the destruction that wastes at noonday. A thousand may fall at your side, ten thousand at your right hand, but it will not come near you. You will only look with your eyes and see the recompense of the wicked. Because you have made the Lord your dwelling place—the Most High, who is my refuge—no evil shall be allowed to befall you, no plague come near your tent. For he will command his angels concerning you to guard you in all your ways. On their hands, they will bear you up, lest you strike your foot against a stone. You will tread on the lion and the adder; the young lion and the serpent you will trample underfoot. Because he holds fast to me in love, I will deliver him; I will protect him, because he knows my name. When he calls to me, I will answer him; I will be with him in trouble; I will rescue him and honor him. With long life I will satisfy him and show him my salvation."
- Isaiah 43:1-2 - "Do not fear, for I have redeemed you; I have summoned you by name; you are mine. When you pass through the waters, I will be with you; and through the rivers, they shall not overwhelm you; when you walk through fire you shall not be burned, and the flame shall not consume you."

Faith-Filled Childbirth

- Psalm 34:18 - "The Lord is near to the brokenhearted and saves the crushed in spirit."
- Jeremiah 29:11 - "For I know the plans I have for you," declares the Lord, "plans to prosper you and not to harm you, plans to give you hope and a future."
- Psalm 139:13-14 - "You made all the delicate, inner parts of my body and knit me together in my mother's womb. Thank you for making me so wonderfully complex! Your workmanship is marvelous—how well I know it. You watched me as I was being formed in utter seclusion, as I was woven together in the dark of the womb. You saw me before I was born. Every day of my life was recorded in your book. Every moment was laid out before a single day had passed. How precious are your thoughts about me, O God. They cannot be numbered! I can't even count them; they outnumber the grains of sand! And when I wake up, you are still with me!"
- Psalm 94:18-19 - "When I said, 'My foot is slipping,' your unfailing love, Lord, supported me. When anxiety was great within me, your consolation brought me joy."
- Jeremiah 1:5 - "I knew you before I formed you in your mother's womb. Before you were born I set you apart and appointed you as my prophet to the nations."
- Matthew 10:29-31 - "Are not two sparrows sold for a penny? Yet not one of them will fall to the ground outside your Father's care. And even the very hairs of your head are all numbered. So don't be afraid; you are worth more than many sparrows."
- Psalm 63:4-8 - "I will praise you as long as I live, lifting up my hands to you in prayer. I lie awake thinking of you, meditating on you through the night. Because you are my helper, I sing for joy in the shadow of your wings. I cling to you; your strong right hand holds me securely."
- John 14:27 - "Peace I leave with you; my peace I give you. I

do not give to you as the world gives. Do not let your hearts be troubled and do not be afraid."
- Isaiah 40:29-31 - "He gives power to the weak and strength to the powerless. Even youths will become weak and tired, and young men will fall in exhaustion. But those who trust in the Lord will find new strength. They will soar high on wings like eagles. They will run and not grow weary. They will walk and not faint."
- Psalm 40:1-5 - "I waited patiently for the Lord to help me, and he turned to me and heard my cry. He lifted me out of the pit of despair, out of the mud and the mire. He set my feet on solid ground and steadied me as I walked along. He has given me a new song to sing, a hymn of praise to our God. Many will see what he has done and be amazed. They will put their trust in the Lord. Oh, the joys of those who trust the Lord, who have no confidence in the proud or in those who worship idols. O Lord my God, you have performed many wonders for us. Your plans for us are too numerous to list. You have no equal. If I tried to recite all your wonderful deeds, I would never come to the end of them."
- Genesis 17:16 - "I will bless her, and indeed I will give you a son by her. Then I will bless her, and she shall be a mother of nations; kings of peoples will come from her."
- Psalm 113:9 - "He makes the barren woman abide in the house as a joyful mother of children."
- Matthew 11:28 - "Come to me, all you who are weary and burdened, and I will give you rest."
- Psalm 40:16 - "But may all who search for you be filled with joy and gladness in you. May those who love your salvation repeatedly shout, 'The Lord is great!'"
- Matthew 6:31-33 - "So don't worry about these things, saying, 'What will we eat? What will we drink? What will we wear?' These things dominate the thoughts of unbelievers, but your heavenly Father already knows all

your needs. Seek the Kingdom of God above all else, and live righteously, and he will give you everything you need."
- Psalm 84:11 - "For the LORD God is our sun and our shield. He gives us grace and glory. The LORD will withhold no good thing from those who do what is right. O LORD of Heaven's Armies, what joy for those who trust in you."
- Proverbs 23:25 - "May your father and your mother have joy; may she who bore you rejoice."

THE CHALLENGE RESPONSE

With all the talk of relaxation and positivity, we can sometimes fall prey to the idea that all stress is bad for us and/or birth, which can make us stressed about making sure we're not stressed! While relaxation, feeling safe, and minimal disturbance are all really important for the body to work as it's designed to during birth, there are times we can meet unexpected challenges, and in those moments, it's good to remember that if we can remain confident, some stress can actually be good for us. I talked about this briefly in the first chapter, and feel it's important to mention it again because we can become very fixated on doing things perfectly and having a very specific image of our perfect birth.

This all-or-nothing attitude actually makes it far more likely that a small change of plans could have a big negative impact on our birth. If, instead, we adopt the attitude that no matter what happens, *I get to choose how I react and what I focus on*, then a change in plans becomes an opportunity to focus on our breathing and lean deeper into trusting God and accepting the path he has for this birth. Athletes and performers who feel confident in themselves and go into a challenge response, are able to operate in the sympathetic nervous system under enormous pressure without the negative effects of fight or flight, and this consistently shows better performance results than those who go into a threat state.[31] Building our confidence that God is with us through all that we face is a great way to help increase the likelihood that if challenges arose, we would be able to go into a challenge response as opposed to a threat response.

> *"Have I not commanded you? Be strong and courageous. Do not be afraid; do not be discouraged, for the L*ORD *your God will be with you wherever you go."*
> – Joshua 1:9

While I would love everyone to have a totally peaceful birth with no distractions or disturbances, the reality is that won't be possible a lot of the time. With bright lights, beeping machines, and many disturbances, the hospital environment is almost the total opposite of the ideal environment needed to support physiological birth. But even for women giving birth at home in a really relaxed environment with darkness, fairy lights, and a midwife who is able to monitor mom and baby with minimal disturbance, there is still the possibility of stressors—a dog barking, other children crying or wanting attention, birth not progressing in the way we had imagined, needing to transfer to the hospital. There are all kinds of things that can happen that might not be part of our plan. But the great news is we have access to a kind of superpower—*a peace that surpasses all understanding*. For me, this peace comes from knowing that even when things don't go according to my plan, I can trust him. I'm not saying that it's easy because there have been some incredibly tough times, which I really struggled with, but I'm always amazed when I look back and see how God used those times of hardship to ultimately strengthen me, help me learn the power of forgiveness and empathy, and in some cases even to turn me back toward him, when I had turned away.

A wonderful metaphor for what I'm trying to describe is what happened to trees that were planted in a giant biodome. Biosphere 2 was a project that was created as a research tool to study the earth's living systems in a controlled environment with purified air and water, healthy soil, and filtered light. In this environment, the trees that were planted grew big quickly, but scientists were baffled when they began to fall over. They realized that they had forgotten to include the natural element of wind. It is the wind that pushes against the trees that encourages the trees to grow deep, strong roots, which support them as they grow taller. With no wind to push against them, the trees had short roots and fell. While we may want everything to be easy all the time, the reality is that having to push against obstacles and challenges can sometimes help us grow stronger and may even lead us to a life of far richer meaning and purpose.

The challenge response is about choosing how we will react when we face unexpected circumstances. In those instances, remembering to just control the controllables can make a big difference. What can I control? My breath. I can breathe in for four and out for seven. What else? My focus. Instead of just focusing on what's wrong, I can choose to focus on what's right. I can pray, work to make the best decision possible in these new circumstances, and continue to trust in God's plans. I can remember that I am not facing these challenges alone.

It may be worth reflecting on some of the times in your life that were hard, but that have ultimately led you to becoming the amazing human being that you are now. What did you learn from those experiences? How did they help you to grow? How have they helped you to be able to help others? Just as you overcame those challenges, God willing, you will overcome any challenges that arise in the future. In John 16:33, Jesus says, "I have told you these things, so that in me you may have peace. In this world, you will have trouble. But take heart! I have overcome the world." When we know and accept that challenges, problems and changes of plan are all a normal part of life, but instead of despairing, we do our best to embrace them, learn from them, and even be grateful for them–then whatever happens, we become unshakeable. We build our house upon the rock.

FORGIVENESS

"Therefore, as God's chosen people, holy and dearly loved, clothe yourselves with compassion, kindness, humility, gentleness, and patience. Bear with each other and forgive one another... And over all these virtues put on love, which binds them all together in perfect unity."
– Colossians 3:12

Forgiveness may seem like a surprising tool to add to this list, but its effects can be profound and have a really positive impact on pregnancy and birth. It's easy to think that forgiveness just benefits the person we're forgiving, but actually, the true benefit of forgiveness is our own freedom and healing. Nelson Mandela said, "Resentment is like drinking poison and then hoping it will kill your enemies." When we hold on to anger and resentment toward someone, it usually ends up harming us far more than it harms them.

You may have heard of something called a neural pathway, which is a series of connected neurons that send signals from one part of the brain to another. When we think the same thoughts over and over, we strengthen that neural pathway, so if we regularly think about something that someone did or said that makes us angry and resentful, it becomes very easy for us to get into that angry/resentful state, which then affects the hormones our body releases. We basically create a highway in the mind that gets us straight to feeling bad. This doesn't just impact us, but our baby as well. Whereas each time we make the effort to forgive and let go, we are changing those neural pathways and creating new ones that more effortlessly flow to love, joy, and compassion, which again release different hormones in our body, helping us (and our baby) to feel good.

I'd like to note that forgiving others does not mean letting them get away with it. There are laws in this world, and when they're not obeyed, there are consequences. So too are there consequences when someone has hurt you. You can forgive, but you may still need to enforce strong boundaries to protect yourself if they are necessary.

I'm certainly not suggesting that anyone allows themselves to continue to be hurt, but that through forgiveness, we free ourselves from the mental torment of holding onto hurt and pain from the past. When we live our life in a state of anger and resentment, it takes from our energy stores, drains us, and can leave us with very little joy. Forgiveness, on the other hand, lightens our hearts and gives us back our joy. Where we previously had nothing more to give, forgiveness allows us once more to be "for-giving."

FORGIVENESS EXERCISE

Please feel free to adapt this exercise and use the words that feel right for you. To ease you into this exercise, start off by thinking about someone you care about deeply, think about that person you love, and say something like, "Father, thank you for (insert name). May they be happy and healthy."

This time, try thinking about someone who vaguely annoyed you, maybe someone who cut in front of you in traffic; think of that person and say something like, "Father, may that person who (insert annoying thing here) be happy and healthy."

Now bring to mind that person that really deeply hurt you and say something like, "Father, thank you for (the person); may they be happy and healthy."

I've tried to make this exercise as simple as possible, but if you'd like to go deeper with it, then please feel free to put it in your own words and make it your own.

There was a time when I was so filled with anger about things that had happened in my childhood I could hardly function. Words like forgiveness, in the context of the Bible, were extremely triggering for me and would bring up feelings of injustice and hate. Funnily enough, it was listening to a podcast where a woman talked about the Buddhist principle of "letting go of the hot coal that keeps burning you" that helped me realize that holding onto all that anger was damaging me. This was a big part of opening my heart toward healing, which helped me find my way back to Jesus and to understand what I believe his true message is, which is one of love.

The interesting thing about this is that when we do what Jesus commanded us to, which is to love God, love others, and love ourselves (Mark 12:30), we feel so much better, and life becomes so much more joyful. Even though we will undoubtedly experience hardships in our lives at times, if we can train our minds to find love and connection with God, others, and ourselves, we will naturally spend less time in anger and frustration and more time in that love and peace.

As difficult as forgiveness can be, I've found the more I practice praying for and sending love to all people, remembering that we are all human beings and we have all made mistakes, the more room I have in my heart to love God. As social activist Dorothy Day said, "I really only love God as much as the person I love the least."

Today, thanks to cancel culture, the message of forgiveness definitely seems counter-cultural. But nonetheless, it is what we have been asked to do. In Matthew 5:44, Jesus says, "Love your enemies and pray for those who persecute you." This deep and hard work may just be one of the greatest gifts we can give ourselves and our baby. And this isn't just about people who have really hurt us; this could be about finding peace as we sit in traffic instead of allowing our bodies to flood with adrenaline when someone cuts us off, being able to let it wash off, put on our favorite music, or a podcast and enjoy the passing of time. During pregnancy, the more we practice keeping that beautiful peace at our center no matter what happens around us, the more likely we'll be able to keep that same peace through birth and into postpartum.

Lastly, it's also important to forgive ourselves. Often, we can hold on to things we've done wrong and feel guilt for years, carrying it around like an enormous weight. Sometimes, this guilt even leads us to do the same destructive behaviors again and again. Interestingly, the word *repent* comes from the Greek word *metanoeo*, which more directly translates to "an internal change of mind and heart." When Jesus invites us to repent, I don't believe he's asking for any kind of self-flagellation but is instead inviting us to change and bring our hearts and minds back into alignment with him. We all mess up, and apologizing is a beautiful way to repair, but we don't then need to continue feeling bad, beating ourselves up over and over. Instead, we have this amazing opportunity to accept God's gift of forgiveness, forgive others, and also forgive ourselves.

I used to find apologizing quite difficult, as it felt like an admission of weakness, but over the years, as I've practiced it more and more, it's become easier, and it allows us to heal as a family so much faster. I see how much it means to my husband and kids when I apologize to them if I've lost my temper, and realize that if I expect them to be kind and apologize, then I also need to model that behavior. I see how it helps my kids to regulate themselves when, instead of getting frustrated if they're very angry or upset, I can breathe, offer a long hug and we can calm down together. I no longer see apologizing as a weakness, but realize that it's actually a great strength. It takes courage to be vulnerable and to be willing to change our behavior. While we'll never be able to do everything perfectly, each day, we get a new opportunity to keep changing our hearts and minds back toward Jesus and the example he's set for us.

Sometimes, when I think that I couldn't possibly forgive someone, I think about Jesus hanging on the cross, having been beaten and tortured by people he came to save, and as he watched them casting lots for his belongings and scorning him, he didn't ask God for vengeance, he looked upward and said, "Father, forgive them, for they know not what they do" (Luke 23:34). There are many times when people don't know the truth, and they wouldn't behave the way they do if they did. Remembering this can help us to be kind, gracious, and to forgive.

POSITIVE AFFIRMATIONS

Just as forgiveness helps change those neural pathways that were previously highways to feeling anger and resentment, affirmations are a great way to help create new neural pathways that get you on the highway to feeling positive and peaceful. As mentioned earlier in the book, words are powerful. The words we listen to, and say over and over, impact how we feel, which impacts our hormones, which impact our birth. The following affirmations are from the "Positive Affirmations" track on the Christian Hypnobirthing app, which is available for free when you create an account in the app. These affirmations are designed to help you feel relaxed, confident, and connected to God as you prepare for and during birth. Feel free to write out your favorites and put them up as visual reminders.

- I give this birth over to our Heavenly Father, Lord Jesus, and Holy Spirit.
- I trust in the Lord, knowing that I have been perfectly designed to do this.
- I relax, I breathe slowly, and I open gently.
- I am strong. I am brave. I am a spiritual warrior.
- Each wave and each contraction brings me closer to our baby.
- I trust in our Heavenly Father, Lord Jesus, and Holy Spirit. I know that they are with me throughout this birth and always.
- My body has been designed by God, and knows how to give birth.
- I trust that our baby's birth has its own perfect timescale, and that God's hand is upon this birth.

- I inhale deeply and fully to meet each surge; I exhale to release.
- I let go of anything that I don't need.
- I accept the path God has for our baby's birth.
- I relax and release completely.
- I accept the sensations of each contraction, knowing that each one brings us closer to meeting our baby.
- I step into God's grace, feeling his warmth and presence around me.
- I feel strength and confidence.
- I am more and more relaxed and at ease.
- I ask our Lord Jesus for help, strength, and spiritual protection.
- I am in a state of wonder at how perfectly God has designed my body for birth.
- I ride each sensation and trust in the Lord.
- I loosen, open, and release.
- I feel God's love pouring into me and into our baby.
- I feel nurtured by God and by those around me.
- I can do this.
- My body softens, expands, and opens.
- I am strong, and I am powerful.
- I hand control over to God and my body, which has been designed to give birth.
- I allow the birthing instincts that God has given me to come to the surface.
- I let go, release, relax, and flow through birth.
- I go with God and with the natural flow of my body.
- I breathe deeply, I breathe fully, I release, and let go.
- I am designed to do this and I can do this.
- Lord Jesus, please continue to help me, strengthen me, and give me all the support I need, Lord.
- Birth is a wonderful, safe experience designed by our Heavenly Father.

- I can feel God's love surrounding me and strengthening me.
- Our baby has been designed by our Father and knows how to be born.
- I feel confident, I feel safe, I feel secure.
- I give this birth over to our Father.
- I know that all things are possible with God.
- I have an unlimited strength that comes from our Father, Lord Jesus, and Holy Spirit.
- I am relaxed and happy knowing that I will see our baby soon.
- I can feel the Holy Spirit surrounding us and keeping us safe.
- My mind is relaxed; my body is relaxed.
- I welcome this opportunity to grow and change.
- I am more and more relaxed and at ease.
- I wonder at the amazing strength and wisdom God has given to my body.
- I ride each sensation and trust in our Heavenly Father.
- I am doing an amazing job.
- Women all over the world are birthing with me.
- I feel timeless strength and courage.
- I allow love to flood through me.
- When the time is right, I surrender to increasingly downward sensations and allow our baby to move downwards.
- Our baby effortlessly moves through the birth canal, guided safely by our Heavenly Father.
- I breathe down to my belly and our baby.
- I welcome our baby with open arms and an open heart.
- I connect with our baby, imagining their journey.
- I go deeper and deeper into relaxation and gratefulness.
- I am open to and grateful for the birth journey.
- I embrace the rhythm of birth and am fully open to this journey.

- I am filled with unlimited strength and power that comes from our Heavenly Father.
- I am excited and happy to meet our baby soon.

NUTRITION

During my pregnancy with my first son, my aunty said to me, "Pregnancy is the one time in life when you can eat whatever you want." As someone who had struggled with feelings around my weight for years, I finally felt free to eat as much as I wanted and whatever I wanted. I gained 50 pounds over the course of my pregnancy, and I felt absolutely terrible. By the end of pregnancy, no matter how I sat or stood, I felt like I could hardly breathe. Because I'm already hypermobile, the extra relaxin (a hormone which loosens and relaxes our ligaments, muscles, and joints during pregnancy, helping our body stretch) in my body, combined with the excess weight, caused a huge amount of pain in my pelvis. Understandably, this also impacted my birth, as movement was more uncomfortable, and I felt less free in my body to move around, and also recovery felt long and slow.

During my pregnancy with my second son, after losing most of the weight I'd gained in my previous pregnancy, I was determined to eat healthier and move more this time around. The difference was considerable. Not only did I have a lot more energy and virtually none of the breathlessness and pain in my previous pregnancy, but birth and recovery were much easier, too. Obviously, there are multiple factors that contributed to having an easier pregnancy and birth with my second son, but I learned first-hand that what you eat during pregnancy has a truly important impact on you and your baby. Choosing to eat healthily is also the single most important factor you have control over that can help you avoid pregnancy complications like gestational diabetes and preeclampsia.[33]

I think one of the biggest problems with saying things like "you're eating for two" or "pregnancy is the one time you can eat as much as you want" is that the focus is on quantity instead of quality. In wealthy countries like Australia and the U.S., despite a lot of the population eating more than the required calorie intake, a huge portion of the population is actually malnourished. This is because such a big percentage of the food being eaten has little to no nutritional value. This is called hidden hunger (officially known as micronutrient deficiency) and deeply affects babies and children. Babies are very vulnerable to this deficiency up to the age of two, as their body is in a period of intense growth. There is no way for them to catch up later in their lives. If they are not given that initial nutrition, children may deal with physical and mental deficits for the rest of their lives.[32]

I wish globally we could stop focusing so much on aesthetics and realize that eating well in pregnancy and postpartum is not about staying in shape or bouncing back; it's about making sure you and your baby have the nutrients needed to flourish. For instance, many women don't realize that if we are not getting enough calcium during pregnancy, our body will start leaching it from our bones to give it to the baby! Sorry, I'm just going to say that again—leaching it from our bones! We need to be giving our body enough nutrient-dense, nourishing foods to make sure our body and our baby have everything they need to grow well, and feel great.

Personally, when it comes to what to eat during pregnancy, my favorite resource that I've found so far is the book *Real Food for Pregnancy* by Lily Nichols. A lot of information out there on nutrition during pregnancy isn't evidence-based, and some mothers (particularly those diagnosed with gestational diabetes) may even be given advice that's harmful. The main idea in *Real Food for Pregnancy* is to focus on applying the wisdom from ancestral diets and traditional cultures and, where possible, eat food that's obtained locally, in season, and unprocessed. Do your best to avoid eating refined carbohydrates, added sugars, and foods that require a lot of modern processing (like refined vegetable oil and food additives). Generally, eating real food means eating vegetables and fruits, meat (nose-to-tail, including naturally occurring fat and organ meats), poultry, fish/seafood, eggs, dairy, nuts and seeds, whole grains, and legumes. There's no one-size-fits-all about exactly what you should or shouldn't eat. I'm also not saying never to eat ice cream or chocolate. When I'm making sure that I'm hydrated and eating enough nutrient-dense foods, I don't tend to crave unhealthy foods because I'm already satiated. So instead of focusing on what I shouldn't have, I try to focus on what delicious foods I can eat that are nourishing and nutrient-dense, and make sure I'm eating enough of them. Then, if I still feel like having a piece of cake, of course, I'm allowed to have it, but I often find I don't even want it anymore.

A way of eating that makes us feel deprived is not likely to last, so finding recipes that bring us joy and leave us satiated will help make eating nutrient-dense foods more sustainable. Some of my personal favorite foods are berries with Bircher muesli and Greek yogurt, poached eggs on sourdough with (real) butter and homemade guacamole, slow-cooked stews with meat and vegetables, or homemade soups, salads with eggs, feta cheese, or avocado, chili con carne and rice, basic meat and three-veg meals like chicken or steak with oven-roasted potatoes, pumpkin, or sweet potato, beans, or broccoli. These are not difficult to make, but I really enjoy them. If I find myself wanting something as a sweet treat, my go-to is hot chocolate made with cacao powder, maple syrup, a scoop of collagen, a pinch of pink Himalayan salt, half a teaspoon of vanilla extract, and whole milk (some people also love this hot chocolate with bone broth if they want the extra nutrients!)

Sweets are really important to me, so I'll share one of my favorite sweet treats, which are also relatively good for you in moderation. I call them "date balls," and they may even be beneficial for labor. Some small studies have shown that women who ate six dates a day for four weeks had a shorter first stage of labor, a higher mean cervical dilatation, and more had intact membranes upon arrival at the hospital. Also, 96 percent of the women who ate dates experienced spontaneous labor, compared with only 79 percent of the women who didn't eat dates. In another small study, researchers found that the date eaters had significantly less need for medical intervention to induce or expedite labor compared to those who didn't eat any dates. So, there's a chance eating dates could reduce the need for labor induction, but more research is needed to confirm whether it would benefit all women.[34] Personally, I would eat them regardless of whether they have any other benefits because I think they're a delicious natural alternative to highly processed sugary foods. Here's my date ball recipe.

TARA'S PREGNANCY DATE BALLS
    2 cups pitted dates
    ½ cup cashews
    ½ cup macadamias
    ½ teaspoon vanilla essence
    Pinch of Pink Himalayan salt
    ½ tablespoon coconut oil
    ½ tablespoon nut butter
    Method: Use a food processor to blend, roll into balls, then store in an airtight container in the fridge.

One of the challenges that can come up when wanting to eat more nutrient-dense foods is the cost. For the first few years of our marriage, our budget was so tight we had to buy almost everything secondhand (Facebook Marketplace was my friend), and while we did our best to buy organic, grass-fed, or pasture-raised foods, we were always trying to find ways to make it more affordable. One of the things we've done to manage the extra cost is buy our organic meat in bulk directly from farmers. We have a big chest freezer (which you can also find for a reasonable price secondhand), and we will buy a quarter of a cow and a whole lamb and deep freeze them.

Compared to buying conventionally raised cuts of meat individually at the supermarket (which may have been pumped full of hormones and fed grains), buying organic grass-fed meat in bulk direct from farmers works out to be similar in price, but means you are getting meat that likely has healthier omega-3 fatty acids, omega-6 fatty acid, and antioxidant vitamins such as vitamin E. We go to the farmers markets on the weekend to buy organic veggies and fruits and get a weekly veggie/fruit box filled with seasonal produce. We also buy other products (like milk, maple syrup, oats, frozen organic berries, and kids' snacks for school) in bulk directly from an organic wholesaler. I know some friend groups form buying clubs or co-ops and build relationships with different local farmers, buy in bulk, and then split the produce, which also seems like a great idea.

Some people argue against the need to eat organic food, as there have been some studies that say non-organically farmed foods contain the same amount of nutrients. While that may be true, that's not actually the issue. The issue is the exposure to pesticides. The American Academy of Pediatrics has made the statement that children are particularly susceptible to pesticide toxicity. There are studies linking pesticides with decreased cognitive function, pediatric cancers, and behavioral problems.[98] While buying everything organically may not be realistic, there is a list called "the dirty dozen," which includes the fruits and vegetables found to have the highest levels of pesticides. So if you can only buy some foods organically, they're the ones to prioritize. Then there's the "clean fifteen," which is a list of the fruits and vegetables containing the least amount of pesticide, so if you can't buy organic, they're a good option if you'd like to reduce exposure to chemicals. Feel free to google what the list is currently, but I'll share this year's list below.

"DIRTY DOZEN"

• Strawberries	• Grapes	• Nectarines	• Cherries
• Spinach	• Peaches	• Apples	• Blueberries
• Collard greens, kale, and mustard greens	• Pears	• Bell peppers and hot peppers	• Green beans

"CLEAN FIFTEEN"

• Avocados	• Frozen sweet peas	• Watermelon
• Sweet corn	• Asparagus	• Mushrooms
• Pineapple	• Honeydew melon	• Mangoes
• Onions	• Kiwi	• Sweet potatoes
• Papaya	• Cabbage	• Carrots

Since reading *Real Food for Pregnancy* by Lily Nichols, I've also become more aware of limiting the use of plastics, using safe cookware, and opting for cleaner personal care products. Obviously, when it comes to exposure to toxins, a lot is beyond our control (like air pollution), but there are small lifestyle choices we can make each day that lessen our exposure (and our baby's exposure), and every little thing helps.

While there's a lot of science and data out there to support eating nutrient-dense real foods, it's just logical. A huge percentage of what's being put into processed food today didn't exist fifty years ago. So, when I find myself wondering if I should eat something, I try to think about whether it's actually food. Does it come from the land? Does it have a mother? If the answer is no, then it's probably not real food. If it was created in a lab, it doesn't go bad (excluding honey, which lasts for thousands of years!), or if I'm unable to pronounce the ingredients, then it's probably not real food. Personally, I believe God designed us to eat real food. I also believe that when we take time to cook nutrient-dense food, we sit together at the dinner table, say grace, and talk about our day—it is nourishing not only for our bodies but also for our souls.

SUPPLEMENTS

When we work to meet our nutritional needs by choosing nutrient-dense foods, we give our body minerals and vitamins in their most bioavailable form, which means they are more easily absorbed. So, I would always recommend making sure you're getting as many nutrients as you can from the foods you eat first, as opposed to just taking supplements. But there are some vitamins and minerals that you still may need to supplement even with a nutrient-dense diet. Over the years, many of our Christian Hypnobirthing mamas have asked me what prenatal I would recommend, and I've never felt confident recommending one until recently. The reason is that so many of the prenatals out there actually lack critical nutrients like Omega-3 DHA + EPA, certain B vitamins, choline, and magnesium.

A little while ago, I heard about a company that combines science with ancient traditions and wisdom to provide women with the nutritional fertility support they really need. It leaves out all the harmful fillers found in some other prenatals, and provides sustainably sourced vitamins and minerals that can actually be absorbed. For instance, you may have heard about the importance of folic acid before and during pregnancy, but it's actually estimated that 40 to 60 percent of women can't absorb it in that form, whereas this company uses folate, which has all the same benefits as folic acid, but is more easily absorbed. Because products and companies can change over time, I'm not going to list the company here, but please see the Store section in the Christian Hypnobirthing app for the most up-to-date recommendations we have for supplements. Alternatively, I'd suggest speaking to a naturopath or your care provider to make sure you're getting the vitamins and minerals you need throughout your pregnancy, postpartum, and beyond.

MOVEMENT DURING PREGNANCY AND BIRTH

Moving our bodies regularly throughout pregnancy helps us feel good and can even help prepare our bodies for labor. Working out during pregnancy has been shown to reduce backaches, constipation, and swelling, as well as improving sleep, giving us more energy, enhancing our mood, and improving overall health. Some studies also suggest that an expecting mother's fitness level can result in a shorter labor, fewer medical interventions, and less exhaustion during labor.[35] Generally speaking, exercises like walking, swimming with your belly down (e.g., breaststroke), prenatal yoga, weight training, and aerobics can be beneficial during pregnancy, but there are also exercises that more specifically help with labor.

Walking can increase stamina, is a good cardiovascular exercise, and is relatively easy on your joints. It can also help the baby descend toward the end of pregnancy. Squatting is often mentioned in birth books as an ideal exercise to prepare for birth, as it strengthens your thighs and helps open your pelvis. There is an infamous quote from midwife Ina May Gaskin: "Squat 300 times a day, and you are going to give birth quicker." Personally, I'd start with ten squats and then see how I went. I'm pretty sure I wouldn't be able to walk if I did three hundred! (As with everything in this book, please use wisdom and be sure to check with your midwife or care provider before implementing new exercises).

Squatting can also be a wonderful position for birth. For those of us who have only ever seen images of women giving birth on their backs with their legs in stirrups, the thought of giving birth squatting can seem strange, but it's actually a much more logical position. Imagine you were walking out in a forest, and suddenly, you needed to have a bowel movement. Would you lie down on the ground? No! You would most likely squat (while desperately hoping you remembered to put toilet paper in your backpack). Because squatting elongates the pelvic floor muscles, it makes it easier for a stool (or a baby) to come out. Squatting may also lead to less tearing of the perineum, reduced need for episiotomy or instrumental delivery, and a shorter, easier, and more comfortable pushing experience.[36] It can also make it easier for you to reach down and catch your baby if that's something you'd like to do.

Faith-Filled Childbirth

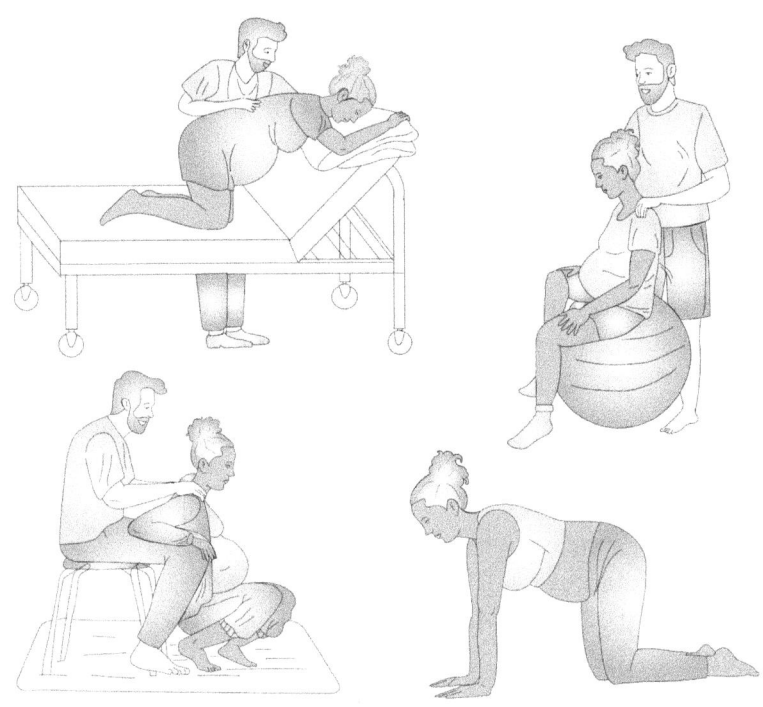

Squatting may not be for everyone, but generally speaking, giving birth in upright positions like hands and knees, kneeling, using a U-shaped birthing seat, or standing allows gravity to help the baby move down the birth passage, lessens the risk of compressing your aorta (which allows more oxygen to flow to the baby, lowers the risk of abnormal fetal heart tones and the risk of emergency cesarean), allows the uterus to contract more efficiently, helps with better positioning for the baby to pass through the pelvis, and is more comfortable. Whereas, when lying on your back, the baby has to go *against* gravity, the pelvic outlet is reduced, and the coccyx isn't able to move as freely, making spontaneous birth (birth without the use of vacuum, forceps, or surgery) less likely. "Why on earth would anyone give birth on their back then?" I hear you cry! For most of history, they didn't. They gave birth in upright positions because, instinctively, they're the positions that make the most sense.

I've heard multiple stories on why this stopped, one of them being that when King Louis XIV ruled France, he apparently liked watching women give birth but didn't like having his view obstructed and wanted women to give birth lying down with their legs spread so he could watch. According to Professor Lauren Dundes, who wrote a paper in the *American Journal of Public Health*[37] on the matter, "Since Louis XIV reportedly enjoyed watching women giving birth, he became frustrated by the obscured view of birth when it occurred on a birthing stool, and promoted the new reclining position." This new way of birthing is said to have initially influenced the upper class and then the lower classes. Dundes continued, "The influence of the King's policy is unknown, although the behavior of royalty must have affected the populace to some degree." The assumption is that if the royals are doing it, then it must be better.

While this fairly creepy story about King Louis may be the reason women started giving birth lying down, why are we still doing it so many years later, despite all the current research showing it's not evidence-based? It seems to boil down to care provider convenience, care provider training, and the ability to manage birth. While giving birth lying down on our backs isn't easier for us, in most cases, it's easier for care providers, and it's how they've been trained. It's easier for them to monitor the baby using continuous fetal monitoring, to rub or stretch the vagina, and perform an episiotomy (a surgical cut to widen the vagina), all of which are not evidence-based in most cases.[38] So, if you'd like to protect your perineum, one of the best things you can do is birth in an upright position, breathe, and follow your body's cues. One exception I'd like to note is that it probably won't be possible to birth in an upright position if the mother has received an epidural. Very occasionally, I hear of mothers being given *walking epidurals*, but as far as I'm aware, this is not the norm, and even in these cases, they often still aren't able to actually walk or move around freely. In most cases, when mothers receive epidurals, they are unable to get themselves into upright positions without assistance, and will usually give birth lying on their backs. There are benefits and risks to epidural use, but I will discuss those in more detail later in the book. If you decide to get an epidural, a peanut ball can be a really useful tool for creating space in the pelvis throughout labor.

It's now common for most of us to live more sedentary lives than we used to, and spend a lot of time leaning back (on sofas, car seats, etc.), which may make it harder for our baby to move into the left occiput anterior position, which is generally considered the optimal position for labor. It's not that positions like occiput posterior (when the baby's back is to mama's back) or breech (baby's bottom is down) are bad, as they are still considered variations of normal. However, in a posterior position, the baby's head is angled, so it measures slightly larger because the top of the head molds less than the crown, and when a baby is breech, most providers automatically recommend a cesarean (unless they are trained to support breech birth, and legally allowed to). Some mothers get very worried about their baby's position even early in pregnancy, but it's good to keep in mind that most babies do turn to the anterior position, often even during labor.

On a positive note, I'd like to share this feedback we got from one of our course members:

"I discovered this course and app at 36 weeks. I started right away and completed the course in a few days while listening to the tracks daily. My first birth was a little traumatic because my son was sunny side up and the back labor was horrendous. So even though I did my best to relax and manage, I ended up having to get the epidural because of lack of progress. I swore if this baby was sunny side up I was going to get the epidural up front. But through the tracks, listening to the powerful affirmations and Word of the Lord spoken through Tara's soothing and calm voice, I was able to manage my contractions so well that I did not know I was having back labor [again]. I knew it was hard and I wanted to give up during the transition, but I persevered. In the end, I just couldn't relax enough to push him out in the tub, so my doula suggested to

try the toilet since we naturally relax our bottom halves there. My son was born on the toilet and I had no tearing! I know I only did it through Christ!"

I absolutely love that this mama swore she'd get the epidural if she had another posterior baby, and then she was so relaxed she didn't even realize it was another back labor. Feeling relaxed and connected to God makes such a difference, no matter what kind of birth you're having.

While babies can be in many kinds of positions and still have totally healthy, normal births, by making small changes to the way we sit, as well as incorporating regular physical activity, we may be able to help support the baby into one of the more optimal starting positions, such as left occiput transverse before labor begins. Below are some helpful maternal positions for pregnancy from Spinning Babies®:

- Sitting with your hips level or higher than your knees.
- Sitting with your back straight and your rib cage lifted off your middle.
- Sitting on a firm exercise ball that allows your hips to be level with your knees or higher than your knees.
- Laying with your navel, aiming lower than your spine, so your belly is a hammock for your baby, then so that an imagined light beam coming from your navel would eventually find the floor.
- Brief forward-leaning inversions, once a day.
- Anterior pelvic tilts with knees bent in a half squat, the tailbone flares out (don't go low enough that the tailbone begins to tuck).
- Walking briskly, daily, with your chin back so your head is over your hips and widening your shoulders.

To read the full article on their website, visit: spinningbabies.

com/about/maternal-positioning/. They are also one of the most well-known resources for helping to turn breech, transverse (sideways), or posterior babies.

Practicing prenatal yoga regularly throughout pregnancy may also be helpful for moving the baby into an ideal position for birth, and is a great way to keep active. I've also heard a lot of positive things about The Miles Circuit, which is a series of movements, generally recommended from 37 weeks onwards. As the first two positions are held for quite a long time (30 minutes each), many of our app users share that they love listening to the Christian Hypnobirthing tracks while practicing the steps of the circuit, so it can be great to take some time for yourself to consciously practice the relaxation exercises, while going through the different movements. You may also find it more comfortable to be on your bed while holding the positions, as some people find them uncomfortable on the floor. The Miles Circuit can be used both before labor begins to help the baby get into an ideal position and if some corrections need to be made during labor. To learn more, visit milescircuit.com/the-circuit.

One other position I'd like to mention is "knees in, calves out" (often referred to as KICO), where you bring your knees together and have your heels apart. As unlikely as it may seem, this helps open the pelvic outlet. Please note that this is best used when the baby is low in the pelvis; if the baby is high and still needs to move through the bend of the pelvis or under the bone, then opening your knees may be more suitable.

While all these movements and positions may seem like a lot to remember, the goal of sharing this information isn't to remember positions. It's really about freeing up our minds from the conditioning that we have to be lying or sitting on a bed to give birth just because that's what we've seen on TV. Once we let go of that conditioning, it's so much easier to trust our God-given birthing instincts and move as we feel to move. You may feel like lying on your side and resting for parts of labor, in other parts, you may feel like dancing (which can be a wonderful way to increase oxytocin and help the baby move down), rolling your hips from side to side on a birth ball, pushing on a wall, pulling on a rope or birth sling, or moving between cat and cow poses while on all fours. The purpose of sharing these different movements is to help empower you to listen to your birthing instincts, which will be the most helpful thing you can do to guide you to the birthing position that is right for you and your baby.

The following video is called "The Dutch Pelvis." This is a really useful video to demonstrate the baby's journey through the pelvis, and how important it is to create extra space by being upright while pushing (if possible) and moving instinctually to the position that feels right to you. It also shows how it is so important to go with your breath, allowing that rotation to happen instead of doing forced pushing.

Dutch Pelvis Intro - Upright Birth Video

SCAN THE QR CODE:

NATURAL COMFORT MEASURES

As discussed in multiple sections throughout this book, creating a calm, warm, and dimly lit environment, using the exercises from the Christian Hypnobirthing app, listening to worship music, and movement, can all increase oxytocin and endorphins, naturally helping birth to be as comfortable and efficient as possible. However, there are some physical tools that I'm going to list below that can also make a significant difference in increasing comfort levels during labor:

- **Warm water** – The use of warm water in a bath, birth pool, or shower can provide significant comfort during labor and birth. Studies have shown that using water for labor and birth is safe and can lead to less need for other kinds of pain relief (including epidurals) and increased maternal satisfaction. Despite this evidence, some organizations do not recommend water births. As with all decisions around birth, this is why it's important to make informed decisions and talk to your care provider about what's right for you personally. A review by researchers in Oxford, England, comparing 36 different studies, found that water immersion significantly reduced the use of epidural and injected opioids, episiotomy, maternal pain, and postpartum hemorrhage. There was an increase in maternal satisfaction and odds of an intact perineum with water immersion.[39] It's great to remember that you can use warm water whether you plan to give birth in a birth pool or not, and even though it's often associated with home and birth center births, thankfully, it's also becoming more and more common in hospital births too.

- **Touch** – Touch causes our brains to release oxytocin, which also stimulates the release of other feel-good hormones like dopamine and serotonin. At the same time, it reduces stress hormones, such as cortisol and adrenaline.[40] Massage can also increase endorphins, providing natural pain relief during labor. Immediately after birth, having your birth partner or doula perform massage on you can help increase feelings of safety and relaxation which may reduce the risk of excess bleeding by increasing oxytocin, which causes the uterus to clamp down on the bleeding blood vessels where the placenta has detached from the uterine wall. There are lots of videos on YouTube demonstrating how to do light touch massage, which you can practice with your birth partner while listening to the Christian Hypnobirthing tracks in the weeks leading up to birth.

- **Birth Comb** – In recent years, holding onto a birth comb during labor has become a popular natural pain reliever.

According to Gate Control Theory, our brain can only process a limited number of sensations simultaneously. So as the sensations of surges increase in intensity, by pressing a comb into the palm of your hand, you introduce another signal which can divert the brain's attention and reduce the perceived intensity of the surge. Many of our app users have shared that squeezing on a comb helped, but others have shared that it didn't do much for them. Regardless, it's worth giving it a try if you'd like to! Some people buy fancy birth combs with beautiful affirmations on them, but honestly, almost any comb will do; you may just prefer to use a wooden one or a plastic comb with more rounded teeth, as sharp teeth could damage your skin. It's best to hold the comb with the teeth pointing just under where your fingers meet your palm, as this hits an acupressure point that can help calm the mind. When you start to feel a surge coming, close your fist around the birth comb and press the teeth into your upper palm. Use as much or as little pressure as feels right for you, and combine with the up breathing for extra relaxation and focus.

- **TENS Machine** – A TENS (transcutaneous electrical nerve stimulation) machine is a small hand-held device, which is normally battery operated, that sends electrical pulses to the lower part of the back. These pulses send messages to the birthing mother's brain, which helps increase comfort through Gate Control Theory (similar to the birthing comb). So, when the brain's focus is directed to the tingling sensation from the TENS machine, it reduces the brain's perception of surges. It also increases comfort through Diffuse Noxious Inhibitory Theory, whereby if the mother chooses to increase the electrical pulses on the TENS machine during labor, it causes her body to release endorphins which work to relieve pain. For maximum benefit, it's best to use the TENS machine starting in early labor. The pads must be removed if the mother wants to immerse in water, but can be reapplied if/when she decides to get out of the water.

SUNLIGHT, SLEEP, AND SCREENS

Growing up in Australia with fair skin, I was constantly warned about the dangers of the sun, so from a young age, I was always covered in sunscreen, a hat, and long sleeves. It's only in recent years that I've learned more about how important sunlight is for our health. While getting sunburnt may increase your risk of skin cancer, there are huge benefits to regular exposure to the sun for a limited and safe amount of time, which will vary depending on your skin tone. Sunlight provides vitamin D, which supports our bones and muscles, helps regulate our blood pressure, immune system, and blood sugar levels, and keeps our brain working well. It also improves sleep quality by maintaining our body's internal clock (also known as circadian rhythm), as exposure to sunlight in the morning increases our melatonin levels.[41] Melatonin is not only important for sleep and regulating our circadian rhythms, but is also a really important hormone for birth as it can help boost oxytocin levels. Exposure to artificial blue light (from fluorescent lights or phone screens) in the hours before bed can suppress the body's release of melatonin, which can hinder sleep and can also impact labor. There are lots of demonstrations on YouTube on how to turn your phone screen red. And if you're heading to the hospital to give birth, wear blue blocking glasses (those orange ones that make you look like Bono), set up a few LED candles, and dim or turn the lights off as soon as you get into your room.

Since incorporating more time in the sun into my daily life, I've noticed that I sleep better and feel more relaxed. While I don't do these activities perfectly every day, here are a few of the things I'm working to incorporate daily to help my sunlight exposure and sleep:

- Walking outside first thing in the morning, grounding my feet on the earth and letting natural light hit my eyes before artificial light.
- Going for daily walks outdoors no matter the weather.
- Taking a ten-minute break in the middle of the day to go and lie down in the sun in my backyard with as much skin exposed as possible.
- After sunset, limiting screen use and turning all our lights orange or red (we have smart lights that change color, but you can also buy warmer light bulbs for lamps and not use overhead lights) to support melatonin production, and improve sleep quality.
- Have tech-free days with our kids where we get outside in nature, play board games, bake, or do chores around the house and garden together.

There is more and more evidence showing that our phones and social media have a significant negative impact on our health. Smartphones are leading to social deprivation, as we spend less and less time with our family and friends in person, sleep deprivation due to the blue light from screens, impaired focus as we are constantly interrupted, and addiction thanks to the dopamine rush from constant notifications. Thankfully, there are things we can do to improve our health when it comes to phone use. A study by the University of Pennsylvania found that reducing social media use to 30 minutes a day resulted in a reduction in anxiety, depression, loneliness, and sleep issues.[42]

There is currently a huge amount of talk around how damaging it is for our children and teenagers to be using smartphones and social media, and I would really recommend reading Jonathan Haidt's book, *The Anxious Generation*, to fully understand the impact technology is having, and what we can do about it. It's important to note that the damage isn't just from a child's direct use, but also from parent use. Evidence suggests that the more parents use their smartphones in front of their children, the lower the child's emotional intelligence.[43] Often, when we use our phones in front of our kids, our faces are totally blank. Children are constantly observing our facial expressions to understand emotional nuances and learn how to regulate their own emotions, and as a result of the high use of smartphones, they aren't able to do this as well. I understand that being a parent can be tiring, and many parents seek a break or some stimulation, particularly when they're spending all day alone with a baby. This section is not about making anyone feel bad for using technology, but more just to bring a level of awareness to the impact it is having on our children and us, so we can be more mindful about how and when we use our phones.

The answer doesn't have to be moving to the top of a mountain with no Wi-Fi. When you're newly postpartum, you might want to just be relaxing on the couch watching a movie, and the good news is, watching a movie together as a family is not associated with lowering emotional intelligence, and may even improve mental well-being. It is the highly interactive and alienating nature of smartphone use specifically that is so concerning. If social media and smartphone use are causing us to feel anxious and impacting our sleep, then it will also be impacting our hormones, which affect our baby, our pregnancy, birth, and postpartum. So, it's worth checking in with how you're feeling, and what impact you feel technology is having on you personally.

There can be benefits to social media, for instance, being able to connect with other moms in our private Christian Hypnobirthing Community on Facebook, where we see mamas praying for each other, answering each other's questions, and in some cases, even making friends and catching up in person. Another benefit is that we are able to share positive birth videos on our Instagram, so instead of only being able to see negative depictions of birth on TV and film, women can now be exposed to encouraging and faith-filled birth content. Despite some of the benefits, it may still be worth taking a break, setting a time limit for use on certain apps, or limiting screen time before bed and seeing whether it has any impact on your sleep and overall well-being.

Since I've turned off all my social media notifications and deleted certain apps, I've noticed a reduction in anxiety and an overall improvement in my mood. While I feel grateful for aspects of technology, I also feel a lot of concern about how it is affecting us. As babies breastfeed, those moments of love and connection through eye contact and gentle touch, which help increase oxytocin, bonding, and milk supply, are often being interrupted or missed completely, thanks to smartphones. We have been told that we can multi-task and do it all, but we actually can't. Evidence shows that multitasking increases stress levels and is associated with symptoms of depression and anxiety.[44] It also doesn't necessarily mean we're achieving more; in fact, we may be achieving less.

In Colossians 3:23, Paul writes, "Whatever you do, work at it with all your heart, as working for the Lord, not for men." There are obviously times when we need to be able to do multiple things at once, but what a gift to free ourselves from the mental burden of having to try to squeeze every ounce of productivity out of every moment and instead be present for what it is that we're doing, and work at it with all our heart. If that's being in a work meeting, listening wholeheartedly instead of simultaneously texting and answering emails; if it's breastfeeding, letting go of other tasks and getting lost in our baby's beautiful eyes; if it's watching a movie with our spouse, putting our phone away, holding their hand, and laughing together; and if it's eating a meal, turning the TV off and asking our kids what their favorite part of the day was.

I share these suggestions as one of the biggest multi-taskers around, who has tried to get every ounce of productivity from every second, and as a result, I feel like I've missed so many precious moments. I fully understand how difficult it is in the world we live in, but as I make the effort to be more mindful and present and give myself permission to do one thing at a time properly, I truly feel more satisfaction and joy each day. I also feel more connection to God. When I'm rushing, I don't notice the beautiful light pouring through the leaves in the trees as I walk our dog, or the smell of the fresh coffee my husband made for me first thing this morning, or how incredibly beautiful my son's eyes are as he gives me a kiss goodbye before school. But when I slow down, not only do I notice them, but I feel like I see God in all of them, too. I see how he's constantly working in and through everything, and is always inviting us into love and connection with him if we'd just take a moment to notice him. But first, we have to give ourselves permission to slow down and stop doing so much. To be still. *Rapha*. I let go. I release.

BIRTH ART AND JOURNALING

No matter what you think about your creative abilities, you can create art. You could do it as a child, and you can still do it now. It doesn't have to be pretty; it doesn't have to stay within lines. Creating birth art is a wonderful way to explore unconscious beliefs that we hold around pregnancy and birth, and can invite us to learn more about ourselves and our baby. When we are preparing for birth, a lot of the learning we do is intellectual, which is associated with the left brain, whereas during labor, when we enter labor land, the more intuitive and creative right brain takes over. So, creating art is a beautiful way to explore that side of the brain and can help us prepare for birth in ways that intellectual learning can't. There are birth art classes (like *Birthing from Within*) in some areas, and if it's something you're interested in, you may want to seek one out. However, it can be as simple as gathering together some paper and pens, paint, or chalk pastels and allowing yourself some space and time to get creative.

Take a few moments to close your eyes and ask yourself a question like, *What does birth mean to me?* or *What does pregnancy mean to me?* Then just start drawing or painting. It doesn't have to make sense intellectually. It could literally be a dot on a page. Don't judge, just start. Keep going and see where it takes you. When you feel that it's complete, take a few moments to pause, look at what you've created, and notice how you feel. What does this piece of art say to you? How did you feel while you were making it? Was there anything that surprised you? It doesn't have to be positive or negative; just let it be whatever it is.

You may also want to do some journaling to further process any feelings that came up for you. Allow yourself to write with complete freedom. Just start writing, and don't judge what you write. Do your best to write fast, in a state of flow, literally anything that comes to mind, without editing it or trying to make it make sense. Art and journaling can be an amazing way to reach the unconscious mind, and with that information, we give ourselves the opportunity to see how we can better support ourselves. Is there a part of me that needs more nurturing? Is there a fear that I need to research further to help build my confidence? Are there new questions for my midwife or care provider? It will be different for everyone, as we are all unique, and even if you don't have any profound realizations, it can still be a really fun exercise to allow yourself to do something different and explore your own creativity. It can also be a wonderful exercise for your birth partner to do as well.

ICE ICE BABY

Once you've practiced the up breathing regularly, and you're starting to feel confident that you have it down pat, using ice can be a really great way to test your skills! For the sake of seeing the difference relaxation can make, you can try this exercise in two different ways. The first time, hold an ice cube in your hand, set a timer for one minute, and focus on the feeling in your hand. How cold is it—uncomfortable, or difficult? Once the minute is up, give yourself a minute break. Set the timer for another minute, and this time, just focus on your breath. Breathe in for four and out for seven. Keep your focus soft and relaxed. If you want, you can also bring to mind any affirmations that resonate with you, maybe something like "I can do anything for 60 seconds," and just keep focusing on your breath. Once the minute is up, notice how that felt compared to when you focused on the discomfort. Was there a difference? If you want to make the exercise more challenging, you can add more ice cubes.

Another way to test your relaxation skills is to go somewhere busy, like a mall cafeteria, put your headphones in, and practice the hypnobirthing exercises there. Being able to focus on your breath in all kinds of environments isn't just great training for birth, but also for motherhood. When trying to settle a colicky baby, or stay calm as your toddler throws a tantrum on the shopping center floor, or your teenager slams the door while shouting that you never loved them, your breath is always available to help you find that place of peace within, no matter what the outside circumstances. And when we can be that place of calm for ourselves, then we can be it for our children, too.

B.R.A.I.N.

It is surprising how often suggestions are made to women throughout pregnancy without a full breakdown of the risks and benefits of those suggestions. The BRAIN acronym is a useful tool taught by many childbirth educators worldwide to help you gather information that can support you in making an informed choice.

Please feel free to note down the following acronym and what it stands for, and bring it with you to appointments to help remind you of useful questions to ask:

B. Benefits – What are the benefits of this decision?
R. Risks – What are the risks involved?
A. Alternatives – Are there any alternatives?
I. Intuition – What is my intuition telling me?
N. Nothing – What if we do nothing (or wait it out)?

You can ask these questions in whatever order feels right for you, and they can be adapted to suit your needs in the specific situation. For instance, you may want to start with "What if we do nothing?" to know how much time you have to make decisions. Or you may want to hear the risks before you hear the benefits. You can ask your provider about their views on the risks, benefits, and alternatives, but then, if you have time, you may also want to do some more independent research, or even get a second opinion, as all providers will have their own biases based on their unique experiences and perspective. Often, just the process of asking questions can open up conversations that mean suddenly you're presented with alternatives that wouldn't have been presented otherwise. That's why it's so important to ask questions instead of just accepting what's offered, particularly if it doesn't sit right with you.

Make sure your birth partner is also aware of these questions so they can support you in asking them if necessary. Unless something is a genuine emergency, there's often time for you to think about things. Before making important decisions, it can be helpful to sleep on it and make sure you're in a positive headspace before you decide. We don't tend to make the best choices when we feel stressed, scared, or rushed into something. So as long as there's time, go home and have a nice relaxing bath or shower, eat a nourishing meal, watch your favorite comedy sitcom, and go to bed early. Then, in the morning, when you feel rested and refreshed, do a breathing exercise, get connected to what you feel grateful for, and then come back to the decision. Pray together, and reflect on what you intuitively feel is right for you and your baby.

If you're struggling to tap into your intuition, feel free to try this little intuition exercise. It's very simple, but it helps you to identify what feels true for you. Put your hands on your heart, breathe, then say the words "I am" and then a name that's not yours. After that, try saying the words "I am" and then your real name. Notice how it feels in your body when you say something that isn't true versus how it feels when you say what is true. Now you have that feeling of what feels true you can use that as you approach these decisions. If you're comfortable praying, then ask God for help and guidance in this decision, then put your hands on your heart again, breathe deeply, and say the different options. Notice how you feel in your body. What intuitively feels true or right?

When I was first taught about the B.R.A.I.N. acronym, the instructor added "S" onto the end for Smile, as it releases oxytocin. So, she wrote it as B.R.A.I.N.S. Most childbirth educators don't add this as it can be a bit patronizing, particularly if someone is facing a really difficult decision. Nevertheless, I often think about her saying, "Smile, it releases oxytocin," and then I smile, and I do feel like it

Faith-Filled Childbirth

makes me feel happier. So even though I'm not officially adding it to the acronym, feel free to add it if you want to.

The tools I've shared in this section are ones I use, as do thousands of our app users and course members. They make a genuine difference in helping you experience a more confident, relaxed, and faith-filled birth (and life). Taking care of ourselves, being kind to ourselves, and nourishing our bodies and hearts extends beyond us and into future generations. This is deep and important work. I pray that these tools help you throughout your pregnancy, birth, and forevermore. In the coming chapters, as I discuss some of the more difficult subject matter around interventions, please feel free to come back to these tools at any time. One thing I try to keep in mind is that I don't have to do things perfectly; all I have to do is *try*. In fact, I often say that as an affirmation when I'm doing something that feels difficult: "Just try, just try."

To help make sure you practice regularly, habit stacking (where you pair a habit you're trying to start with a habit you already do every day) can help it become automatic. For instance, listening to the tracks on the app every time you take a nap, bathe, or as you're falling asleep each night. Practicing the down breathing every time you have a bowel movement. Thinking of three things you're grateful for as you drink your tea each morning. Taking a look at your affirmation cards as you brush your teeth. Listening to positive birth podcasts while you walk your dog. Make a list of a few of your favorite tools in this section and a few habits you already do daily that you could stack them with.

An effective way of ensuring you follow through on a new commitment is to make a promise. So if you're happy to, make a promise to yourself and to your baby about the specific things you're going to do to help prepare for a faith-filled birth and when and how often you're going to do them. Something like, "I promise myself, and you baby, that I will practice up breathing for one minute when I get into bed each night." I really recommend writing this promise down on a piece of paper and putting it somewhere you can see it. When you do this, you significantly increase the chance of following through on this commitment because you're the kind of person who keeps your promises. The reason this is so important is because understanding these concepts intellectually won't make that much of a difference to your birth experience; it is the *execution* of these tools, putting them into action, and practicing them regularly that will make the difference. So to stack the odds in your favor of following through and using these tools, decide which habits you can stack together, write down the specifics of when and how you'll do them, and make a promise that you'll follow through.

– BIRTH STORY –

DAWN'S FAITH-FILLED VBAC

(This is a transcript from Dawn's incredible birth and testimonial video, which really has to be watched via the QR code below to understand just how amazing and redemptive this birth experience was for her).

Dawn's Faith-Filled VBAC

SCAN THE QR CODE:

My first was born via C-section. I was induced at 40 weeks and 5 days because my OB was concerned that my belly was measuring big and he was afraid of meconium aspiration or stillbirth going overdue (which here in the United States is 40 weeks). I'm from Columbus, Ohio. I wasn't able to tolerate the strong contractions from the Pitocin, so I ended up getting an epidural that really limited my ability to push. And I pushed for four hours and wasn't able to push her out.

With my second, I knew that I wanted to do an all-natural VBAC. So I switched OB providers. I hired a doula. I went to chiropractic care. I went to a pelvic floor PT. I was eating healthy, I was walking every day, and I also wanted to take a hypnobirthing class, but I wanted it to be faith-based because I'm a Christian. So I just Google searched "Christian Hypnobirthing" and came across the Christian Hypnobirthing course and the app and tracks. I bought the course, downloaded the app, and I started listening to the tracks nightly just to fill my mind with positivity, to kind of combat the trauma from my last birth, and just make this pregnancy as positive as possible.

Around 25 weeks, I started getting really anxious, and I feared that I was going to end up in another C-section, so on my walks, I would just pray to God every day and ask him, "What can I do, Lord? What should I do?" and every day I just felt him saying, "Home birth." I didn't want to believe it because I'm a medical professional. I do anesthesia for a living, so my job is to make sure people don't have pain. So the thought of having an all-natural birth was kind of crazy in the anesthesia world. But I really felt like the epidural just hindered me from pushing. And I didn't want that again. So then having a home birth was like way out of the norm. People in the medical profession don't do that because we know all the risks and scary things that can happen, but I just felt like the Lord was telling me to do it.

I didn't want to believe him, thought the devil was speaking to me, but again and again, he said, "Home birth." So finally, I surrendered, and I said, "Okay, home birth it is." And I just continued to listen to the Christian Hypnobirthing tracks every single night and some of the ones that really stood out to me and just had a really big influence on me were "All Things Are Possible With God." "I have been perfectly designed by God to do this." "Each wave brings me closer to our baby." "I trust in the Lord. I know that he is with me during this birth and always." "My body has been perfectly designed by God and knows how to give birth." That one really stood out to me because I felt that my body was inadequate for birth... And the other one was, "Our baby has been designed by our Father and knows how to be born," which is another cool thing I didn't think about. It is just always like the mom having to push the baby out, but also the baby has to work their way down, and they have a part in this too. And the last one that really helped me through the pushing phase was "I have unlimited strength that comes from God."

So I ended up switching to midwife care. I had an amazing midwife, Amy, an amazing doula, Jen, and a great birth photographer, Colleen. My best friend (who is also a CRNA), Sam, was there, and I really felt the Lord's presence and that he was with me. And I just want to say thank you for the Christian Hypnobirthing course and all of the positive tracks that played a big part in me having my HBAC. Thanks.

4

Where Should I Give Birth?

"Behold, I am with you and will keep you wherever you go."
– Genesis 28:15

The birth that you experience is heavily influenced by how you feel and your environment. To help optimize our hormones for birth, it's crucial that we feel completely safe, so that our body can fully relax. So, for a lot of people, feeling safe will automatically mean the hospital, which is completely understandable. At first glance, the hospital always seems to be the safest place because that's what we've always been told. It may surprise you to learn that for women who have healthy, normal pregnancies giving birth with a qualified and experienced midwife and the option to transfer to a hospital if needed, there have been multiple studies showing home birth can be just as safe as hospital birth, and often results in fewer interventions.[88] In the following sections, I'll look at some of the benefits and risks of the different birth locations. Because every pregnancy and birth is totally unique, I have no opinion on where you personally should give birth, and I recommend that you seek out advice from a medical professional for your specific needs. The hospital may indeed be the safest place for you. This is offered as general information to help you better understand the impact that environment can have on birth.

HOME BIRTH

A study of births in Victoria (Australia) by the Consultative Council for Obstetric and Pediatric Mortality and Morbidity found that "In women with normal pregnancies, there were no differences in the rates of perinatal death between those who planned a home birth and hospital birth." The evidence also showed that for healthy women with a healthy pregnancy, home birth was associated with lower rates of unplanned cesarean section, epidural, and episiotomy, and higher rates of spontaneous vaginal birth than similar women who gave birth in the hospital.[8] High-quality research on planned home births worldwide with studies from The Netherlands,[9] the UK,[10] and North America[11] all support the safety of home birth for healthy normal pregnancies as comparable to hospital birth, and also show fewer medical interventions than for women with similar risk factors in a hospital setting.

In 2019, there was a large systematic review and meta-analysis published in *The Lancet*.[11] It looked at 14 studies, including data from around half a million intended home births. The authors found that "The risk of perinatal or neonatal mortality was not different when birth was intended at home or in the hospital." This research is significant because of the scale of this study, but is also reflected in the many smaller studies mentioned above. So, to put it plainly, if you have a healthy normal pregnancy, this data suggests that you're just as safe giving birth at home with a qualified midwife and the option to transfer to hospital if needed, as you would be in the hospital, and you're also less likely to experience medical intervention.

Now studies are important, but they're really just showing us numbers. On paper, a woman may have had a birth classed as safe in the hospital because both she and her baby are alive, but that doesn't tell us anything about the actual birth experience. Numbers don't show us how a mother was treated in her prenatal appointments, how much time or support she was given, or whether her questions were answered. They don't tell us how supported she felt during labor, or whether she was given enough information to make fully informed choices. They also don't tell us whether she felt pushed into unnecessary interventions.

Most people feel relaxed in their homes because it's their safe place. Again, please forgive this comparison, but when considering where to give birth, it might be a good idea to think about how comfortable you are having a bowel movement outside of your home. Many people won't feel the need to go to the toilet the whole day, but the instant they get home, they need to go because their body finally feels able to relax. Some years ago, I went on a holiday with a friend, and we stayed in a small apartment with one bathroom that had no windows. My friend felt so self-conscious about going to the bathroom that she literally couldn't do a bowel movement for a whole week. That is not an exaggeration. She was genuinely starting to feel unwell. I told her I was going out for a few hours, as I felt she needed some proper privacy if she was ever going to go. And thankfully, that did the trick. The reason I use this comparison is because, just like with having a bowel movement, when we give birth, we are expelling something from our body (in this case, a baby), and feeling a high enough level of privacy and safety will help our body to relax and release.

Mothers are often surprised by the fact that contractions may become more uncomfortable, slow down, or even completely stop when they get in the car and go to the hospital. But our bodies are not machines. Even though logically, we know that we're getting in the car to go to the hospital to have our baby, that's not how our limbic system works. The limbic system is the part of our brain that's involved in our emotional and behavioral responses, especially those behaviors needed for survival. As I talked about earlier in the book, that is our fight-or-flight response versus our rest-and-digest response. We cannot just logic ourselves out of these responses. Just as my friend didn't feel relaxed enough to go to the bathroom in a space that didn't feel private, if we do not feel relaxed and safe, our body will do what it can to preserve both our life and our baby's life by slowing down labor and giving us time to get away from this perceived threat.

So, if you have a healthy, normal pregnancy, this is something to take into consideration when deciding on where to give birth. The benefit of giving birth at home is that you get to be in your own environment, feel more relaxed and comfortable, have more privacy, and you will have a much higher chance of continuity of care (as you'll likely see the same midwife multiple times throughout your pregnancy). This means you'll probably feel more supported and comfortable with your care provider, and you'll have a higher chance of a vaginal birth, a lower chance of intervention, and a higher chance of breastfeeding. You can also choose when you want to eat or drink during labor, take baths or showers whenever you want, and create your birth space exactly as you want it to be with the use of fairy lights, affirmation cards, or aromatherapy. One of the things women often say to me that they loved about having a home birth was that afterward, the midwives cleaned everything up, got them all comfortable, and tucked them into bed before leaving. No sitting for hours in a sterile environment waiting to be discharged. The immediate comfort of home.

What are the downsides? There are certain factors that will make it safer to be in the hospital, like type 1 diabetes, preeclampsia, or other health conditions or factors. There's also a chance of needing to transfer to the hospital, particularly for first-time moms. According to the Birthplace Study[10] (done in the UK), while the risk of an adverse outcome was actually lower in a home birth setting for second (or subsequent) babies of mothers with healthy normal pregnancies, for first-time moms, the risk increased very slightly from five in 1,000 in an obstetric unit, to nine in 1,000 within the home birth setting, but the risk of intervention for first-time mothers was still lowest at home. It also showed that around 45 percent of first-time moms intending to give birth at home transferred to the hospital, versus around 10 percent of moms giving birth for the second (or subsequent) time. It's important to note that most transfers are not emergencies. The most common reasons for transfer include wanting an epidural, not dilating as quickly as anticipated, exhaustion, meconium in the baby's waters, or other signs that it could be beneficial for the baby to have continuous monitoring. I think it's so important to know that all those reasons are completely valid for transferring. In fact, just wanting to go to the hospital because you feel that's where you'd like to be, is a completely valid reason to transfer, and I hope that any mother reading this book will feel empowered in making that decision to transfer if necessary.

As I've said previously, words are so important, so instead of using the term "failed home birth," I would say "successful home birth transfer." Finding providers who will support you in this attitude is so beneficial. Some hospitals and obstetricians are very happy to partner with home birth midwives, supporting them if a transfer is needed, which can make a massive difference to how the mother feels during that process. For some women, arriving at the hospital to be met with snide comments about home birth from staff members can be very upsetting, so if you are having a home birth, it's worth taking this into consideration and seeing if your midwife has a hospital/obstetrician that she has a good relationship with when it comes to transferring.

Another thing to consider when deciding where to give birth is that it's much easier to change your mind from a home birth to a hospital birth than it is to change your mind from a hospital birth to a home birth. If you've planned a home birth and then at the last minute decide that you'd actually rather give birth in the hospital, it's usually quite an easy process to just decide to go to the hospital. Whereas if you are planning a hospital birth and when you get to hospital you decide you'd rather be at home, the odds of being able to arrange a home birth midwife at the last minute are probably quite low, and you'd also miss out on the benefit of that continued supportive relationship with your midwife in the months leading up to birth, which has been shown to reduce intervention, increase the likelihood of spontaneous labor, and tends to lead to greater confidence and better outcomes for moms and babies. Not to mention it's quite nice to be cared for by someone you like and have a good relationship with during birth.

Where to give birth can be quite a tricky question to navigate, especially if you decide to give birth at home and have to deal with comments like "That's risky" or "You're brave." One of the most common things people say is, "Well, I'd rather be in the hospital just in case something goes wrong." While, obviously, we would all rather be in the hospital if something were to go wrong, that statement doesn't give the full picture. If we look at those studies mentioned and the fact that women with healthy normal pregnancies are more likely to experience a forceps, vacuum, or cesarean birth just by being in the hospital (no other increased risk factors), then it begs the question, "What if it went wrong *because* I was in the hospital?"

Wherever you choose to give birth, overall, the findings from the Birthplace Study[10] show that for women with healthy, normal pregnancies, adverse perinatal outcomes were low (4.3 events per 1000 births) and that giving birth is generally very safe. Which is so important to remember.

BIRTH CENTERS

Something to consider if a home birth isn't for you is whether you would like to give birth in a birth center/midwife-led unit. Birth centers can be freestanding or attached to a hospital. They are midwife-led and normally set up in a way that is designed to support physiological birth with low lighting, birth pools, comfortable beds, and a calm, peaceful environment. A birth center may feel like a nice middle ground between a hospital and a home birth, particularly for first-time mothers with healthy, normal pregnancies who would have liked to be at home but didn't feel comfortable with the very small increase in risk. Or it might be suitable for parents who live a long way from the hospital and would like the benefits of a relaxed environment while knowing that they're closer to the hospital if a transfer is necessary.

What's available in a birth center and the care you will receive is likely very similar to what you would have received in a home birth setting with midwives who will likely have similar equipment and training. There are also similar limitations in that they will not be able to provide epidurals (which require an anesthetist) or cesareans, so a transfer to the hospital would be necessary in those cases. The Birthplace Study[10] showed that for a second-time mom with a healthy, normal pregnancy, giving birth in a midwife-led unit/birthing center substantially reduced the odds of having a cesarean, instrumental delivery, or episiotomy.

One of the really big benefits of birthing in a birth center (like home birth with a midwife) is you have a much higher chance of continuity of care. Whereas when a woman is being cared for by a stranger or someone she doesn't feel particularly comfortable with, she is less likely to feel safe and relaxed, which can impact her labor.

The downside of giving birth in a birth center is that there's a small chance it could be full (as the birth centers were in both of my sons' births), but if you're going to a private birth center, this may not be the case, so be sure to ask. There also may be a limited number of birth pools, which you may want to consider if a water birth is important to you (giving birth at home with your own birth pool is the only way to guarantee access to one). There's also the inconvenience of having to travel to the birth center during labor and having to travel home afterward. In most cases, the mom and the baby can go home four to six hours after birth, but if you want to stay the night, you may need to transfer to a hospital maternity ward.

On the whole, if you have a healthy, normal pregnancy, then

giving birth in a birth center or midwife-led unit reduces your risk of intervention and increases the likelihood of good outcomes for babies and moms when compared to a hospital birth.[10]

HOSPITAL BIRTH

For mamas who have a medical condition (or develop one in pregnancy, such as pre-eclampsia), a breech baby or twins, go into labor before 37 weeks, have a low-lying placenta, their baby's growth is restricted, have bled throughout pregnancy, have extreme anemia, or whose waters break and are stained with meconium, the recommendation will generally be that hospital is the safest place to be. If you are unsure whether the hospital is the safest place for you to give birth, I'd recommend doing a quick search on Evidence Based Birth, or the NICE guidelines on your specific factors.

For some, it may still be possible to have a home birth (with breech or multiples), but it really depends on whether there are licensed and skilled providers in your area. Many people assume that breech birth is dangerous because the standard response to breech positioning tends to be an automatic C-section; however, breech vaginal birth can be a safe option for many women. What makes it dangerous is the lack of providers who are trained with the skills to assist a breech delivery. The laws also differ for different countries and states as to what providers are allowed to assist with, so if vaginal birth is important to you, be sure to research whether there are certified providers with those skills and qualifications in your area.

I don't really like the term "high risk," as I think having that label can add an unnecessary level of stress and potentially lead to a *nocebo effect*, as described by Dr. Michel Odent, which is essentially the opposite of a placebo effect. It is the impact of the belief in a negative outcome. So, if a mother feels her baby could be at risk (even if that risk is very small), the level of worry that it causes may be more harmful than the original risk factor. For this reason, no matter what labels you are given by any care provider, it is so important to protect and continue to build your faith-filled birth mindset. This doesn't necessarily mean everyone around you must change their language, but instead, having a deep inner knowing of how God sees you and your baby. You may even want to create a word or phrase that you think of whenever a label is mentioned that reminds you of how loved and precious you and your baby are to God. That way, someone mentioning a high-risk label becomes a lovely reminder to relax and draw near to God.

While I may not like the term high risk, it's important to acknowledge there are certain factors that make the hospital the safest place to be and that we can be so grateful for the specialized care of obstetricians where it is necessary. For the mamas who may feel disappointed if they've been risked out of midwife-led care, I want to provide some gentle reassurance that it's still possible to have a wonderful, faith-filled birth in the hospital (I have experienced it myself) and there are multiple things I will share to help give you the best chance of experiencing that too.

Also, for the moms with healthy, normal pregnancies who want to have a hospital birth just because that's where they feel to be, I want to encourage you to feel empowered in making that decision. It is so important that you choose the place that is right for you and your baby, and that will be different for everyone. Some women would be so fearful of giving birth at home that the downsides of the fear then outweigh the benefits of being at home or at a birth center. If, after looking at the evidence and understanding the risks and benefits of the different places to give birth, you feel the hospital is the right place for you to be, then it most likely is.

When selecting the hospital you want to give birth in, you may want to check if birth pools are available if you want a water birth. Even if birth pools aren't available, many rooms in hospital labor wards now have baths or showers. So even if you can't give birth in the water, it's often still possible to use warm water as a comfort measure.

One of the downsides of giving birth in the hospital is that as soon as you get in the car to leave for the hospital, your hormones will be impacted, as you will likely feel nervous or excited about going. For this reason, you may want to listen to the tracks from the Christian Hypnobirthing app as you drive to the hospital to help keep you calm and relaxed. Getting to the hospital before 4cm dilation has been shown to increase the risk of intervention,[13] so to give yourself the best chance of a physiological birth, if you can (and it's safe to do so), stay at home until you're in established labor. Many midwives and doulas recommend the 411 Rule, which means that you would go to the hospital when your contractions are regularly coming four minutes apart, each one lasting for at least one minute, and that they've been following this pattern for about an hour. It's good to remember that this is a general rule and will differ for everyone based on how far you are from the hospital.

When it comes to influencing our hormones for birth, it's great to think about the ***five senses***: ***sight***, ***smell***, ***sound***, ***touch***, **and** ***taste***. Obviously, there's a lot in the hospital that is beyond our control in terms of these senses, but there's also a lot we can do to influence them. Wearing blue-blocking glasses as you walk into the hospital can help to minimize the effects of the fluorescent strip lights (which some studies have suggested can increase anxiety and may impact hormones like melatonin).[14]

The hospital may say that you have to have a vaginal examination to establish whether you're in active labor, so you can be admitted. While it may be hospital policy, they must have your consent to perform one, and whether you consent or not is totally up to you. This may be a sensitive subject for some women, particularly those who have experienced sexual trauma, and if that is the case for you, I'd really recommend speaking to a doula, midwife, or other specialist about this, and also your birth partner so they know how you feel and can advocate for you. If you do consent to having one, you may want to practice the breathing exercise from the Christian Hypnobirthing app while it is being performed, to help you to relax. This made a huge difference to my experience in my second birth, and it was so much more comfortable than my first birth.

Once admitted and into your room, I would go back to thinking about the senses. I like to think about old-school churches or cathe-

Faith-Filled Childbirth

drals where they swing incense, have candles burning, and the sound of Gregorian chants drift over you. They're creating an environment that helps you feel the Holy Spirit. And you can do this with your birth space (maybe minus the Gregorian chant). So, starting with *sight*, as soon as you get in the room, turn the overhead lights off (as dark or dim lighting can help with feelings of privacy and increase melatonin). You may want to bring some LED candles or fairy lights. Although, try to go for more dim/warmly lit options if possible, as bright white lights may again be disruptive to hormones. You may also want to put up some positive affirmation cards (we have printable affirmation cards in the store section of the app) or a photo of loved ones. Some kind of positive visual reminder to help you feel focused and happy. Maybe write down your favorite scripture on a Post-it note.

When thinking about *smell*, the smell of antibacterial cleaning products in hospitals probably isn't going to help you feel super relaxed, so using aromatherapy can be really beneficial. We brought a diffuser into the hospital with us and used frankincense oil, which was lovely. Otherwise, you could use an essential oil roller, misting spray, or even just put some on a tissue that you hold under your nose. In one study, using mandarin essential oil in combination with four other essential oils (Clary sage, Roman chamomile, lavender, and frankincense) has been shown to significantly decrease labor pain and anxiety.[15] Clary sage should not be used before 37 weeks as it could potentially induce labor, and should also not be used if you are having a VBAC or have had previous uterine surgery. If in doubt, check first with your care provider.

Sound is another helpful tool in aiding relaxation in the hospital, so think ahead about what you'd like to listen to and bring a listening device. You may want to have the Christian Hypnobirthing tracks playing or worship music, or you may prefer silence—just go with what feels right to you. *Touch* could come from your birth partner doing a light massage if that feels good, a birth comb or tens machine or from the warm water of the shower or bath. For *taste*, it can be really nice to bring your favorite chocolates as a special treat (it's a celebration!), as well as healthy snacks and drinks that will help you to feel energized and hydrated throughout labor. In some hospitals, it is against hospital policy to allow a laboring woman to eat or drink. This is not evidence-based[89] and is based on outdated nothing-by-mouth policies from the mid-1900s, when anesthesia methods were crude and unsafe, in an attempt to prevent aspiration with general anesthesia. Since then, the safety of anesthesia has improved greatly, and hospital policies should be rewritten to be in line with current evidence. Giving your body the nourishment it needs should be a human right. That said, you may not feel hungry in labor, in which case you can listen to your body, and only eat if you feel like it.

Once admitted, many hospitals will want to do further vaginal examinations to chart progress against the traditional standard of cervical dilation (based on Friedman's curve), which is 1cm per hour. If dilation is slower than that, there may be pressure to augment (speed up) labor. One of the issues with this standard is that cervical dilation time can vary dramatically from individual to individual, which is normally understood and respected by independent midwives, or midwives in birth centers, but seems less understood by a lot of hospital staff. Whether this is because of a lack of beds, understaffing, or financial reasons, I can't say, but it is my own lived experience that there can be an enormous amount of pressure to move things along, and if that causes you stress, then your body may want to do the opposite.

If you're giving birth in the hospital, make sure your birth partner is fully aware of your wishes for your birth and can advocate for you. I highly recommend they read this book or do an antenatal education course with you if possible. Also be sure to have written birth preferences (multiple copies) to give to the hospital staff, and also consider hiring a doula.

My final comment on giving birth in a hospital is that you can have a faith-filled birth experience, but it will likely take more preparation and advocacy than giving birth at home or in a birth center. There is a short film called *The Performance* on YouTube created by @FreedomForBirthRAG, based on what it would be like if making love was interfered with in the same way birth is in most hospitals. And it's a really good comparison to make, as oxytocin (often referred to as the love hormone) is pivotal in both orgasm and birth. Environment and feeling safe is key to the release of oxytocin. If we think of the environment we normally want to make love in, it's probably fairly dark and private. Would we want to make love in a brightly lit room, with our feet up in stirrups, with people putting monitors on us, and charting our progress? Probably not.

For this reason, be sure to practice the tools from the Faith-Filled Toolbox regularly in the lead-up to birth. Listen to at least one track on the Christian Hypnobirthing app a few times a week from 30 weeks and every day from 36 weeks. Once you feel that you've trained your mind and body to relax, test yourself by going somewhere busy (maybe a brightly lit/busy shopping center), putting on your headphones, and practicing the breathing and visualization exercises. Once you've finished this book, write down your birth preferences (we have a template in the "Extra Resources" section at the end of the book) and discuss them in detail with your birth partner. Watch positive birth videos and practice light touch massage with your birth partner. And train your brain to find the joy, the fun, and the laughter, even in stressful situations. One of the greatest gifts to me in my last hospital birth was laughing at silly things with my husband between contractions in early labor. If you feel stressed after antenatal appointments, put on your favorite comedy series, listen to worship music, listen to the Christian Hypnobirthing app, get a pregnancy massage, and read your favorite scriptures. And more than anything, know that wherever you give birth, God will be with you and that all things are possible with him (Matthew 19:26), including a wonderful, faith-filled hospital birth.

UNPLANNED UNASSISTED BIRTH

Over the years, a few of our Christian Hypnobirthing mamas have had unplanned, unassisted births at home because they were so relaxed they didn't realize they were in active labor. Thankfully, all the mothers and babies were totally fine (in fact, most of the mothers were quite excited about it). Their midwife (or the ambulance) arrived soon afterward, and all was well. Here are some suggestions for what to do in those instances.

In the case that your baby was to come earlier than expected (for instance, before the midwife was able to arrive or before getting in the car to go to the hospital), it's good to know that most healthy babies can pretty much deliver themselves. It's really important for mom and birth partner to stay calm. Call the ambulance and/or midwife and unlatch the door so they can let themselves in. If it's winter, be sure to boost the heating and grab some blankets, as it's important for the mom and baby to stay warm after birth. The birth partner should encourage the mother to breathe slowly and deeply as her body pushes the baby out. As the baby's head emerges, the birth partner (or mom) can hold their hands just under the baby's head (do not pull on the baby's head). As the baby's body emerges, the birth partner can support and hold the baby with their hands and offer mom words of reassurance. If the umbilical cord is around the baby's neck, ease it over their head slowly or loosen it enough to form a loop so the rest of their body can slip through.

Once fully emerged, place the baby on Mom's chest for immediate skin-to-skin contact (which will help to regulate the baby's temperature) and cover the mom and baby with blankets to keep them warm. Do not tie or attempt to cut the cord, as the cord will continue to give baby blood and oxygen as it pulsates over the next few minutes. Some babies can be a little blue at first, but most healthy babies will "pink up" fairly quickly after birth. If the baby seems a bit stunned from their swift entrance, simply rub the baby's back, or tap the soles of the baby's feet. If the towels or blankets become wet, replace them with fresh ones. If the mom then births the placenta, it can be placed next to her. Having skin-to-skin contact and breastfeeding after the placenta comes out can help Mom's uterus continue to contract, which can help control bleeding. If the baby doesn't nurse right away, manually stimulating Mom's nipples can help release oxytocin. Keep Mom and the baby warm, take some deep breaths, and do your best to stay calm and relaxed as you wait for the midwife and/or paramedics to arrive.

CAR BIRTH

For those who don't make it to the birth center or hospital, calmly put your hazard lights on, pull over, and call the ambulance. It's important for Mom and the baby to be warm after birth, so turn the heat up in the car. Help Mom take off her pants/underwear. Stay calm and offer Mom words of reassurance, encourage her to breathe slowly and deeply as her body pushes the baby out. As the baby's head emerges (do not pull on the baby's head), gently place your hands ready to catch the baby, then place the baby on Mom's chest for skin-to-skin contact and cover them with a blanket/towel or clothes you have available in the car (you may want to store a few blankets/towels in the car for this reason). As above, leave the cord intact so the baby can continue to receive blood and oxygen from it, and if the baby is a bit stunned, then rub their back and/or tap the soles of their feet. Having skin-to-skin contact and breastfeeding after the placenta comes out can help Mom's uterus continue to contract, which can help control bleeding. If the baby doesn't nurse right away, manually stimulating Mom's nipples can help release oxytocin. Do your best to stay calm and warm as you wait for the paramedics to arrive.

SUMMARY

Everyone will have their own bias when it comes to giving birth and the choices around it (including me) based on their experiences, research, and intuition. Once you have weighed the risks and benefits, and feel you're able to make an informed decision, I recommend spending some time in prayer about it and seeking where God is leading you. While we can never eliminate all risk, keeping risk in perspective can help you to feel more relaxed throughout your pregnancy as you approach your birth, which we know generates feel-good hormones, which are good for us and our baby.

Many people would love to swim in the ocean but they don't because of the fear of sharks, so they sit on the shore making sand castles instead. You'll probably be surprised to learn that there is a higher risk of being killed by a sandcastle than by a shark. Sounds crazy, but it's true. More people are killed falling down holes and tunnels under sandcastles, than by sharks.[93] Yet no one fears sandcastles. Isn't that an incredibly sad thought, that someone who longs to swim in the sea would spend a lifetime on the shore out of fear?

I was shocked recently when I read that the odds of dying in a car crash are one in 93![12] That means the likelihood of dying in a car crash is around ten times higher than the likelihood of our birth having an adverse outcome, but most of us will jump in our cars and drive to work every day without a second thought about safety. We just trust that fellow commuters driving at high speeds toward us will stay on their side of the road, despite the only thing separating us being a tiny white line. However, when it comes to labor, we seem to have so little trust that we can birth our babies, even though our bodies have been miraculously and wonderfully designed to do it.

One of the reasons I feel we so confidently drive our cars without fear each day is because of two things: the illusion of control, and practice. We think we're in control of the vehicle, which means we think we must be safe, but of course the reality is there are thousands of factors beyond our control. We also practice every single day, multiple times a day, which significantly increases our confidence. The reason I believe we fear birth so much is because of the opposite: we feel we have no control, and we don't believe there's a way to practice. But that's not necessarily true. Yes, there are lots of things beyond our control, but there are also lots of things within our control. We can control whether we choose to educate ourselves, eat nourishing foods, move regularly, practice relaxation daily, the location of our birth, who to have as our care provider, and many, many other things to set ourselves up for the best birth possible. And when it comes to practice, while we can't literally give birth every day, we can vividly rehearse our birth every day in our minds through visualization, building our mental confidence and strength, which has been shown to have positive results on physical performance. Wherever you choose to give birth, once you've made the decision, I encourage you to embrace it and choose to focus on making it the most positive, faith-filled experience it can be.

– BIRTH STORY –

KATIE'S FAITH-FILLED INDUCTION

Let me start by saying it doesn't matter how a woman brings a child into this world. Every form is beautiful in its own way. Ten years ago, it was questionable if I would ever be able to have children due to countless x-rays, MRIs, and just the trauma overall to my body due to scoliosis. I had six back surgeries, and my spine is fused all the way down. My orthopedic surgeon told me that whenever I decide to have kids, to be completely ready, it would not be easy and that an epidural wouldn't be an option. For years, the thought of kids scared me because I didn't think it was possible for me, and I thought if it did happen, it would be a miserable experience - but then God. God always makes something so beautiful out of our trials. My entire journey with scoliosis, I have held on to Matthew 19:26, "Jesus looked at them and said, with man this is impossible, but with God all things are possible." At the young age of 15, this scripture spoke to me through the pain, tears, scars and fear. Ten years later, this scripture got me through birthing my child. I was induced at 8 p.m. with Cytotec, used before Pitocin. Not dilated at this point. They were planning on giving me Pitocin the next morning, but God had a better plan. My water broke at 12 that night. I then quickly dilated to a four, and by 2 a.m. I was at a ten and ready to push. Audrey made her arrival at 2:30 a.m.

During my labor, I spent a lot of time in God's presence. I prayed and spoke the affirmations that Christian Hypnobirthing taught me. It goes down as the closest I have ever felt to Jesus. I can't help but think God intervened and blessed me with a short labor, knowing I wouldn't receive an epidural. He gave me power, he gave me confidence, he gave me peace. Looking back on Audrey's birth, it was everything that the doctor 10 years ago said it wouldn't be. It was beautiful. It was powerful. It was magical. Jesus has used one of the hardest things I have ever been through (scoliosis), and turned it into so many different testimonies. Thank you, Christian Hypnobirthing, for guiding me and teaching me how to navigate through my birth in the most spiritual way.

5

Who's Looking After You?

"Cast all your anxiety on him because he cares for you."
— 1 Peter 5:7

Feeling supported, understood, and cared for during pregnancy and birth deeply impacts mothers and their overall experience. Having continuity of care has been linked to better, more positive birth outcomes, less intervention, and more positive feelings associated with pregnancy. So, who you choose as your care provider is another one of those incredibly important decisions. You can have all the tools in the world to help you feel relaxed and confident, but if the person who's with you during your birth isn't supportive of the kind of birth you want and doesn't listen to you, then the odds of you feeling relaxed and safe enough for your body to work as it's been designed to will be significantly reduced.

In the sections below, I discuss different care providers, their skill sets, and do my best to help you weigh up the pros and cons of which care provider is right for you. It's important to remember that all care providers are unique, and it's best to go with someone you feel comfortable with. Midwives, obstetricians, and doulas can vary dramatically depending on their background and experience, so it's important to ask questions. For instance, if you're looking to have a vaginal birth, even though, generally speaking, midwives are viewed as the experts in physiological birth, there are midwives out there who are very medicalized, and may still be quick to push interventions before they're needed. On the opposite end of things, even though obstetricians are generally viewed as having a very medicalized view of birth, there are some OBs who care deeply about supporting physiological birth, and may even support mothers at a home birth. For this reason, I have included some questions that you could take to your interviews to ask your care provider and see how your values line up. If you feel they are not on the same page as you, and aren't going to help you feel safe and relaxed during your birth, then it's great to know that you can usually change providers, even late in pregnancy.

MIDWIVES

Midwives are highly skilled health professionals trained to support and care for women during pregnancy, labor, birth, and postpartum, and are often referred to as "the experts in physiological birth." The term midwife comes from the Middle English *mid* and *wif,* which translates to "with woman." Throughout the ages, midwives have been the wise women who cared for members of the community, both as they entered into this world, and as they left it. They understood how to use herbs for medicine and healing, and the power of words to help soothe and support a woman as she labored. They were a source of comfort and wisdom as a mother learned to nurse her baby and healed postpartum.

Today, midwifery training can vary dramatically across cultures. In countries like Canada, the UK, and Australia, midwives undergo extensive medical training, while in other parts of the world, training may be less formal. In the U.S., there are quite a few different types of midwives (CNMs, CMs, CPMs, and unlicensed or lay midwives).[99] As this has been confusing for some of our app users over the years, I will go over these different types in more detail.

CNMs are Certified Nurse Midwives who have completed nursing school and have a graduate degree in midwifery. In addition to caring for women during pregnancy and birth, they can provide general reproductive care, prescribe medications, diagnose conditions, and order lab tests. They're qualified to work in homes, birthing centers, and hospitals. They are certified by the American Midwifery Certification Board and work in all 50 states and the District of Columbia.

CMs are Certified Midwives and have a master's degree in midwifery, but haven't completed nursing school. CMs also have an undergraduate degree in something other than nursing. They are certified by the American Midwifery Certification Board and are able to prescribe medications. CMs are licensed to practice in nine states.

CPMs are Certified Professional Midwives and work at birth centers or in homes. They are certified by the North American Registry of Midwives after they have completed coursework. CPMs aren't licensed to practice in all states and cannot prescribe medications.

Lay midwives, or unlicensed midwives, are not medical professionals and don't have certification or a license to practice. They are normally self-taught or have done an apprenticeship or other kind of training. Unlicensed midwives normally only work in homes.

Please note that when I talk about midwives, I am referring to certified/licensed midwives (not lay or unlicensed midwives). While midwives vary considerably in their approaches based on their training, experience, and background (whether they work in hospitals, birth centers, or homes), overall, they tend to take a more holistic approach to maternity care, viewing birth as a natural, physiological process that occasionally requires medical assistance, as opposed to a medical condition that needs to be medically managed. Midwives are unable to be the sole care providers for women with high-risk pregnancies and cannot provide epidurals or perform surgical interventions like C-sections (though a midwife may be able to accompany a mother during a cesarean birth for extra support).

One of the really beautiful things that mothers often mention to me about having an independent/home birth midwife is how much time they were given. While it is common for prenatal appointments with an obstetrician to last less than 10 minutes, normally, prenatal visits or appointments with a home birth midwife can be half an hour or even longer, giving mothers plenty of time to ask questions, talk about any concerns they may have, and build a connection with their care provider.

Another wonderful thing about experienced home birth and birth center midwives is that they normally understand how to best support physiological labor. They know how to honor the environment that helps a woman feel safe—with darkness, warmth, and feelings of privacy. Allowing her to move as she feels to move, giving her words of encouragement when needed, and observing as much as possible with minimal interference. They will normally be able to monitor the baby's heart tones, and keep a close eye on the mother to make sure things are progressing as they should, with enough sensitivity and subtlety to not disturb the incredibly important balance of hormones unless necessary.

If birth begins to go off course, a midwife has the skills and tools to bring it back on course or to recognize if extra help will be necessary and suggest a transfer. They normally carry synthetic oxytocin in the case of hemorrhage, resuscitation equipment if the baby needs extra help breathing, IV fluids, oxygen, antibiotics, RhoGAM (a shot to prevent mothers who are Rh negative from developing antibodies to their baby's blood), the Vitamin K shot, and antibiotic eye ointment. Please note that different countries and states have different allowances for what home-birth midwives are allowed to carry with them, so be sure to check this with the midwives that you interview and check the laws in your area.

As mentioned earlier, studies across the world have shown that for women with healthy, normal pregnancies, delivering at home with an experienced certified midwife (and the option to transfer to hospital if needed), the rates of adverse outcomes are the same as delivering in a hospital,[11] and the likelihood of intervention is significantly reduced.[19] One thing that has been brought to my attention, though, is that the studies on home birth in the U.S. are not quite as favorable.[90] Often people assume this is because midwifery care in the U.S. isn't standardized for all midwives, and there is such a variety in the level of training. While that may be the case, I recently read that it's also important to take into consideration that the U.S. doesn't have national health care. This means that in some cases, there may be mothers who are classed as high-risk and need special medical care, but choose to stay at home because they don't have insurance and can't afford to go to the hospital. There are also cases where mothers have denied transfer to a hospital when the midwife has suggested it because they haven't had insurance. This leads to a higher rate of adverse outcomes, which is then counted against the safety of home birth.

There is, to my knowledge, no current data on home birth in the U.S. that only includes women with healthy, normal pregnancies being attended by a certified midwife, with the option to transfer to the hospital if medically necessary. So taking that into account, if you decide to give birth at home and want to ensure your birth is as safe as possible, it's important to confirm that your midwife is highly qualified, highly experienced, carries all the necessary medical equipment, is monitoring how you and baby are handling labor, is willing to transfer you to the hospital if medically necessary and that you are willing to be transferred. If, alternatively, you choose to give birth unassisted or with a lay (uncertified) midwife or birthkeeper, then that is your legal and autonomous right, but I do not have access to data to verify the safety or risks.

If you choose to have midwifery care in a hospital, then it's worth knowing that it can be quite different to independent midwifery care. From my own personal experience, the midwives I've seen working in hospital labor wards tend to have a more medicalized view of birth. When I was sent to the labor ward at my first birth, the midwife seemed to have no skills whatsoever when it came to offering words of encouragement. She knew I wanted to give birth unmedicated but kept saying that I'd "need drugs" and told me how "hard it would be."

I also didn't want interventions, but felt she pushed me into getting my waters broken, having continuous fetal monitoring, and being hooked up to an IV, all of which made the contractions feel considerably more painful as I wasn't able to move and felt more and more tense. I got the impression she wanted me to have the epidural, as it might have made her job easier. Over the years, many mothers have shared similar stories of highly medicalized midwives who work in labor wards pushing unwanted interventions on them and not giving them the kind of care they were expecting from a midwife (you may have seen posts on social media referring to midwives like this as "medwives"). And while women definitely deserve better, before placing blame on an individual, I think it's really important to look at why this might be happening.

Most birth professionals working in hospitals are doing their best to work in a system that was never set up to support the physiology of birth. It is set up for efficiency because they are dealing with thousands of people, and processes are standardized for that reason. They are also working in an environment with higher and higher expectations of healthcare, and less and less tolerance of risk. Seemingly there is an expectation that all adverse outcomes can be prevented with enough monitoring and medical intervention. Midwives in a labor ward are often looking after six (or even more) mothers at one time and have to spend more time checking monitors and filling in charts than being *with women*. In maternity care (just like in so many areas of our lives), we are attempting to replace human connection, support, care, and wisdom with the use of technology and then wondering why so many mothers are left feeling unsupported and even traumatized.

As much as the following data may seem startling, I feel it's important to share it, as there is still a widespread assumption that it's safer to give birth in the hospital with obstetric-led care than it is to give birth in a birth center or at home with a midwife. In the U.S. currently, more than 98 percent of women give birth in hospitals, and there are almost triple the number of obstetricians to midwives, yet the U.S. has the highest maternal mortality rate of any high income country in the world.[21] In the following graphs, you can see that in the U.S. and Canada, the number of OB-Gyns greatly outnumber midwives, yet in most of the other high income countries, midwives greatly outnumber OB-Gyns. The countries with the lowest maternal mortality rates also tend to have the highest number of midwives.

Maternal Mortality Ratios in Selected Countries

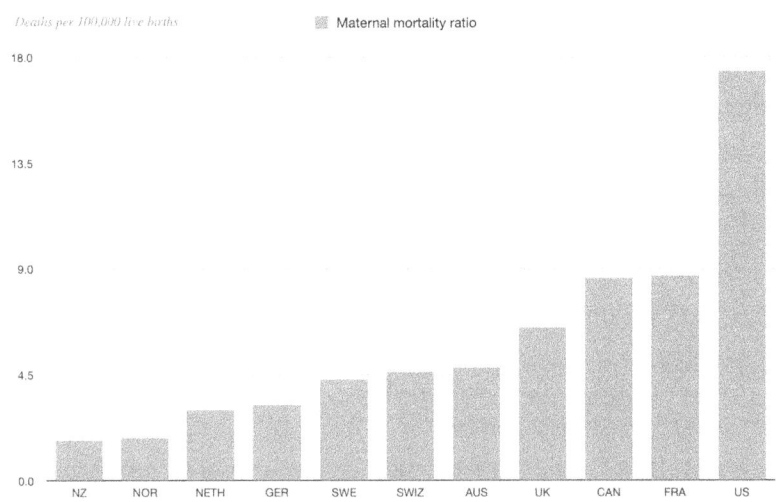

Maternal Care Workforce: Supply of Midwives and Ob-Gyns

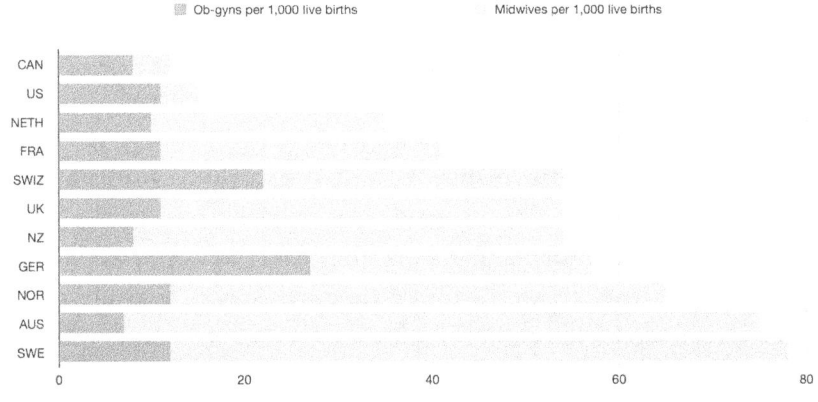

(Source: Roosa Tikkanen et al.)

When trying to understand these figures, I think it's also really important to note that the U.S. is the only one of these countries that doesn't have midwifery-led care covered by national insurance, guaranteed paid maternity leave, or guaranteed access to home visits postpartum. To me, these numbers really highlight the difference that midwifery care can make for the majority of pregnant, birthing, and postpartum women. The World Health Organization (WHO) has recommended midwives as an evidence-based approach to improving outcomes for women and reducing maternal mortality.

According to the Commonwealth Fund's study on maternal mortality,[21] several systematic reviews have found that midwifery-led care for women with healthy pregnancies is comparable or preferable to physician-led care in terms of:

- Mother and baby outcomes, including lower rates of maternal mortality, reduced stillbirths, and preterm births.
- Lower use of interventions like C-sections, epidurals, and instrument-assisted births.
- Improved patient satisfaction and maternal well-being outcomes, including those for postpartum depression.

Some experts[21] note that "high-income countries with the lowest intervention rates, best outcomes, and lowest costs have integrated midwifery-led care" into their health care systems.

Unfortunately, at this stage, we are experiencing a global shortage of midwives. So, it's not realistic to think that we could suddenly have the whole population giving birth at home, or in birth centers. But we can work to shift the way the world views birth, and midwifery care. We can honor midwives and show them the huge respect they deserve for the truly life-changing work they are doing. We can stop talking about them as if they are doctors' assistants and see them for the highly skilled professionals they are, the experts in helping to facilitate healthy, normal births. We can write to our governments and insurance companies, telling them the kind of care we want, asking them to fund midwifery programs, and cover midwife-led care. Maybe then we'll see a resurgence of midwives, and with that, far better birth outcomes for mothers and babies globally.

While it's obvious that I deeply appreciate and advocate for midwifery-led care where possible, I think an ability to look at birth from a balanced perspective is essential. I am grateful to live in a country where medical care is available 24/7 when it is needed. That is a privilege many people don't have, and I don't take that lightly. Unfortunately, in maternity care, the phenomenon of *too much too soon* and *too little too late* is still very much prevalent. We see two extremes: the routine overuse of non-evidence-based interventions in upper-income areas, and a lack of access to life-saving medical care and resources in lower-income areas when they are needed. It is my prayer that, worldwide, we will see the implementation of respectful, evidence-based maternity care for all. Women deserve to feel safe, cared for, respected, and listened to during their pregnancy and birth, and they also deserve to have access to medical assistance where it is needed.

So, after all that, if you have a healthy normal pregnancy, are in a position where you can choose midwife-led care, and that's what you would like, what's important to you? I've included some questions below to help you find out if the midwife you're interviewing is on the same page as you. Feel free to add, remove, or change any based on what's right for you. If you can, it's great to meet prospective midwives in person so you can get a feel for them. I recommend leaning into your God-given maternal instincts (or your gut feeling) about them. Just like with any important decision, if there's something that doesn't sit right with you, don't ignore it. Who you choose as your care provider will deeply impact your birth experience.

It's also worth having your birth partner with you so they can ask any questions they may have as well, and provide support. When you know you have a great midwife who offers kind reassurance, wise guidance, and treats you like a friend—while also being highly experienced and capable of handling any issues that may arise—it helps you relax fully, optimizing your hormones for birth and giving your body the best chance to work as it was miraculously designed to.

Questions for potential midwives:

- What are your philosophies and beliefs when it comes to childbirth?
- What kind of training and experience do you have?
- How long have you been a midwife, and how many births have you attended?
- What prenatal care do you provide?
- Do you work with other midwives, and will they also be caring for me during my pregnancy and birth? If so, am I likely to meet them?
- What backup arrangements do you have if you were unable to attend my birth?
- What kind of tests or screenings do you perform during pregnancy?
- Does insurance cover any of the cost?
- Do you work with any local OB-Gyns?
- What care and observations will you be doing during my labor?
- Are there laws or regulations that may influence the care you can offer me?
- What medical equipment do you carry?
- What kind of assistance do you provide if labor is difficult or prolonged?
- Are you experienced in the resuscitation of both mother and baby, administering Pitocin in the case of hemorrhage, and can you suture (stitch) tears at home?
- Do you have experience with unexpected complications like shoulder dystocia, or unexpected breech birth?
- What's the process if I need to transfer to the hospital?

- What are your rates of hospital transfer, interventions, perineal tears, and postpartum hemorrhage?
- Do you provide care postpartum?
- Do you have children yourself, and if so, what was your birth experience like?
- Do you offer any alternative skills such as homeopathy, massage, herbs, acupuncture, or aromatherapy?

OBSTETRICIANS

Obstetricians (often referred to as OBs or OB-Gyns if they also specialize in gynecology) are doctors who specialize in caring for women during pregnancy, birth, and postpartum. They are highly trained and skilled professionals who have normally completed at least four years of medical school and three additional years of specialized training.

They specialize in managing high-risk pregnancy conditions (like diabetes, preeclampsia, epilepsy, heart disease, and multiples) and are experts in surgical birth. If you need or want to have a cesarean, an obstetrician will need to perform it.

There are some truly wonderful obstetricians out there who do what they can to support the physiology of birth, and there are even some who will attend home births, or support vaginal breech births (although this will vary depending on their training and the laws in their area). There are also some OBs who are happy to share care with a midwife as a backup option in the case of a home birth transfer. Many of our Christian Hypnobirthing mamas have managed to find a home birth midwife with a great relationship with an obstetrician and have been cared for by both. This meant that in the cases where a transfer to the hospital was necessary, it was a much easier and supportive process than it might have been otherwise. So that may be something to look into if you are interested.

In my experience talking to hundreds (if not thousands) of women about their births over the years, most obstetricians tend to view birth as a medical event that needs to be treated and managed, as opposed to something that we've been miraculously designed to do, which occasionally requires medical intervention. Before criticizing this approach, though, just as I said in the section on midwives, I think it's really important to think about where it comes from and why.

Birth is one of the most litigious industries in the world, which means a huge number of medical professionals have to perform their jobs with the constant pressure of minimizing liability, as opposed to giving the mother and baby the best birth experience possible. For instance, it is common for many obstetricians to routinely use continuous electronic fetal monitoring in the labors of women with healthy normal pregnancies, despite the fact that it's not evidence-based, because it can be a defense against malpractice claims.[17]

So just to break that down, continuous electronic fetal monitoring has not been proven to improve outcomes for the mother and baby (in women with healthy, normal pregnancies), and using it will likely mean that the mother is restricted to the bed, and unable to move during her labor. Movement during labor can help enormously with the baby's positioning and increasing comfort. So, despite the fact that we don't see an improvement in outcomes for the mom and baby, and the mother's experience of labor will possibly be longer and more painful (as she's unable to move around), this is being used routinely as it can protect the doctor or hospital from being sued in the case of adverse outcomes.

I like to keep this in mind when I think about many of the routine procedures I hear of that make no sense to me from the perspective of supporting the physiology of birth. I think it's really important to remember that most hospitals were not set up to support healthy, normal births but to support sick people or people requiring urgent medical care, and many current practices are still based on tradition, fear of litigation, and convenience rather than evidence. They are also dealing with a high number of patients and processes are standardized to make care as efficient as possible.

I always want to think the best of people, and it's my belief that most obstetricians are doing their best to operate in a system that isn't set up to support our physiology for birth. Bright lights, beeping machines, the smell of disinfectant, and people wearing masks and rushing to support emergencies is not an environment geared toward making you feel really relaxed, safe, and comfortable. In the holistic birth community, it can feel like we are often quick to criticize obstetricians for the increase in interventions used and their mistrust of a woman's ability to give birth, but I wonder if it's fair to blame them when they're educated and operating in a system where it's rare to see normal physiological labor.

If what you're used to seeing is women coming into the hospital, labor slowing down and becoming more painful, getting an epidural, requiring synthetic oxytocin to re-start or speed up labor, babies going into distress because they can't tolerate the intensity of synthetic-oxytocin-induced contractions and requiring forceps or an unplanned cesarean, then I imagine that soon becomes your new normal. And if you are an obstetrician, and you have to do this every day, how are you going to feel about birth? Are you going to see birth as something women have been miraculously designed to do? Or are you going to see it as something dangerous and full of risks that need to be managed and controlled?

In both my hospital births, I had nurses remark to me that they'd "never seen a birth like it" simply because I didn't have an epidural or any Pitocin (synthetic oxytocin) during or after birth. Many of our app users have shared similar experiences, with comments from hospital staff being *amazed* that they were able to give birth without interventions. There's a moment in the documentary *The Business of Being Born* (which I really recommend watching) where they ask, "How often do you get to see a fully natural birth?" and the medical staff answer, "Almost never." To me, this kind of sums up just how unusual it is for staff on labor wards to see births that are unmedicated, without interventions.

If you opt for an obstetrician and you're planning a vaginal birth, I'd recommend asking them what their cesarean rate is, as that will likely impact your chance of having a cesarean more than your health factors. It's been really interesting for me giving birth in the

UK through the NHS (public National Health Service) with midwife-led maternity care, then moving home to Australia, where most of my friends with private health insurance opted for obstetric care. Of my friends in Australia who had obstetric care, almost every single one ended up with a C-section. Whereas, when I lived in the UK, most of my friends who gave birth through the NHS supported by midwives gave birth vaginally, with only one needing a cesarean. Obviously, I can't base anything on my friend group, but there was a study done in Australia of over 300,000 women that showed that private obstetric care increased the chance of cesarean birth regardless of health needs and wishes.[18] And it's possible that there may be financial incentives for some obstetricians who are paid more for cesarean births than they are for vaginal births.

The World Health Organization's recommended rate for cesarean is between 10-15 percent, but some obstetricians have cesarean rates as high as 60 percent or even higher. So, for this reason, it is so important to ask your hospital or your obstetrician what their C-section rate is, as that will likely reveal your odds of having one if you choose them as your provider. If they won't share their intervention/C-section rates, they are dismissive of your thoughts and opinions, or they just treat you in a way that makes you feel uncomfortable, you may want to change care providers. Feeling supported and listened to by your provider during your pregnancy, birth, and postpartum will drastically increase the likelihood of you having a positive experience. Also, it's never too late to change! One of our app users literally changed care providers during labor. She felt that her obstetrician wasn't supporting her during birth, so she fired her, managed to have one of the hospital midwives come in for the rest of her labor, and overall had a really positive experience.

So, is an obstetrician the right provider for you? There are certainly times when obstetricians will be the safest and best option as your care provider. My best friend has Type 1 Diabetes, and toward the end of her pregnancy, her blood pressure started increasing. After her cesarean, her blood pressure continued to rise, and she had to be rushed to the ICU due to preeclampsia. If it wasn't for the lifesaving work of her obstetrician and medical team, my beautiful friend wouldn't be here today. I feel such enormous gratitude that we have access to the lifesaving skills of obstetricians where they are medically necessary.

If I were pregnant again and my risk factors made it safer for me to have obstetric care, then I would absolutely choose that and incorporate all my tools for a faith-filled birth. I would also make sure my obstetrician was aware of my wishes, paying attention to how they responded to my questions and whether they seemed supportive. One mama recently told me that as she lay on the operating table about to have a cesarean, she was feeling nervous, so she asked if someone could play some music, and her OB replied, "This is my surgery, not a concert hall." (I'm sure you can imagine what I'd like to say to this obstetrician, but I won't be writing it here...) For this reason, I cannot overemphasize the importance of finding a provider who shares your values. And if you can't, make sure your birth partner or doula knows your wishes and is ready to advocate for you. It is reassuring to remember that if a cesarean is necessary there are lots of ways to make it a more connected and faith-filled experience, and I go into more detail about that in the next chapter.

Below are some questions for your obstetrician that can help you determine if your values align. Please remove or add any as you wish. A couple of things to look out for are whether they view birth as a risky event that needs to be medically managed, or whether they view birth as a natural, physiological event that occasionally requires medical assistance. Does their view of birth match up with yours? Do they use phrases like "I will not allow" in reference to things like eating and drinking in labor, not having continuous fetal monitoring, or going over 39 weeks of pregnancy? It's good to remember that your care provider can make recommendations, but they are not actually allowed to *not* allow you. You have the right to make informed, autonomous decisions about your body and your birth. How do they feel about your birth preferences/plan? Do they seem supportive? As I said in the midwife section, it's great if your birth partner is also able to be there to support you and ask questions. Again, it's great to lean into your God-given maternal instincts. What is your intuition telling you about this person, and whether they are the right person to care for you and your baby?

Questions for potential obstetricians:

- What are your philosophies or values when it comes to childbirth?
- What kind of training and experience do you have? How many births have you attended?
- What percentage of women under your care have spontaneous vaginal births? What percentage are induced? Have instrumental deliveries? What is your C-section rate?
- Are there any things you won't allow me to do?
- How would you feel about me declining certain procedures?
- What backup arrangements do you have if you were unable to attend my birth?
- Would you consider sharing my care with a midwife if I wanted to have a home birth?
- Are there circumstances under which you'd recommend induction?
- What happens if I go over my estimated due date?
- What are your recommendations for monitoring during labor?
- Do you support vaginal breech births? What happens if my baby is breech?
- What comfort measures do you offer and recommend during labor?
- Under what circumstances do you recommend cesarean, and what is your cesarean rate?
- Do you support gentle, family-centered, or maternal-assisted cesareans?

- During birth, do you allow for restitution (waiting for baby to rotate), or do you pull on the baby's head as soon as it emerges?
- How do you support the third stage of labor? Do you support delayed cord clamping? Do you support Expectant Management (where you wait for the placenta to be birthed naturally) as opposed to Active Management (which often combines an injection of Pitocin, fundal massage, immediate cord clamping, and controlled cord traction)?
- Are you happy for me to have a doula supporting me throughout birth?

DOULAS

A doula is a non-medical companion who can provide support throughout pregnancy, labor, and birth. Having a doula has been shown to improve outcomes for mothers and babies, including reducing the need for cesarean.[22] Doulas are not medically trained and cannot provide medical advice, so they are not a replacement for an obstetrician or a midwife, but they can make a wonderful addition to your birth team. Doulas can vary considerably in their training, views on childbirth, services they provide, and prices they charge, but primarily, their role is to provide the mother with support (which can be emotional, physical, and informational) and to advocate for her wants and needs.

Often doulas share childbirth educational resources and provide tools to help mothers and their birth partners feel calm and confident throughout labor. They may suggest breathing and relaxation techniques for labor, as well as ideas for movement and positioning. They can also provide evidence-based information about different medical procedures, so you feel informed and can make empowered decisions. They can help you put together your birth plan/preferences so they and your birth partner have a clear understanding of your wishes and can help advocate for you. While in some cases they may not be able to advocate for you directly to medical professionals, they can support you and your birth partner by encouraging you, reminding you of decisions you've made, asking you questions, and helping to facilitate a sense of good communication and collaboration with your care providers. This can be of enormous support to your birth partner also, particularly if they are feeling anxious or confused. They may also be able to draw your attention to any potential interventions that are about to be performed and make sure you fully understand them and consent to them. For instance, if a care provider said something like, "Now just hop up on the bed, and we'll examine you" (which doesn't explain what's about to happen or include informed consent), your doula could explain that your care provider wants to do a vaginal examination where they will insert their gloved fingers into your vagina, that the information they'll get from that is how effaced and dilated your cervix is, but that it doesn't tell you how long labor will be (as dilation time varies considerably from individual to individual). Your doula may then also remind you that it's your choice whether you consent to having one or not.

Doulas can offer physical support through light touch massage, counter pressure, hip squeezes, or even just holding hands with you and making eye contact. They may be able to guide you in breathing techniques or visualizations and help to create a calm environment by dimming the lights or setting up aromatherapy, LED candles, or fairy lights. They can also help with practical things such as making sure you have access to food and drinks, walking you to and from the bathroom, helping you change your clothes, applying warm or cold packs, or assisting with filling birth pools. Emotionally, just through their continuous presence, a doula can provide a great sense of reassurance, as well as using words of encouragement and praise. And if you manage to find a Christian doula who is happy to read scriptures and pray over you during labor, that can also provide a particularly special kind of spiritual support.

What's the difference between a doula and a midwife? While some midwives incorporate aspects of emotional, physical, and informational support, most midwives (especially those in the hospital settings) are focused on the medical side of monitoring you and the baby and making sure things are progressing as they should, whereas a doula's primary focus is to provide support. A doula is not medically qualified and does not give medical advice, diagnose conditions, perform cervical exams or fetal heart monitoring, or catch the baby.

While some doulas are trained in advocacy, others are trained that advocacy is not a part of their role. Either way, there are times when it may be very difficult for a doula to speak up, particularly if they are being told not to by someone who is considered more medically qualified than them. When interviewing doulas, having clear communication about your expectations and what you're specifically looking for in a doula gives them the opportunity to let you know whether they are comfortable providing the kind of care you're looking for. For this reason, I've also included questions below to ask potential doulas to make sure they're a good fit for you.

Should you hire a doula? This is a really personal question. The majority of the time, mothers tell me they loved having a doula and that they considered having one a wonderful investment, but I also recently had a mother say that because her husband was such an amazing birth partner, she didn't really feel her doula was necessary. We often have couples who do our Faith-Filled Childbirth Course together, listen to the Christian Hypnobirthing app together nightly in the lead-up to birth, and have done lots of their own research (watched positive birth videos, read books, and listened to podcasts). In these cases, where your birth partner feels really prepared and very confident in supporting you through labor, you may not feel like a doula is necessary, but it's still good to keep in mind that during labor, your birth partner will need to go to the bathroom, take breaks to rest, eat, and drink and having a doula can mean you have a continuous source of support in those instances. Also, at some stages (particularly if it's their first time being a birth partner) your birth partner may need some encouragement, guidance, and support as well.

When I was pregnant with our first son, things were very tight financially. We didn't feel that we could afford to do a birth course, let alone hire a doula. Looking back, I can't help wondering what kind of impact having a doula would have made on that birth experience. Even though I'd read books and listened to relaxation tracks, I just wasn't prepared for the level of advocacy that myself and my husband would have to do just to stand up for my birth preferences. It would have been so nice to have some extra support for me and my husband as well. Even though he was so wonderful and encouraging during labor, and ultimately was so grateful and excited when our son was born, I think it was a really difficult experience for him, and having the gentle guidance and encouragement of a doula could have really helped.

Here's a quote from a mother who found a doula on our Christian Birth Directory:

"Jessica was truly a Godsend for our family. My husband and I are first time parents and originally had planned to skip hiring a doula for financial reasons. We later changed our minds, and wow I am so glad we did. Jessica was a calm, guiding voice amidst the unknowns of childbirth. She helped us to feel prepared, confident, and at ease. I desired a drug-free birth, and she helped me achieve that. She was our advocate and helped us keep the birth experience in line with our desires when the hospital staff pushed for something different. And most importantly, she kept Christ at the center of this incredible opportunity we get to partner in creation with him. She turned the hospital labor & delivery room into a sanctuary where I felt calm and safe. We have absolutely zero regrets and recommend Jessica without hesitation to any parents, regardless of what type of birth they desire."

Just like with your midwife or obstetrician, asking questions can help you work out whether the person you're interviewing will be a good fit for your birth team. Essentially, you want your doula to be someone who helps you feel safe, confident, and relaxed. While it's great for them to be knowledgeable about birth, they shouldn't feel pushy or as though they are going to want you to give birth in a certain way. Their role is to help support *you* in what *you* want. Pay attention to how they make you feel during your time with them and afterward.

Questions for potential doulas:

- What are your philosophies and beliefs when it comes to childbirth?
- What kind of training and experience do you have?
- How long have you been a doula, and how many births have you attended?
- How would you describe your doula style?
- (If this is important to you) Are you a Christian? Do you offer prayer support during labor?
- What are your fees, and what is included in your doula package?
- What backup arrangements do you have if you were unable to attend my birth?
- What are your beliefs about advocacy in the birth room environment?
- Have you experienced tough situations with advocacy in the past, and what strategies worked best?
- Are there types of advocacy that you do or do not provide?
- Do you provide care postpartum? Or do you have any postpartum doulas you recommend?
- Do you have children yourself, and if so, what was your birth experience like?
- Do you offer any alternative skills, such as massage or aromatherapy?

BIRTH PARTNERS

As I've mentioned multiple times, continuity of care is associated with better outcomes for mothers and babies, but in some situations, it just may not be possible to have a known care provider, and that is when your birth partner is so incredibly important. Whether you're able to have a doula or a provider that you know and trust, a birth partner can provide that continuous, loving support that can make such a difference toward a positive birth experience. Depending on your situation, you may choose to have your spouse, mom, another family member, or close friend as your birth partner. The most important thing is that it is someone you trust, that they help you feel safe, and that they know your wishes and are willing to advocate for you.

My main suggestion is that it is someone you want, not someone you feel pressured to have with you. A while back, one of our course members told me her mother-in-law was putting enormous pressure on her and her husband to be at the birth, and she felt really uncomfortable about it. As much as it may feel difficult to let down relatives, your baby's birth is too important to risk feeling uncomfortable. Just having one extra person in the room who makes you feel tense could inhibit oxytocin production, which will impact your birth. If you're still feeling pressured into having someone at your birth, ask yourself, *Would I let them be there even if I knew it would add ten hours to labor?* Some women want to be surrounded by their mother, sisters, and closest friends, while some want no one other than their midwife and their husband. It is totally up to you. But I would suggest you make sure whoever you have present, you feel totally uninhibited with them, able to move as you feel to move, and make the noises you feel to make. It might be a good idea to ask yourself, *Would I be comfortable going to the bathroom in front of this person? Would I be comfortable being naked in front of them?* If the answer is no, then you might be better off not having them at your birth.

A birth partner's most important role is that of *protector*. A woman is incredibly vulnerable when she is giving birth, so for thousands of years, when a woman was in labor, someone would have stood guard against predators. We see this still sometimes in the animal kingdom, where another animal will look out for or guard the laboring mother. The mother needs to feel safe to allow her body to soften and open. She needs to feel warm, private, and undisturbed. Knowing that she's being protected can help her to do that. While your birth partner may no longer need to fight off predators, they may still need to fight for your preferences, and do their best to limit interruptions that interfere with the very delicate hormonal dance that happens as you prepare to bring your baby into the world.

Something as simple as being interrupted to answer questions, or having to stand up for your birth preferences can activate your prefrontal cortex (the logical/thinking part of the brain) and bring you out of that deeply relaxed state that allows your body to work as it's designed to. Your birth partner is able to act as a kind of buffer between you and the frequent interruptions that can happen, particularly in a busy hospital setting. Obviously, any important decisions would still need to be discussed with you, but a lot of standard questions can be answered by your birth partner, who can also give medical care providers copies of your birth plans/preferences, answer questions about those, and fill in paperwork. This is why it's so important that you go over or make your birth plan/preferences with your birth partner, and they fully understand what your wishes are.

Niles Newton, a perinatal psychologist, studied what happened when pregnant mice were disturbed during their labors. He found that their labors increased in length by up to 70 percent, and some of the mice didn't even end up giving birth.[23] We know that disturbances in labor don't just affect mice; they affect all mammals. When mammals feel threatened, hungry, or cold during labor, their bodies release adrenaline, and adrenaline stops the release of oxytocin, which is the hormone responsible for the uterus contracting. This is a survival strategy that allows them to get away from the threat that's disturbed them. We are mammals, and while we're not getting disturbed by tigers anymore, our nervous system can be just as disturbed by bright lights, vaginal examinations, having to answer questions and fill in paperwork, being hooked up to an IV, continuous fetal monitoring, and the many other interventions routinely used in most hospitals today.

So, it's up to your birth partner to do their best to protect you from as many of these disturbances as possible and create a safe environment. That might look like ensuring you have blue blocker glasses on as you enter the hospital, and telling the hospital that you are declining any vaginal examinations if you don't want them. Once you've been admitted, your birth partner can turn the lights off in your room and put on a few warm-colored LED candles or fairy lights. They can turn your Christian Hypnobirthing app or music playlist on and set up an aromatherapy vaporizer. Your birth partner can make sure you're warm and comfortable and that you have food or drinks if you're hungry or thirsty.

Light touch massage is a really wonderful way your birth partner can help you to relax (if you're enjoying being touched), and is a great comfort measure as it's a fast way of increasing endorphins during labor. Massage can also help increase serotonin and dopamine, which may reduce anxiety. So, if you've experienced something stressful, light touch massage (along with up breathing) could help bring you back into that relaxed rest and digest state. A nice basic light touch massage to practice is your birth partner starting with their fingers at the base of your spine and very gently going up your spine with the backs of their fingers, going out from the spine in a V shape, or crossover S shapes, as they work their way to the top of your spine, then down over your head, your shoulders, and your arms. It should be so light that it has that almost tickly feeling. Firmer massage can also be really useful in releasing tension during labor, in the shoulders, lower back, buttocks and upper thighs, and hands and feet. Hip squeezes may increase comfort in the lower back and pelvis during a contraction as they push the ilia together, which can help relieve pressure on the sacroiliac joint. There are lots of videos on YouTube with visual demonstrations on how to do this, which I'd recommend watching with your birth partner, or you could also ask your midwife or doula if they know how to demonstrate helpful labor massage techniques and hip squeezes to your birth partner.

During pregnancy it's great to practice different kinds of massage while listening to the Christian Hypnobirthing tracks together, and you can also massage your birth partner. This is a wonderful way to connect, increase oxytocin, and also for them to get a really good understanding of what feels good for you. Communication is key, and helping them to understand what helps you relax will be an amazing way for them to support you during labor.

Ideally, in active labor, it's best to have minimal speaking other than words of encouragement, so your birth partner can communicate with medical staff, and also tell care providers the kind of environment you want to create, and ask for them to respect that. In our Faith-Filled Childbirth Course, we have a sign you can print out that says, *"We are practicing Christian Hypnobirthing during our baby's birth. Please help us to keep the atmosphere calm and peaceful. Thank you."* If you don't have the course, you can create your own sign and put it up on the door of your room so that before anyone enters, they will already be aware of the environment you are working to create and hopefully be respectful.

Your birth partner can also alert any medical care providers to the importance of the language they use (see chapter on the power of words) and can gently ask them to use positive language where possible. So instead of asking, "How much pain are you in?" they could ask, "How comfortable are you?' And instead of comments like, "It's so hard, isn't it?" say, "You're doing a wonderful job." To help minimize speaking, it may be worth letting your care provider know if you consent to them coming in and monitoring the baby's heart rate without asking permission, so they don't need to disturb you with questions each time. All of these requests may sound excessive, but when you understand that birth is an involuntary process controlled by hormones from primal parts of the brain (the hypothalamus and the pituitary gland) that can be so easily disturbed and inhibited by any activation of the prefrontal cortex (the thinking part of the brain), it really highlights the importance of environment, and why all this effort is necessary.

When it comes to important questions, for instance, if an intervention is suggested, your birth partner can ask why it's being offered (remembering to go through the BRAIN acronym of Benefits, Risks, Alternatives, Intuition, and Nothing) and then say, "Can we please have a few minutes to discuss this?" If something is not an emergency, then you shouldn't feel rushed to make a decision. Take a few minutes to discuss the options with your birth partner and pray together if you can. When we were being pressured into various interventions during my first birth, I feel such gratitude looking back that we asked the midwife to step out for a few minutes as we prayed together and talked about my birth plans. I had been allowing the circumstances to overwhelm me, and having that space to pray and talk gave me the peace and strength I needed. I feel like God met me in that place, and I was able to work through some of my deepest fears and insecurities and go through to the other side. But if my husband had not been my protector and provided that place of safety to pray with me and help support me through those tough decisions, I feel that birth could have gone in a very different direction.

Doing *nothing* can be *everything*. Sometimes, birth partners can feel unsure of what they're supposed to do, particularly in cases when a mother doesn't want their birth partner to say anything or touch them (which can be common, particularly toward the end of labor). It's so important for your birth partner to know that just their loving presence alone makes a huge impact on providing reassurance and support. This can be difficult for first-time dads who have never seen a birth, as they may feel totally out of their depth, particularly as surges become more powerful. They may feel the need to fix the situation or save the mother from the experience, which may even lead them to push for unnecessary interventions. I would really encourage birth partners to do their best to gain an understanding of the physiology of birth, as that will help them to feel comfortable just being present, knowing that sometimes the most powerful thing they can do is just *be* there.

As I talked about in the Faith-Filled Toolbox chapter, in the verse "Be still and know that I am God" (Psalm 46:10), the words "be still" come from the Hebrew word *rapha,* meaning to "let go, to release, to make yourself weak." This verse isn't just powerful for the mother, who can allow God's design and strength to work through her as she lets go of the need to control, but it's also amazing for the birth partner. If they can accept that they cannot control this birth, and are just able to be present, responding to what the woman needs from them in that moment, then they can provide the most wonderful support.

It can be beneficial to listen to the app together at night as you go to sleep as it helps the tracks to become an anchor for deep relaxation, and listening to the tracks can also help your birth partner get to know some encouraging phrases and affirmations that they can say to you during labor. Saying something as simple as "You're doing an amazing job," "I'm so proud of you," or "I love you" can work wonders.

If your birth partner is also your spouse, then they have a particularly special relationship with you that can help generate more oxytocin. A secret many midwives use when labor has stalled is giving a couple some privacy to get that oxytocin flowing. Remember, "The hormones that got the baby in are the same hormones that get the baby out." Kissing, hugging, and nipple stimulation are all ways of increasing oxytocin. Kissing a woman during labor can also help her relax her face and jaw, which can be connected to holding tension in the pelvic floor area.

So, if labor has slowed down and you start feeling pressured into augmenting labor with synthetic oxytocin, you may want to ask for some privacy and try naturally boosting your natural oxytocin before agreeing to synthetic alternatives. There have been studies that have shown that nipple stimulation has led to shorter labors,[24] and can be a powerful tool for increasing or bringing on surges. One of the reasons for this is when a baby breastfeeds, it increases oxytocin, which is responsible for your let-down reflex and uterine contractions. If you're trying nipple stimulation, you want to try to mimic a baby's latch as closely as you can. A good latch includes a significant amount of the areola (the dark circle that surrounds the nipple), not just the nipple itself. If using your fingers, gently massage from just outside the areola inward toward the nipple, massaging the nipple gently in a rolling motion.

When using fingers, you can also use lubricant or oil to make it more comfortable. It's recommended that you only do one breast at a time to avoid overstimulation and limit stimulation to five minutes, then wait fifteen minutes before trying again. Stop nipple stimulation once surges are three minutes apart or less and one minute or longer. Please ask your provider if you have any concerns or questions.

If the above paragraph made you feel a little uncomfortable, please know that you don't ever need to do anything mentioned in this book that doesn't feel right for you. However, if you feel that your discomfort is coming from a place of shame around your body, I would gently encourage you to investigate whether there's room for healing there. As Christians, many of us were brought up with damaging shame-based messages around our bodies and/or sex, and as a result, many of us feel a sense of awkwardness, fear, embarrassment, or shame when discussing these subjects. Unfortunately, feeling shame around our bodies can have a negative impact on birth, as it may inhibit us from fully letting go and releasing into the experience. During labor, to produce optimum levels of oxytocin and help support baby's descent through the birth canal, we want to feel free and uninhibited in our bodies so we can move as we feel to move, guided by our God-given birthing instincts.

When it comes to shame, I find it helpful to remember that God isn't disapproving of our bodies, or what we're doing in the bedroom. God designed sex, and he designed it to be a good, mutually pleasurable, euphoric experience that bonds us together. If you feel shame, obligation, or any other negative feelings around sex or your body, then I really recommend a book called *The Great Sex Rescue: The Lies You've Been Taught and How to Recover What God Intended* by Sheila Wray Gregoire, online courses from Carlie Palmer-Webb (known as The Christian Sex Educator), and *Call of the Wild* by Kimberly Ann Johnson. As hard as this work can feel at times, when we work to heal the relationship we have with ourselves and our bodies, the ripples go out, and that healing impacts all the different areas of our lives, including how we give birth.

As you go through this book, you should feel more and more clear about what choices feel right for you, and by the end of the book, I suggest putting together your birth preferences/plan with your birth partner (we'll have a template at the end), so they know exactly how you feel about where you want to give birth, who you want as your care provider, what comfort measures you want to use in labor, and the circumstances under which you would be happy to accept different interventions. Whether you and your birth partner do our Faith-Filled Childbirth course or not, I really recommend you do some kind of holistically minded antenatal training course together if you can, as it will help you and your birth partner to know that the two of you, along with your baby, are working together as an amazing team, and should help them feel much more confident in knowing how they can best support you.

Here are a few quotes from our course members who included their birth partner in their preparation for birth:

"I struggled finding a birthing course that was truly for mother and father to learn and grow together in the information provided. Thank you so much for creating a curriculum that appeals to both!!! My husband started asking to watch the next video before I even had to initiate it. My heart is so full knowing we are so much more prepared as a couple after taking this course." - Julie

"I so appreciate the work of Tara and the team at Christian Hypnobirthing. For my second child, I wanted a peaceful, unmedicated birth. By listening to her helpful modules I felt prepared and confident for labor. Her knowledge of what happens to the body, mind and spirit during labor gave me insight that no typical birthing class could offer. My husband listened to a few key lessons as well and was able to be the strong support partner I needed to experience

a truly wonderful delivery. I recommend the app and modules to any expectant mom." - Leigh

"The app has given me so much peace and my husband listens to it as we go to sleep with me! He reminds me every night and quotes the scriptures during the day!" - Alexis

SUMMARY

When I've talked to mothers who were disappointed about their birth experience, it has often come down to something that happened with their provider. Whether they didn't feel listened to, or they felt pushed into decisions, the impact of who they chose as their care provider was one of the biggest influences on their overall feelings about their birth. Often, when speaking to women about this, they've said things like, "I had a bad feeling about them" or "I had some concerns," but for various reasons, they didn't change providers, even when they noticed red flags.

Many of us have been conditioned from a young age to just do as we're told and not hurt anyone's feelings, often to the point where we'll sacrifice our own wants or needs to not ruffle any feathers. Please let this be your reminder that your birth is too important to just do as you're told and stay silent. For most providers, you will just be one of thousands of clients throughout their career, and they will move on to the next birth they have to go to, but this is your one chance of having this birth experience. You may have other births in the future, but *you will only get to have this birth with this baby once*. You have a voice. If something doesn't feel right to you, speak up, and remember, you are always free to get a second, third, or fourth opinion, or change providers.

As difficult as these decisions can feel at times, it can provide such peace to give them over to God, to remember that he loves us, that he covers us, goes before us, and hems us in from behind. We are not faced with these decisions alone. He promises to be with us always. Sometimes, when I'm struggling with a decision, even after weighing up the pros and cons, or the risks and benefits, and spending time in prayer, there comes a time when I have to just make the decision and then trust in God, knowing that even when things don't go to my plan, he is always working for good, through all things. And the peace that comes from trusting him really does surpass all understanding.

I spoke to a mother a while back who had to give birth in the hospital alone during the COVID-19 pandemic. Her husband and doula weren't allowed to enter the hospital because he had tested positive for COVID-19, and due to restrictions, the hospital wasn't allowing doulas in at that time. Not only was this mother birthing without any kind of emotional support, but she also had to wear a mask throughout her whole labor, which must have been unbelievably difficult. She told me that she listened to the Christian Hypnobirthing tracks all throughout labor and that despite all those incredibly challenging circumstances, she felt the Holy Spirit's presence helping her, and she was still able to experience a faith-filled birth. Her story moved me to tears because it reminded me that God is our ultimate provider and will continue to support us even when everything else falls away. Obviously, I pray that you don't have to go through anything like that and that you'll get to have wonderful support and care providers who help you feel safe and cared for all throughout your pregnancy and birth, but I share this story to remind you that he is with us through everything, and he will not forsake us. Even in the most difficult times, we can turn to him, and he will carry us through.

> "Where can I go from your Spirit? Where can I flee from your presence? If I go up to the heavens, you are there; if I make my bed in the depths, you are there. If I rise on the wings of the dawn, if I settle on the far side of the sea, even there your hand will guide me, your right hand will hold me fast. If I say, 'Surely the darkness will hide me and the light become night around me,' even the darkness will not be dark to you; the night will shine like the day, for darkness is as light to you."
> – Psalm 139:7-12

– BIRTH STORY –

SHANNON'S GBS POSITIVE FAITH-FILLED HOSPITAL BIRTH

I wanted to share my positive, unmedicated hospital birth for the moms who are anxious about birthing in the hospital. We knew we wanted to birth at the hospital just in case an emergency were to arise. This was especially important to us after testing GBS positive, but knowing we wanted to decline the antibiotics. I had a wonderful, unmedicated, no intervention experience, and all my wishes were respected.

Here's my story: I used the Christian hypnobirthing app every night leading up to birth. Beginning around 39 weeks, I started having prodromal labor every evening for several hours that would stop around bedtime. At 40 weeks, contractions picked up in strength and consistency, but still eventually stopped later in the night. Our hospital was 37 minutes away, so in order to better understand how much we'd need to rush to the hospital, I had a cervical check at my 40 week appointment. I was 4cm and 80% effaced with my cervix facing far forward and my water bag bulging. My midwife said to leave for the hospital as soon as I had four to five strong contractions in a row. She also said the baby was going to come flying out as soon as my water broke ... At 40 weeks and two days on 6/10, I went to bed at 10 p.m. after timing non-painful contractions seven to ten minutes apart since 6 p.m. Some contractions woke me throughout the night, but I was easily able to return to sleep. They felt slightly stronger than what I had been experiencing throughout the week.

The morning of 6/11 at 40 weeks and three days pregnant, I woke to intense contractions at 2 a.m. I immediately began timing them, and they were two minutes apart. I quickly woke up my husband Steven and told him it was time to go. We called our doula, Lily, to let her know we were headed to the hospital. We headed to the hospital at 2:20 a.m. and arrived at 3:07 a.m.

The drive was one I will not soon forget. We saw five deer, a raccoon, and a fox at such a late hour, and my contractions were so intense and close together, it was all I could do to breathe and hang on. Steven had my worship playlist on, and I tried to focus on the songs and relaxing my body as much as possible through the twisty roads.

I distinctly remember one contraction occurring just as Steven reached a roundabout. I'll never look at roundabouts the same way again! Our doula had perfect timing and met us at the door of the hospital as we were getting out of the car. Our midwife greeted us, checked my cervix, and left. In the rush to get to the hospital and the focus that my contractions required, she said we forgot to call her. Whoops! I was admitted at 6cm dilated, 100% effaced, with strong contractions coming every two minutes. The nurses wanted to insert an IV lock, which I declined. I was also GBS positive, but declined the antibiotics. We eventually made it into our birthing room. It was all I could do to hang on to Steven and Lily as I breathed through strong contractions (in for 4 out for 7).

As soon as the nurses finished their blood draw and 20 minutes of monitoring contractions, I got into the nice, hot birth tub Lily had filled up. It felt amazing!! All but one nurse left the room. I was having a hard time relaxing with the intensity and frequency of contractions. At Lily's suggestion, I got onto all fours with my arms and head resting against Steven/a pillow on the edge of the tub. I remember having to let out a few soft moans and thinking it was early to be needing to moan already. Lily was spraying water down my back. I was trying to concentrate on the worship song that was playing (Available by Elevation Worship).

I felt a pop and involuntary tensing sensation that, at the time, I thought was a bowel movement, but was actually my water breaking and my body beginning to push. I thought to myself that I was not going to tell them I had pooped if they weren't going to say anything! I was then hit with another extremely intense contraction, and I looked at Steven and Lily and said I needed an epidural, there was no way I could keep doing this. Little did I know that this was the very last contraction I'd have before baby was born!

They assured me I could do it and to try and breathe/relax. It was then I started feeling my body pushing (again I thought it was just clearing me out and was another bowel movement). All of a sudden I jerked back with the intensity of my body bearing down, completely out of my control. I felt a little wild! It can only be described as animalistic power running through me. It was not painful at all, but an extremely intense whole-body feeling of pushing everything that was inside of me OUT of me. I didn't know it at the time, but this was the Fetal Ejection Reflex. To my extreme surprise, I felt Baby's head crown and completely come out with a quick gentle, popping sensation, but couldn't speak through the intense sensation of my body bearing down. It wasn't painful at all, which is why I had no realization of what was happening until it was already done because things were moving so quickly.

I started to stand and someone shouted, "That's a baby! I see a head!" I was immediately rushed by nurses and our midwife (who called them? How'd they have time??), with everyone trying to get me out of the tub (hospital births are not allowed in the tub once baby is coming out). I had one leg out of the tub and one leg in the tub as the rest of baby was born into the waiting hands of our midwife. She did not even have time to put gloves on! There was barely any pause between feeling Baby's head come out and the rest of his body being born. I had no control over anything—my body was doing all the work! It happened so quickly. Baby was born at 4:03 a.m. It was less than an hour after arriving at the hospital!

I was slowly coming out of my shock to hear the sweetest little newborn cries and Steven saying, "Oh my gosh, oh my gosh! You did it!" Everyone was SHOCKED! No one had any idea (including me) that I had progressed from 6cm to fully dilated in under an hour and that Baby was on his way out. I was only in the tub for 15-20 min. The midwife and nurses helped me over to the bed and passed Baby between my legs. I laid him on my chest and looked down. He was absolutely perfect. The cord stopped pulsing, and the nurses helped Steven cut it. The midwife assessed me and informed me I *had a first-degree tear. She numbed the area and stitched me up while waiting for the placenta to come out. She asked to give me Pitocin to deliver the placenta, which I declined. I gently pushed it out about 20 minutes after Baby was born, with no complications.*

During that time, I sat soaking in the baby on my chest and the birth we had just completed together! I was in wonder that my body really did do everything it needed to all by itself, just as God designed. Everyone says we are meant to do this, and boy were they right! Baby soon began nursing all on his own. He was 7lbs 9oz and 19 inches long. God answered all my prayers for a quick, low-intervention, unmedicated birth. It was truly an unforgettable labor, and I feel like I could do it all over again tomorrow. We did it!

6

Informed and Empowered

"The excellence of knowledge is that wisdom gives life to those who have it."
– Ecclesiastes 7:12

While it's important to surround yourself with positive birth stories and watch positive birth videos so that you can create a positive, faith-filled birth mindset, it's also important to know the truth about how different interventions work and how they may impact your birth experience. I'll do my best when looking at these interventions to take the B.R.A.I.N. acronym approach and look at the benefits, risks, and alternatives for the different options. While I try to be fairly neutral about the information I share, obviously, I have my own biases based on my experiences, being a hypnobirthing instructor, and also the experiences shared with me by the many women I've interacted with over the years. For this reason, please always ask your own questions, talk to your healthcare provider, and do your own research about what's right for you and your baby.

According to the National Institutes of Health, up to 45 percent of new mothers experience birth trauma.[45] While unnecessary interventions can definitely contribute to birth trauma, it is more likely that a woman will feel traumatized if she doesn't fully understand what is happening to her or feels that she's not an active participant in decision making. Whereas, if a mother is able to feel in control by making decisions with a fuller picture of benefits and risks involved in those choices, even if birth goes a different direction than what was planned, she is more likely to feel positive about her experience.

For that reason, in this next section, I'll be sharing in more detail about different interventions, and despite the fact that it may not seem positive at times, I ask that you stick with it, and read all of it. Some people believe that learning about something will make that thing happen. From my experience, that is totally unhelpful, and can actually lead to the opposite. One mother who did our course a while ago, specifically avoided watching the section on cesareans because she really wanted to have a vaginal birth. When she ended up needing to have an unexpected cesarean, she had none of the knowledge from that section that could have helped her have a far more connected and gentle experience. Remember, often what we *resist–persists*, so instead of pushing against things, or trying to avoid them, embrace learning about these interventions, knowing that it doesn't increase the risk of them happening. If anything, *fear* increases the risks of interventions happening, and learning more about something is one of the best ways to combat fear. So by reading about the interventions in this chapter, you may actually be decreasing the risk of them happening.

MEDICATED PAIN OPTIONS IN LABOR

Throughout this book, I've talked a lot about the benefits of a physiological birth, but it's good to remember that there is a time and a place for medication in childbirth. It's not as black and white as saying "epidurals are bad" or "unmedicated is good." While for one mom, having an epidural early in labor may slow labor down and lead to unnecessary interventions, for another mom who's been laboring at home for 36 hours and is exhausted, deciding to transfer to the hospital and have an epidural may allow her to have the rest she needs, wake up refreshed, and push her baby out. The following information is designed to help you feel more informed about the potential positive and negative effects of different medicated pain relief options.

Nitrous oxide: Often referred to as laughing gas or gas and air, nitrous oxide can be an effective medicated pain reliever during labor. It is breathed in through a mouthpiece (so very easy to administer) and has minimal side effects for the baby. It doesn't limit mobility, so women can continue to move to whatever positions feel best during labor. While some moms experience dizziness or nausea, one of the benefits of nitrous oxide in comparison to other medicated pain relief is that if mom isn't enjoying the feeling, then she can stop using it, and it leaves her system very quickly. Nitrous oxide won't completely eliminate all sensations, but helps to dull them and can also lessen anxiety. Many hospitals, birth centers, and home birth midwives can carry nitrous oxide, so if it's of interest, be sure to discuss availability with your care provider.

Narcotics: Opioids like fentanyl, morphine, or pethidine can provide some pain relief for your body; however, they may pass to the baby and can cause some babies to have temporary breathing and heart issues after birth. If this is the case, they will be given a drug to reverse the effects. Opioids can also cause some mothers to feel nauseous, spaced out, or sleepy.

Epidural: Epidurals are administered by an anesthesiologist injecting pain-blocking medication into a space between the vertebrae. It generally causes numbness between the belly button and the thighs. Usually, the catheter that delivers the drug is left in the epidural space until the baby is born so that the medication can continue to be administered as needed. Depending on the level administered, epidurals can provide temporary pain relief or a temporary lack of feeling. Often, when an epidural is administered, it will restrict a mother's movement as it decreases sensation in the legs, which puts the mother at risk of falling. There's also a possibility that the mother may have issues urinating and require a catheter.

With an epidural, the baby will require constant monitoring, so the mother will usually be restricted to the bed. In some cases, it's possible to request a *walking epidural* (or lower dose) and be supported in more upright positions, but unlike the name suggests, it usually isn't actually possible to walk. As an alternative to upright positions like squatting or all fours, a peanut ball can be useful to help create more space in the pelvis in a side-lying position. Because of the total lack of feeling, epidurals can reduce the laboring mother's release of beta-endorphins,[46] which are associated with the labor land altered state of consciousness that helps women to let go of feeling self-conscious and allows them to move instinctively, make the noises that they feel to make, and contributes to feelings of euphoria during and after birth. The lack of sensation and lower endorphin levels may cause a mother to feel more disconnected from the experience of birth, and can significantly reduce her body's release of oxytocin, leading to an increased need for interventions like the use of synthetic oxytocin and vacuum or forceps deliveries.

In a physiological birth, normally stretch receptors in the lower vagina trigger a major oxytocin peak as the baby's head descends. However, with an epidural, these stretch receptors are numbed. As Dr. Sarah Buckley explains,[47] "A woman laboring with an epidural therefore misses out on the final powerful contractions of labor and must use her own effort, often against gravity, to compensate for this loss. This explains the increased length of the second stage of labor and the increased need for forceps when an epidural is used." This reduction in oxytocin also impacts the major oxytocin peak, which is meant to happen at birth,[48] which is designed to help bond the mother and baby together, and also help with breastfeeding.

Some other potential side effects from an epidural include the mother's blood pressure dropping, which can affect blood flow to the baby and lead to fetal distress. Epidurals may also cause headache, itchiness, fever, nausea, or vomiting, and in rare instances, nerve damage or breathing issues. There are mixed results when it comes to the effect of epidurals on newborns. According to ACOG, it's the use of opioids in epidurals that increases the risk of a baby experiencing a change in heart rate, breathing problems, drowsiness, reduced muscle tone, and reduced breastfeeding.[52] In a 2021 cohort study[49] of over 400,000 mother and baby pairs, researchers found an association between epidurals and neonatal resuscitation, neonatal unit admission, and increased health conditions.

If you're planning to get the epidural, it's worth noting that sometimes epidurals don't work. Different studies have found that epidurals fail between 8-23 percent of the time. Also, in some cases, it may not be possible to get one administered as quickly as you'd like. One mother told me when she arrived at the hospital for her first birth, she wanted the epidural immediately, but an anesthetist wasn't available. Waiting hours for the anesthetist was incredibly traumatic for her because she had no backup methods to cope with the sensations of labor. As you can imagine, all the tension and stress would have increased adrenaline and cortisol and severely impacted her oxytocin and endorphin levels, making labor more and more painful.

I helped coach her in the lead-up to her most recent birth, as she had a lot of fear that it would happen again. Through doing our course and listening to the Christian Hypnobirthing tracks each night, she trained her mind and body to relax and embrace the sensations of birth instead of fighting them, with the goal that she would be able to manage if the epidural was not available. Due to her water breaking and contractions not beginning, she decided to accept an induction. Despite the stronger induced contractions, she used the relaxation techniques so well that she never ended up feeling the need to request the epidural. She shared:

> *"My first birth a year ago had me so traumatized I was petrified of giving birth again, but Christian Hypnobirthing changed everything for me... I breathed through the whole thing–no screaming, no anything. I won't lie and say it was pain-free but it was SOOOO bearable! Conclusion: DO HYPNOBIRTHING AND TRUST THAT GOD GAVE YOU A BODY THAT KNOWS WHAT IT'S DOING."*

So, if you're planning on getting an epidural, it's still always worth incorporating all the tools in this book and practicing the relaxation techniques regularly in the lead-up to birth so that you'll feel confident and equipped to stay calm and positive throughout labor, regardless of whether you have access to an epidural or not. You may also be surprised at how far you get without one.

Something I find deeply frustrating regarding the epidural is when people say things like, "You wouldn't get dental surgery without anesthesia, so why would you give birth without it?" or "There are no medals for giving birth without drugs—just get the epidural." No offense to the people who say this, but it displays a total lack of understanding of the physiology of birth. Getting a tooth pulled is not a physiological process that your body is designed to do, and having anesthesia during dental work doesn't have any major downsides. Meanwhile, the sensations of labor have a purpose. As discussed earlier, when you don't feel those sensations, your body doesn't produce the endorphins to cope with them, which help to drive oxytocin production, which is responsible for contractions, bonding with your baby, your let-down reflex, and so much more. If you eliminate the sensations, you impact the incredibly important balance of hormones. These hormones not only prepare your body for birth and your baby to be born, but they also help prepare you for motherhood.

Having an epidural can be a wonderful option if labor has become exhausting or has stalled, and the sensations are so intense that it is no longer a positive experience. But it's important to know that getting an epidural for birth is not the same as getting pain relief for surgery. The sensations of labor have a purpose. When you know that, then you can make an informed choice about whether it's a positive decision based on your unique circumstances.

My number one piece of advice for someone who has decided to use medicated pain relief is that once they've decided, embrace it and decide to feel positive about it. There's no point in getting an epidural and then beating yourself up, as that will just lower your oxytocin levels. I really encourage finding an empowering meaning in whatever you've chosen to do. So, if someone got an epidural after laboring at home for 24 hours, instead of saying, "I'm so disappointed I got the epidural," they could say, "I'm so proud I managed to labor for 24 hours just using warm water and breathing techniques," or "I'm so proud that I knew what was right for me, and I made the decision to transfer." Also, if you decide to have an epidural, remember to keep using the faith-filled tools! Due to the lack of sensations, it may be tempting to scroll through social media on your phone, stare at the clock, or watch the news, but that won't help your birth hormones. Do your best to create a safe, relaxed environment in the hospital room, dim the lights, have the Christian Hypnobirthing tracks or worship music playing, get support to help you into more upright positions if that's possible, or if you're lying down use a peanut ball to help open the pelvis, and have your birth partner give you a massage and remind you that you're doing an amazing job.

– BIRTH STORY –

STEPH'S EMPOWERED EPIDURAL BIRTH

Whenever people ask me about my birth story and hear I LOVED giving birth, I'm met with a bit of disbelief. I think our society/women have been so conditioned to fear birth. I certainly did for years before even planning to start a family, but listening to Christian Hypnobirthing while pregnant shifted my beliefs. I was truly relaxed before and during birth, choosing faith over fear. The tracks kept me calm and centered because there is truly a strength and a peace that comes from God's word. I gave birth in a hospital, with an epidural during a time of strict lockdowns and I still loved my birth experience. My amazing Grace came into this world with the word of God spoken over her.

I advocated for myself and I thankfully had my doula and my husband there to support me. I remember the nurse said to me while pushing, "I've never seen someone so happy to give birth." I was laughing and excited - truly so much joy in that day. The powerful Christian Hypnobirthing helped me progress in labor even with an epidural (which is known to slow down those hormones we need to get labor moving along). I could relive that day over and over, as I truly had so much joy in giving birth... something I never thought was possible. But, with God all things are possible.

ROUTINE PROCEDURES

In many hospitals today, there are routine practices being performed, despite not necessarily being evidence based for women with healthy normal pregnancies whose labors are progressing normally. The following chart includes some evidence-based alternatives that can be considered. These alternative suggestions won't be appropriate for everyone, so always do your own research and discuss the different options with your care provider when deciding what's most appropriate for you.

Faith-Filled Childbirth

Routine Procedure	Evidence Based Alternative Suggestion
Continuous fetal monitoring with EFM	Intermittent monitoring with a doppler
No food or drink during labor	Eat and drink as wanted
Artifical rupture of waters	Allow waters to release spontaneously
Routine use of Pitocin IV to increase contractions	Try relaxation, cuddling, nipple stimulation, and allow time and space for labor to progress
Coached pushing (also known as purple pushing) on back	Mother leads based on her natural urge to push, in a position of her choice
Episiotomy	Only to be used in emergency situations
Immediate Cord Clamping	"Wait for white" and cord to stop pulsating

There are also a few common routine practices that are more frequently performed in the U.S. than in other high-income countries, which I'd also like to mention.

In the U.S., some obstetricians will pull on the baby's head as soon as it emerges instead of waiting for restitution (where the baby's head rotates to face the mother's thigh so that their shoulders line up with the widest part of the pelvis). Pulling on the head before baby has rotated may cause perineal injury, a shoulder injury to your baby, and increase the risk of shoulder dystocia.[50] It is worth asking your provider about their views on this, and making sure they will honor whatever your wishes are for your birth.

The routine screening and use of antibiotics in labor for Group B streptococcus (GBS) is also not as common elsewhere as it is in the U.S. For instance, in the UK, screening pregnant women for GBS is not recommended by the UK National Screening Committee because:

- *"A woman may have a positive result a few weeks before labor and a negative result when she gives birth*
- *GBS does not cause an infection in every baby—there is no way of telling which babies will be affected*
- *Screening may result in giving many women antibiotics when they do not need them*
- *It is not known if the benefits of screening outweigh the harms for most of the population*
- *The proportion of babies affected by disease in countries where screening is carried out is similar to that in the UK."*[51]

During labor, the routine use of antibiotics is not benign for the mother or her baby; IV treatment impedes physical comfort, interrupts normal labor flow, increases rates of antibiotic resistance (which is a major threat to modern medicine), and also affects the microbiome which is crucial for a baby's healthy development. If a mother is GBS positive during birth, the use of antibiotics does decrease the risk of it being passed to the baby; however, it doesn't eliminate all risk. Regardless of whether you get tested, whether you test positive or negative, or whether you choose to accept antibiotics, it's worth knowing the symptoms to look out for in your newborn, which are: difficulty breathing, breathing too quickly or noisy breathing, being very sleepy and not interested in breastfeeding or drinking from a bottle, vomiting, being too hot or too cold, pale or mottled skin, and floppy arms and legs.

If you are worried your newborn could have GBS, seek urgent medical advice or call an ambulance. While there's currently no way of making 100 percent certain that your baby won't contract GBS (even with antibiotics), most pregnant women who carry GBS have healthy babies, and the risk of passing GBS to the baby during childbirth is small. There are also some things you can do to decrease the over-colonization of the bacteria. You can support your microbiome and influence healthy vaginal flora through:

- Eating nourishing foods (probiotic foods contain beneficial live microbiota that may further alter one's microbiome; these include fermented foods like kefir, yogurt with live active cultures, pickled vegetables, tempeh, kombucha tea, kimchi, miso, and sauerkraut)
- Exercising (recent studies suggest that exercise has a number of benefits for the gut microbiota)
- Taking supplements (some studies suggest that using a probiotic daily in your last trimester may cut your chance of testing positive for GBS by almost half—ask your midwife or provider if they have recommendations on a women's/vaginal health-specific probiotic with a high CFU).

In the U.S., the routine use of antibiotic eye ointment, erythromycin, is another routine procedure that isn't as commonly used in other high-income countries. It's given to newborns to prevent blindness, which is caused by a mother infected with gonorrhea or chlamydia, but is routinely given even when mothers have tested negative for these two sexually transmitted infections. Antibiotics can harm a baby's gut health, which potentially increases their risk of illness later in life. Also, the ointment can cause a baby to have blurred vision, which may interfere with bonding and establishing breastfeeding. If you have tested negative for these sexually transmitted diseases, and you're in a monogamous relationship with no risk of contracting gonorrhea or chlamydia, then it's worth talking to your care provider about what's right for you and whether the eye ointment is necessary.

It's still common for newborns to be bathed within a couple of hours of being born, but bathing a newborn removes vernix caseosa, which is a white, cheese-like substance found on your baby's skin. Vernix protects your baby's skin while in the womb, but it can also be useful outside of the womb. It contains antioxidants, as well as anti-infection and anti-inflammatory properties; it can also help regulate the baby's temperature and moisturize your baby's skin. Many people now delay giving their baby a bath for a week or even longer after birth.

Circumcision is a painful procedure frequently performed on newborn baby boys without using pain relief and has multiple risk factors. The U.S. is currently the only country where the majority of boys are circumcised for non-religious reasons, with a circumcision rate of 71 percent. Whereas in many other countries, circumcision is much less common:[91] Australia (27 percent), the UK (21 percent), France (14 percent), Germany (11 percent), Sweden (5 percent), Italy (3 percent) and Ireland (1 percent). Circumcision has a lifelong impact on your child, so it is worth making an informed choice. If you'd like to know more about the potential risks, visit yourwholebody.org

Babies are currently offered a vitamin K shot shortly after birth, as babies are born with low levels of vitamin K (which is responsible for blood clotting). While bleeding from vitamin K deficiency is rare, it can be life-threatening, and we aren't able to predict which babies will experience it. As someone who is fairly holistically minded, I do struggle to understand this and wonder whether there is a purposeful physiological reason as to why we're born with low levels of vitamin K, but at this stage, research is still unclear on this. According to the currently available evidence, the best practice seems to be to give the vitamin K shot at birth.[85] As an alternative to the shot, some people decide to give vitamin K orally, but it may not be as effective. As always, talk to your care provider about what's right for you.

INDUCTION

In most pregnancies, labor will naturally start spontaneously, sometime between 37 and 42 weeks. Induction of labor is when doctors and midwives encourage the process of labor to start artificially. Induction is becoming a more common procedure, with the rate rising from 9.6 percent in 1990 to 31.7 percent for first-time moms in the U.S. in 2020.[53] Before I discuss some of the risks and benefits of induction, I want you to know that I am not against induction or any intervention where it is medically necessary. I also want you to know that induction certainly doesn't mean you can't use the tools I've discussed throughout this book. If anything, using them will be even more important. Many of our course members who have gone on to have inductions have shared that the affirmations and relaxation exercises helped them to feel encouraged and positive throughout their induction, and in many cases, mothers have even shared that they didn't feel the need for pain medication despite the stronger induced contractions. So, I hope that while reading this, you will keep in mind that if you do need to have an induction, it can still be a positive and faith-filled experience.

There are absolutely legitimate reasons to have an induction, for instance, when the risks of continuing the pregnancy begin to outweigh the benefits. Unfortunately, though it's common to hear of parents being convinced to have an induction with very little knowledge of what it actually entails, often they are just told they'll get to meet their baby sooner, without realizing that it could mean a much more difficult labor than if they'd waited for labor to start on its own. By the end of pregnancy, many women understandably feel tired of being pregnant; their body may feel heavy and achy, breathing may be more difficult, sleep may be illusive, and the thought of getting the baby here sooner may seem like a great idea! But it's important to know that an artificial induction is not the same as spontaneous natural labor, and the effect on your birth experience can be significant.

DUE DATES

There are many reasons someone might opt for an induction; from waters breaking and labor not beginning, or a reduction in fetal movement to medical reasons like diabetes, preeclampsia, or obstetric cholestasis. But more and more commonly, women are being induced for being near or past their due date. An important thing to note is that due dates are estimates. Only around four percent of babies arrive on their due date. By 40 weeks and five days, only 50% of first-time moms will have spontaneously gone into labor.[100] So, telling a first-time mother that her baby is "due" by 40 weeks sets up an expectation that is unrealistic for most. And more and more, mothers tell me they're being pressured to set up an induction date, sometimes as early as 39 weeks. Many women don't realize that you aren't actually considered overdue until after 42 weeks. According to the World Health Organization,[92] if you are between 37 and 42 weeks pregnant, you are perfectly within your due period, not overdue or late.

Personally, I think it would be great to call it a *due month* instead of a *due date*. Because when we become fixated on a date, we put all sorts of pressure on ourselves once we hit that date, thinking that we're now overdue and wondering why the baby isn't here. Relatives start calling regularly, asking if there's any news. Your care provider said they'll book your induction *just in case*, so then you start mentally trying to will yourself into labor so you don't have to be induced. And what is all this most likely doing? Producing stress hormones, which may actually be *preventing* you from going into labor. So, what do I suggest? Take the pressure off and give family and friends a rough guide as opposed to an actual date. If your baby was due on November 3rd, for example, maybe say the baby should be here around mid-November. That way, if the baby arrives earlier, what a lovely surprise, and later, no stressful constant calls.

If your medical care provider wants to book your induction because you're nearing 40 weeks, the following information might help you make an informed decision about what's right for you. Induction is not something to be taken lightly. Multiple studies have shown that induction increases the risk of intervention, with research by Professor Hannah Dahlen[54] showing that compared to spontaneous onset of labor, the induction of labor increased the likelihood of instrumental birth with forceps or vacuum, C-section, epidural, and episiotomy.

Why are so many care providers now recommending induction from around 39 weeks, even when there's no medical indicator? Parents are often told the number of stillbirths increases as the length of pregnancy progresses. Now, on hearing that, it can sound immediately like induction is a great option, as obviously, stillbirth is a tragedy, and we want to prevent as many stillbirths as possible. However, midwife and doctor Sara Wickham (who has a PhD in induction) says,[55] "The claim that induction lowers stillbirth is often not true. It depends on the reason for induction. When it is true, the difference is often tiny. And stillbirth is not the only way to measure harm. Induction causes more medium and long term harms, and more deaths may occur later after induction than after waiting for labor to start on its own." This is a really important point and one worth considering.

For instance, if we induced all women at 39 weeks, then we would, of course, prevent some stillbirths that would have happened after that because the babies are no longer in utero, so they cannot be stillborn. However, if other studies[56] show that induction potentially causes higher rates of neonatal mortality, including SIDS, then are we actually saving the lives of babies by inducing them early? Or are we forcing vast numbers of women with healthy, normal pregnancies to go through a more difficult birth experience, with higher rates of intervention and no genuine benefits?

The language used is incredibly important, as some care providers may use coercive phrases such as, "The risk of stillbirth doubles," or, "Do you want your baby to die?" Dramatic statements like that are an incredibly manipulative way of getting a mother to do whatever she's told. If you experience a care provider saying something like that to you, ask them to put it in writing so you have a record, and then ask them to give you the actual numbers. When the statement "the risk of stillbirth doubles" becomes "the risk of stillbirth goes from 0.61 in 1000 at 41 weeks to 1.08 in 1000 at 42 weeks,"[57] you're then able to make an informed decision based on actual numbers. Feel free to look up the article "Studies That Calculate Risk of Stillbirth by Gestational Age" by Evidence Based Birth to get an idea of the actual risks at different stages of gestation.

INDUCTION DUE TO BIG BABY

Many women are warned about the risks of having a big baby and encouraged to be induced early or schedule a C-section because of the risk of shoulder dystocia (the baby's shoulders getting stuck). While a bigger baby does have a slightly higher risk of shoulder dystocia, around half of babies who have this issue are smaller or normal-weight babies, and it is also not possible to estimate the size of a baby accurately before they are born.[62] If a mother is induced, it increases her likelihood of having an instrumental birth (which is also a risk factor for shoulder dystocia), and it also increases the chance of her requesting an epidural and giving birth on her back, which can make it harder for babies to maneuver through the pelvis. While shoulder dystocia is a medical emergency, it's good to keep in mind that in most cases, the care provider can help handle the situation without any harmful consequences for the baby by helping Mom to change position to facilitate increasing the pelvic outlet. One of the big benefits of unmedicated physiological birth is that when women are free to move around in upright positions throughout labor, they will often instinctively move in ways that support the baby through the pelvis. Sometimes, mothers may do some very strange-looking movements, which often make total sense once the baby emerges, based on the baby's position.

Interestingly, research across multiple studies[60] has shown that a care provider's perception that a baby is big can be more harmful than the baby actually being big. In one of the studies,[61] researchers compared the births of women with suspected big babies (qualified as babies larger than 8lbs 13oz) with the births of women who weren't suspected of having big babies but ended up having one. Shockingly, the group of women who'd been suspected of having a big baby (and ended up having one) had triple the rate of induction, triple the rate of cesarean, and quadruple the rate of maternal complications compared to the group of women who had not been suspected of having a big baby but ended up having one. Most of the complications were due to cesareans and included hemorrhage, wound infection and separation, fever, and need for antibiotics. There was no difference in shoulder dystocia between the two groups. This indicates that a care provider's concern about a baby being big seems to be a higher risk factor than the baby actually being big.

I know the stress of being told your baby is big, as my first baby was 9lbs 8oz, and second baby was 8lbs 15oz. The worry from being told I had a big baby in my first pregnancy was partly what caused me to push so hard in my first birth that I tore very badly. Whereas with my second son, who was also considered big, I allowed my body to push him out, working with my breath and the contractions, and hardly tore at all. One of the reasons I found it so stressful being told I had a big baby is that they didn't tell me about it in the context of our miraculous design for birth. In the lead-up to labor, our body has significantly increased levels of the hormone relaxin, helping to relax our joints and ligaments, working to allow our pelvis to expand and make room for the baby, and by moving and shifting throughout labor, we can also increase space in the pelvis. Another part of our miraculous design is that our baby's head is made up of flexible plates that can overlap as the baby passes through the birth canal, and the flexibility of these plates helps the baby's head to adapt to the size and shape of our pelvis.

You may have seen videos or photos on our Instagram page of babies with cone-shaped heads, showing how their heads have molded during birth and then amazingly returned to their normal shape within a short time after birth. It's great to keep this in mind when faced with these decisions and to know that cephalopelvic disproportion (where a mother's pelvis is genuinely too small to give birth vaginally) is actually very rare. Babies born to mothers with uncontrolled diabetes tend to be larger due to extra sugars in the mother's bloodstream, but management of gestational diabetes (through diet, exercise, or medication) can lower the chance of having a big baby down to normal levels.[63] Some of the dietary advice given to mothers diagnosed with GD may actually be unhelpful, so if diagnosed, I really recommend reading *Real Food for Gestational Diabetes* by Lily Nichols for evidence-based advice on how to manage it. If your care provider wants to induce you because of the size of your baby, be sure to discuss the risks and alternatives based on international best practices, not just the benefits.

THE DIFFERENCE BETWEEN SYNTHETIC OXYTOCIN AND NATURAL OXYTOCIN

In a recent study,[59] researchers found that "infusions of synthetic oxytocin in labor change uterine contraction patterns. This may influence uterine blood flow and maternal autonomic nervous system activity, potentially harming the fetus and increasing maternal pain and stress." In a natural, spontaneous labor, oxytocin is naturally regulated, with peaks and troughs gradually building throughout labor. After a surge finishes, usually both the mother and baby get a complete break before the next one, where they can fully rest. Alternatively, synthetic oxytocin (commonly called *Pitocin* or *Syntocinon,* depending on your location) induced contractions begin and become stronger more quickly, and the uterine muscle never totally relaxes between contractions, meaning the mother and baby don't get that total rest period afterward. This can increase stress on both the uterus and the baby.

The increased risks for the uterus and the baby mean that continuous electronic fetal monitoring is needed. The monitor, along with the IV, makes movement during labor more difficult. Because synthetic oxytocin doesn't cross the blood-brain barrier the way naturally occurring oxytocin does, endorphins are not released in response to the contractions, which can make them feel more painful.[58] With the increased intensity of induced contractions and the lack of endorphins to help, mothers may end up requesting an epidural. Once administered, while a mother no longer feels the intensity of the contractions, the baby is still fully experiencing them, and if there are too many strong continuous contractions in a row, this can lower the baby's oxygen supply, potentially leading to fetal distress. There's also an increased risk of postpartum hemorrhage as induction increases the risk that the uterine muscles won't contract the way they should after birth. In very rare instances, induced contractions can cause uterine rupture, which is a serious complication requiring an emergency cesarean and potentially requiring the removal of the uterus.

I am not sharing this information to scare anyone, but to make sure that you're fully aware that natural oxytocin and synthetic oxytocin are not the same thing. It really saddens me when I speak to mothers who ended up with an unexpected cesarean after being induced, who say things like, "I guess I just wasn't designed to give birth" because they think their body couldn't handle labor. The reality is that their body or their baby couldn't handle *artificially induced* labor, which is not the same as spontaneous natural labor. The truth is, we don't know how their body would have handled physiological labor because that's not what they experienced.

WHEN TO BE INDUCED, AND WHAT INDUCTION LOOKS LIKE

There are times when the risks of continuing to be pregnant outweigh the benefits. I can't tell you the point at which that will be, as everyone has different levels of risk tolerance. But as an example, if a mother has preeclampsia, the only way to cure it is for the baby and placenta to be born, so she may consider being induced as a beneficial alternative to a cesarean birth. In the cases that an induction is necessary, being aware of the process can help mothers to feel more relaxed about what will happen and to prepare for a positive, faith-filled experience.

Different hospitals have different policies, but for many women being induced, they will offer a prostaglandin pessary or gel to help ripen the cervix, which means that it helps to thin (efface) and open (dilate) the cervix. The pessary is inserted up into the vagina and positioned at the opening of the cervix, whereas the gel is spread internally around the cervix. Normally, at this point, you'll be left alone and then re-examined about six hours later. If there is no change, they may offer another pessary with another six-hour wait.

It's worth asking if you can go home to rest during this six-hour wait, as many hospitals will allow it. Regardless of whether you go home or not, the main things to do are rest, eat, and stay hydrated. In some cases, a Foley bulb, a catheter-like device with a balloon-like end, is used to put pressure on your cervix and encourage it to open.

Certain care providers may offer or use Misoprostol (Cytotec), which has been associated with some high-profile cases. It's always worth chatting with your care provider about what medications they use and researching them to make sure you feel comfortable with what's being offered. Just like in unmedicated labor, you want to help generate as much oxytocin as possible so you can help support your body in getting labor started. If you're not able to go home, think about what will help you feel as relaxed as possible while in the labor ward. Maybe that's dimming the lights, putting on your comfy clothes, listening to the Christian Hypnobirthing tracks, wearing an eye mask and earplugs, snuggling down with a pillow and a blanket from home, and getting some rest.

If the previous options have not started labor, then the next part of induction is likely to be the artificial rupture of membranes (more commonly called breaking your waters), where the midwife inserts a plastic instrument called an amni-hook to nick the amniotic sac. The waters will gush and trickle out and will continue to do so, so it's a great idea to bring a few pairs of underpants and maternity pads.

The next and final step of the induction is normally the use of synthetic oxytocin (Syntocinon or Pitocin) administered via a drip to push the uterus to contract longer and more frequently. As discussed in the section above, because the contractions are artificially stimulated, they can be stronger and more frequent than your body's natural contractions. So constant monitoring will normally be required to make sure the baby is tolerating the stronger contractions. Being hooked up to an IV, as well as constant fetal monitoring, can restrict your ability to move around, but you can still adopt upright positions and remember to keep practicing your breathing and listening to the tracks, play worship music, and consider hiring a doula for extra support. Doulas aren't just great for unmedicated births. They can also be incredibly encouraging throughout inductions or cesareans, and a wonderful source of continuous support if you're in a sterile environment like a hospital. Remember to bring things from home that will help you feel cozy and comfortable, like a photo of someone you love or your pet, your favorite essential oil for relaxation in an essential oil diffuser, or even just dabbed on a tissue that you smell when you want to.

SYNTHETIC OXYTOCIN FOR SPEEDING UP LABOR OR STOPPING POSTPARTUM HEMORRHAGE

Labor can slow down for a variety of reasons, and based on what we know about the nervous system and how it impacts birth, it's possible that if labor slows down, the mother may be feeling unsafe, stressed, fearful, or exhausted. If labor stalls, mothers are often offered synthetic oxytocin to help encourage contractions. Before agreeing, so long as the mom and baby are handling labor well, it may be worth trying the options mentioned in the birth partner section (having some privacy to snuggle or try nipple stimulation), a back rub or massage, a nap, changing position, walking (as movement can encourage contractions), having something to eat or drink, or a warm shower or bath. Sometimes, mothers just need some extra time. However, if active labor has stalled for a prolonged period and none of the above suggestions are helping, it may be worth considering synthetic oxytocin to help restart contractions. Discuss the risks and benefits with your care provider, and remember that when modern medicine is necessary, we should never feel bad about using it, and we can be grateful that it's available.

The same goes for the use of synthetic oxytocin after a baby is born. When babies are born, in many countries, Active Management of the third stage (the delivery of the placenta) is used, where synthetic oxytocin (or another uterotonic) is routinely injected into the mother's thigh to avoid postpartum hemorrhage. When there is excess bleeding, this can be lifesaving. However, when synthetic oxytocin is injected, it is usually combined with immediate cord clamping and controlled cord traction (where traction is applied to the cord with counterpressure on the uterus to help deliver the placenta). This rush to remove the placenta is necessary because the oxytocic injection will cause very strong uterine contractions that could trap the placenta, making it necessary to have an operation to manually remove it. Despite often being standard practice, there is some evidence that immediate clamping of the umbilical cord contributes to postpartum hemorrhage and retained placenta by trapping extra blood within the placenta, making it more difficult to expel.[101] It's also standard practice in many U.S. hospitals to perform fundal massage (massaging the uterus) as part of Active Management, which many mothers have told me they found more uncomfortable than giving birth.

As an alternative to Active Management, some care providers practice Expectant Management, which is a more physiological approach to managing the third stage of labor. This approach is more popular in midwife-led births and involves the care provider waiting (while the mom's uterus contracts) for the placenta to separate from the uterus and be born naturally. Instead of preventatively giving synthetic oxytocin, the care provider waits to see whether it is necessary. Care providers who take this approach may also take actions to help support the mother's natural release of oxytocin immediately after birth by helping to facilitate immediate skin-to-skin contact (where baby is placed straight onto the mother's bare chest) and breastfeeding, massaging her feet or legs and ensuring that the environment is warm, calm, and private. They may also support the mother into more upright positions so that gravity can also aid the uterus in birthing the placenta.

TO INDUCE OR NOT TO INDUCE?

The Bishop's score is a somewhat subjective scoring system to help determine how successful an induction of labor might be, with a higher score meaning it's more likely to be successful and a lower score meaning it could be a more challenging birth. In instances

Faith-Filled Childbirth

where it is medically necessary for the baby to be born quickly (if someone has a very low Bishop score), it may be worth considering a planned cesarean, as that would be a lot less stressful than going through multiple days of induced labor only to end in an unplanned or emergency cesarean. If a mom's body really isn't ready to go into labor, then trying to force it into labor artificially may do more harm than good. On the other hand, if the mom has a high Bishop score and is considered *ripe for induction*, it's more likely that the induction will be successful, and it will be an easier experience for both the mom and baby. Be sure to discuss this with your care provider to work out what's best for you.

It's also worth knowing that sometimes providers may schedule inductions for their own convenience. For instance, in many parts of the world, Christmas is the least popular day to be born, followed by New Year's. If your provider wants to be home enjoying the holidays with their family, it's much easier for them to set you up for an induction a week or so before Christmas than risk you naturally going into labor on Christmas Eve. When it comes to being induced for non-medical reasons (like your provider not wanting to miss out on Christmas pudding), it's worth remembering that no one can force you to have an induction. They cannot show up at your house and drag you to the hospital. So, if you and the baby are both healthy and there's no medical reason for it, but your provider says, "I'm scheduling your induction," it's within your rights to say you're not going, and not show up. When you are faced with the decision of induction, be sure to go over the B.R.A.I.N. acronym, and know that a possible alternative may be to have increased monitoring to make sure you and the baby are both doing well.

Sometimes, induction really is the best choice. My number one piece of advice to mamas who decide to be induced is to embrace it. Even if it's not how you envisioned your birth going, you can still have a positive, faith-filled experience by accepting the new circumstances, knowing that God is with you no matter how you give birth, continuing to listen to the tracks, and doing your best to support your birth hormones. By practicing relaxation techniques and naturally supporting your oxytocin levels, you help to increase the likelihood that an induction will be successful.

– BIRTH STORY –

JESS'S POSITIVE INDUCTION DUE TO PREECLAMPSIA

I wanted to share my birth story and experience with the Christian Hypnobirthing App to hopefully encourage anyone whose birth plan didn't/doesn't go exactly to plan. I'm a first-time mom and had an emergency induction due to preeclampsia. I managed to have an unmedicated water birth, which was so beautiful.

On 06/27 I had my 37-week appointment and was sent to triage with high blood pressure. After running tests, my midwife told me I was right on the edge of being preeclamptic. She knew my birth plan and said she was comfortable waiting another week to see if anything changed.

On 07/03 I had my 38-week appointment. Within five minutes of being there, my midwife came in and told me it was time to have a baby. My blood pressure had skyrocketed and I had been feeling super off all week. Leading up to my 38-week appointment, I had dealt with five to twelve hours of prodromal labor every night for about a week and was miserable. I hated the idea of an induction as it was my worst fear and the thing I thought would stand in the way of an unmedicated childbirth. That being said, I knew that a healthy mom and baby was the ultimate goal.

My induction started at 1 p.m. on July 3rd. I was extremely nervous for what was to come but prayed that God would protect us and give me energy for the long night ahead. I was already dilated to 4cm and was 70 percent effaced before my induction. The first tightenings began very shortly after the Pitocin was started. They started as very mild Braxton Hicks. Within a few minutes, the contractions became regular and were four and a half to five and a half minutes apart. I walked the halls for a little while then moved to the birthing ball to do hip circles.

The Pitocin was upped 2ccs every 30 minutes until I requested to stop upping the amount to see what my body would do. At 5:15 p.m. my midwife checked me and did a stretch and sweep. I felt discouraged because she was trying to pressure me to up the Pitocin and have my water broken. I was still only 4-5cm, but knew that the centimeters meant nothing. I just closed my eyes and reminded myself to remain relaxed and positive.

The contractions picked up in intensity immediately after the membrane sweep, and I started walking the halls again. Every time I got a contraction, I would get into a deep squat and sway back and forth. At 7:30ish, I started considering having my water broken because the contractions weren't picking up in intensity or duration. I talked to my nurse for a while about it and weighed the pros and cons. Due to the prodromal labor, I hadn't really been able to sleep for days, which left me exhausted. On one hand, I wanted to try to let my body progress as naturally as possible and avoid all other interventions. On the other hand, I wanted to have enough energy to go through transition and pushing. I decided to lie down to rest in an exaggerated side-lying position for 30 minutes on each side in hopes of getting some rest. After that, I decided to continue moving and requested to have my water broken at 10:30 p.m.

She checked me and I was still at 4-5cm. My midwife questioned this and said this is exactly why she wanted me to continue turning the Pitocin up. This upset me because she was being really pushy about progressing my labor quickly. Mind you... I was already at 16ccs, which is not a small number... Although I felt discouraged when she said this, I closed my eyes and prayed, reminding myself that my body was built for birth and that the centimeter dilation meant nothing. She tried to sweep my membrane first, then tried to break my water with her nail. After that failed, she tried to break it with a tool meant to poke the sack. She was still unsuccessful and tried two more times. She said she would try one more time if I was up for it, otherwise she was going to give up and crank up the Pitocin. Finally, at around 10:30, my water finally broke.

I had another contraction immediately after it broke and it was way more intense. I could no longer talk through contractions and needed my husband to apply counter pressure on every contraction along with heating pads to my back. By 11 p.m., my contractions were two to three and a half minutes apart.

My mom arrived around 12:15 a.m. My midwife told me I had hours to go before I was anywhere near pushing then hours of pushing. I had a gut feeling that things would progress a lot quicker than she thought and told my mom to get there anyway. At this point, I was vocalizing through every contraction. It felt best to lean forward and sway with counter pressure on my hips. I got in the bath at 12:34 a.m. and was moaning through each contraction. They were less than a minute apart and one and a half to two minutes long.

At around 12:45 a.m., my midwife walked into the bathroom and said, "Alright Jess, are you going to cave and get the epidural, or are you doing this thing?"

I said, "Oh, I'm in this. I'm doing it."

She offered to get a birthing pool set up for me so I could have a water birth. I was over the moon because I had risked out of the birthing center and had mentally prepared to not have a water birth like I wanted. At 1:07 a.m., I got into the tub and immediately felt my muscles release. Although this intensified the pain, I knew it was more effective and focused on relaxing every muscle in my body. Every contraction made me want to clench up, but I moaned lowly and did a mental scan of my body every contraction to ensure I was relaxed. By 1:30ish my contractions were only 20-30 seconds apart and never fully released.

At 2:10 a.m., I experienced intense pressure. Felt like I was starting to push. My nurse checked me and said I had a ways to go and was nowhere near pushing. I was 6cm. My contractions were 5 seconds apart and lasted one to two minutes. At 2:42 a.m., I asked my mom to call the nurse in again. She checked and I was at 8cm. My body was already trying to bear down. At this point, my body was in a constant contraction. As soon as one would peak and start to die down, it would pick right back up. I was utilizing horse breathing to prevent myself from pushing and kept whispering "loose and open" over and over again to try to keep my muscles from pushing.

2:48 a.m., my mom called the nurse back in and I told the nurse I had to start pushing. She told me it wasn't time. Fetal ejection kicked in and I started pushing anyway in spite of her telling me not to. My husband bowed his head and whispered into my ear. "Baby, trust your body. If it's telling you it's time to push, it's time. You have got this." The nurse wanted to check me again, but I was in a constant contraction. 2:52 a.m. I finally *laid back for her to check me. I was crying out to God for strength, and then the nurse pulled away and quickly walked off. Although I was extremely upset at her in the moment, I found out she had rushed to get my midwife and was taking her badge, pager, phone, etc out of her pocket because she thought she was going to have to climb in behind me to catch my baby. I was 10cm and fully effaced, with his head about an inch away from my vaginal opening.*

2:55 a.m., finally, I let my body push and started to J breath to encourage my muscles to push my baby out. I barely had to do anything. It was such a relief to finally push. My midwife arrived at 3:02 a.m. As his head began to crown, my nurse tried to coach me to push, which I really didn't want to do. Instead, I waited for a contraction and I breathed him out; it wasn't until the last contraction that I held my breath and pushed him out. His head and body were delivered in one contraction, and at 3:15 a.m., July 4th, he was in my arms! He came out with his eyes wide open. He wasn't crying but I could tell he was taking air in. I rubbed the bottom of his feet and his back, and he let out a small cry. The water was cold at this point, so my midwife wanted to cut the cord so they could get him warmed up. I agreed that this was the best move as I was already shaking from the coldness. They brought him over to the warmer and wrapped him up. He was pink and looked perfect. He was on my chest by 3:21 and had only been apart from me for 2 minutes.

I used the Christian Hypnobirthing app and the course throughout my whole pregnancy, starting in the first trimester. I used the tracks to visualize my birth and the calmness and peace I would have. I went into preterm labor at 27 weeks and was admitted to the hospital at 33 weeks. I was on bed rest until I was full term and continued to meditate using the tracks and breathing exercises the entire time. I truly believe this was the only reason my birth went the way it did. The funny thing was that I only had the tracks playing for 10 minutes during the whole labor. I forgot I had my phone and was too focused to use them. That being said, my husband has been around me while I listened to them during pregnancy and was coaching me through each contraction just like the tracks do. He reminded me to be loose and open. He encouraged me to embrace the tightenings because each one brought me closer to meeting my son. He coached me through breathing and honestly ended up being my own personal doula.

He told our nurses at the beginning of the induction that we would not be using the word pain to describe my labor and that he would appreciate if they respected that. Instead, he asked them to use the words intense, effective, and productive. Anytime anyone (including myself) would slip up, he would interrupt and gently remind us that they were effective and doing exactly what my body needed them to do. He also reminded everyone that the use of the word "epidural" was not to be mentioned at all. I cannot recommend this course enough. I got my dream birth in spite of getting an induction, which was my worst fear. Immediately after giving birth, I told my husband I wanted to do it again and was so excited to go naturally without the use of Pitocin.

CESAREAN BIRTH

By this stage in the book you likely have a pretty good understanding of our miraculous design, the benefits of physiological birth, and how to best support it. However, it's important to recognize that sometimes cesareans are medically necessary, and in those cases we can be grateful for their availability. It's also good to know that if you need to have a cesarean there are multiple ways to make it a more connected and gentle experience. First, I'm going to review some of the risks and benefits so you can make an informed choice, particularly if considering an elective cesarean.

Much like inductions, the percentage of cesareans being performed today has increased significantly in recent years. In countries like the UK, USA, and Australia the C-section rate is now more than 30% and in some other countries like Brazil and Turkey C-sections now outnumber vaginal births. A reason for this may be that it's becoming more common for women to view cesarean birth as safer than vaginal birth, despite scientific evidence to the contrary. Except in situations where cesarean is the only safe option—for instance baby is sideways (transverse) or the placenta is blocking the cervix (placenta previa)—in the majority of cases, vaginal birth is safer than cesarean birth for most women.[64] A cesarean is a major abdominal surgery, carrying various risks to the mother, sometimes leading to breathing problems for baby after birth[65] and the mother's recovery is considerably more difficult than after a vaginal birth.

There is also research that suggests C-sections can affect the long-term health of children, with a higher risk of developing chronic childhood diseases like asthma, child-onset diabetes, allergies, and obesity.[66] Babies born vaginally come into contact with bacteria in their mother's vagina, which helps them to grow bacteria in their gut. These bacteria help to form their microbiome, which helps to keep them healthy and fight disease. The fact that babies born by C-section miss out on this bacterium may be what's responsible for the increased risk of disease.

Some mothers electing to have a cesarean may see the ability to know their baby's date of birth as a benefit as it allows them to schedule and plan. Waiting for spontaneous labor may feel out of control for some mothers, and this can apply to care providers, too. If they schedule an induction or a cesarean then it can provide a feeling of control. Some providers also encourage a cesarean if they themselves are not skilled in a specific area of vaginal birth, for instance breech or multiples. And in certain cases, there may be financial incentives for providers to encourage cesareans as they are usually more profitable for hospitals than vaginal births.

One of the issues that concerns me the most about cesarean births is that they create a hormonal gap. As discussed throughout this book, there are so many important hormonal processes that are going on in both the mother and the baby during labor and birth, and when a mother has a scheduled cesarean before labor has begun, these hormonal processes are totally missed. The stress hormones released in a baby as they go through the birth canal help to clear their lungs and prepare them to breathe, as well as ensuring that they are alert at birth and ready to initiate breastfeeding. The incredibly important oxytocin peak that mothers experience during and after birth is also missed, potentially leading to issues with bonding and breastfeeding. Thankfully, there are lots of ways to help close these hormonal gaps by choosing a gentler form of cesarean, as well as doing skin-to-skin contact and breastfeeding, so please be sure to read the next section so you can include them in your birth preferences (regardless of what kind of birth you're planning).

WHEN A CESAREAN IS NEEDED - TRADITIONAL VS. GENTLE

Sometimes, despite all our efforts to prepare for a vaginal birth, it just isn't possible. In the instances where a baby is transverse (sideways) and won't turn, or the mom or baby are at risk for any reason, we can be so grateful that we have access to cesareans. As I mentioned earlier in the book, how we look back at our birth experience has a lot more to do with how we felt during the birth than the actual mechanics of how our baby was born. So, if you need to have a cesarean for medical reasons, it's good to know that there are multiple ways to make it a more connected and spiritual experience than they have been traditionally.

A cesarean normally takes between 30 and 60 minutes and will involve the doctor making a cut into the mother's abdomen and uterus, which the baby is then lifted through. In traditional cesareans, babies are often immediately taken straight for routine procedures like cleaning and weighing, sometimes not being reunited with their mother for as long as half an hour. This can be a distressing experience for the mother, but it's even worse from the baby's perspective, after spending their entire life in warm, liquid darkness, constantly hearing their mother's heartbeat and her loving voice, then suddenly being thrust into a brightly lit room, having to breathe air on their own for the first time, have hands rubbing them down and being put on a cold surface. It must be incredibly stressful. We know now that the greatest comfort for a baby is immediate skin-to-skin contact with their mother, which is also incredibly important with regard to establishing bonding between mother and baby, lowering the risk of postpartum depression, reducing blood loss after birth, and increasing rates of successful breastfeeding.

Thankfully, things are changing. Step by step, more and more hospitals are starting to offer what are called *gentle*, *family centered* or *natural* cesareans. And in some hospitals, they're even starting to implement *maternal assisted* cesareans, where the mother helps pull the baby out and lifts them immediately to her chest. This may not be for everyone, but for some women who really want a vaginal birth, this can be an empowering and beautiful alternative. A gentle cesarean can involve some or all of the following:

- Instead of wearing a hospital gown, a mother may be able to wear her own clothes.
- She may be able to play music or have the Christian Hypnobirthing tracks playing (we have a track called "Faith-Filled Cesarean" on the app).
- It's sometimes possible to have just a spotlight over the incision, with the lights in the rest of the room dimmed to aid relaxation.
- Babies may be walked out of the uterus, meaning they wriggle out of the opening in the abdomen as opposed to being pulled straight out. The benefit of this is that it is more similar to how they are squeezed in the birth canal, which can help them in clearing the fluid from their lungs.
- Instead of the cord being immediately clamped, it may be possible to request delayed cord clamping.
- Instead of the baby being taken for routine weighing and monitoring immediately, the baby can immediately go to Mom's chest for skin-to-skin contact and breastfeeding (with routine assessments being done later).
- A mother may have the opportunity to seed her baby's microbiome (which I'll talk more about shortly).

Hospital policies vary, but if any or all of these alternative practices to a traditional cesarean are important to you, then be sure to speak to your medical care provider about it. Many obstetricians are happy to facilitate a more connected and gentle experience. If you get the impression that your care provider isn't supportive, remember you can always change care providers at any point during your pregnancy. This is your baby, your body, your choice. And for this to be a positive experience, where possible, I really recommend choosing a care provider who is fully on board with your preferences.

Allowing your baby to have a more gentle, connected cesarean birth, which also helps facilitate immediate skin-to-skin contact and breastfeeding, will help generate oxytocin and close those hormonal gaps I mentioned earlier. If the baby cannot be placed on the mom's chest, the cheek-to-cheek position is a beautiful alternative. I can't help but feel deeply moved when I see videos of babies crying after being born via cesarean, placed cheek-to-cheek with their mother, and then stopping as soon as they hear their mother's voice. What they need and want is *you*.

SEEDING THE BABY'S MICROBIOME

As I mentioned earlier, when a baby is born through the vaginal canal, they pick up microbes along the way that help them establish their own healthy gut bacteria. Babies who are born via cesarean miss out on those microbes, which, according to some research, may put them at greater risk of developing some health conditions.[66]

It is now being suggested that the microbiomes of babies born by C-section look quite different to those born vaginally, with lower numbers of the good bacteria Lactobacillus, Escherichia, and Bacteroides in their guts, which are very important for growth and could protect against asthma, allergies, obesity, and autoimmune disorders. To help restore the microbiomes of babies born by C-section, researchers tried something called vaginal seeding, where babies were swabbed with bacteria from their mother's vagina shortly after being born. This was clinically tested by Jose Clemente, a geneticist at the Icahn School of Medicine at Mount Sinai, and Maria Gloria Dominguez Bello, a microbial ecologist at Rutgers University, who found the procedure was successful in restoring the microbes that C-section babies lacked.[68]

If your hospital doesn't facilitate seeding, some women, before going into the operating room, take samples of their vaginal fluid with their fingers and place it around their nipples so the baby is exposed to that good bacteria as soon as possible. To help put into perspective whether this can make any difference, just one milliliter of vaginal fluid contains around 100 million microorganisms from five to 10 species, 95 percent of which are from the genus *Lactobacillus*.

There is some debate on whether seeding is safe for a baby born to a mom who is GBS positive or has other infections, so talk to your care provider about whether it's right for you. It's great to also keep in mind that breastfeeding is another wonderful way to help seed your baby's microbiome.

– BIRTH STORY –

SARAH'S PLANNED HOME BIRTH TURNED GENTLE CESAREAN BIRTH

Labor started the afternoon of 06/13 around 2:45 p.m. while I was bouncing on the labor ball, cleaning out my desk. Funnily enough, this was the last thing I wanted to mark off my list before the baby. I texted Ted and told him I thought I was having contractions. Then after he got home, he went ahead and put air in the birth pool.

As the evening went on, contractions started to get more and more intense and closer together. Our midwife and doula came around 8 p.m. and got everything else set up. I labored all night long until the evening of 06/14, moving from the pool to the floor, to the toilet, to the bed, doing whatever felt comfortable. Thankfully, I'd lost all track of time and felt totally in the labor zone, because Ted had the best birth playlist going, rotating it with the Christian Hypnobirthing tracks. The lights were low, it was calm, and I was supported. At around 5:30 that evening, we knew something was up. I'd been at eight to 8.5 centimeters for hours and in labor for 26 at that point. They'd pulled out all the tricks to help the baby boy move farther down and it just wasn't happening. I was beyond exhausted mentally and physically.

After a few conversations and tears, we decided to transfer to the hospital at that point. I was upset, sad, and defeated, but realized the best thing I could do was surrender my plan for the Lord's. I held on to the affirmation, "I accept the path God has for our baby's birth." On the ride to the hospital, I remember thinking I was in a dream, that this couldn't be happening.

My (Type A) plan was perfect, my pregnancy was perfect, how could this be? We get to the hospital and my OB is already there waiting on us and angel labor and delivery nurse, Emily Campbell, too. Much to their surprise that I was there - they had both cheered me on my entire pregnancy and supported our decision to do a home birth. We ended up having a gentle C-section with my OB. We came to find out during the cesarean that baby boy couldn't move any farther down the birth canal because his cord was wrapped under one thigh and around the other. Over 24 hours in natural labor trying to move him down was the most exhausting, hardest thing I've ever done in my life. Not at all what we had planned but in the end it worked out and I'm at peace about it because I know we did everything we could have possibly done and my body labored perfectly. I'm so thankful to have been able to naturally labor at home and make it as far as we did... I was in the most pain from surgery and the most exhausted I've ever been in my whole life, but he's worth it and I know it's temporary. This is something I'm very much still processing and taking a day at a time. Although we did have a gentle C-section plan just in case, this recovery is not something I had planned or prepared for, so that's another thing we are navigating. Labor and birth is the most spiritual thing I've ever experienced. The presence of the Lord was so evident. I've learned that labor, birth, and motherhood are all about surrendering.

THE MEANING WE CHOOSE

To finalize this chapter, I'd like to talk about the meaning we give to events and how important it is to choose an empowering meaning. Even though we have the power to influence events in our life (for instance, through where we choose to give birth and who we choose as our care provider), there are still things that can happen that are beyond our control. How we choose to respond to these circumstances will impact the quality of our lives and the actions we then take. For example, two people may both experience the exact same difficult event, and one person may choose to think, *This is God punishing me because I'm a bad person,* and the other may choose to think, *This is God challenging me and helping me to grow.* Even though they both experienced the exact same thing, how they feel, and the actions they will likely take are vastly different.

Everything in this book is designed to help you set yourself up for the most positive, faith-filled birth experience possible, and that includes when plans have to change. It's in those moments that we have a choice. We get to choose the meaning we give to anything that happens, and whether we will keep trusting in God's plan for us. I really suggest practicing finding a meaning that empowers you.

EMPOWERING MEANING EXERCISE

I'm going to start a few sentences that could initially be perceived as negative and then finish them with an empowering meaning, and I encourage you to think of some examples from your own life (they don't have to be birth or pregnancy-related). Practice writing something that didn't go to plan and then a positive and empowering meaning you could give to it.

UNEXPECTED EVENT

Unexpected Event	Empowering Meaning
I had to have an unplanned cesarean because my baby was transverse and wouldn't turn during labor.	But it's so wonderful that my baby could be born safely and was still able to experience the benefits associated with spontaneous labor.
I need to be induced tomorrow due to preeclampsia.	But thankfully, I have a high Bishop's Score and will likely have a successful vaginal birth.
I wanted a home birth, but after a long labor, I decided to transfer to get the epidural.	But it helped me have a rest and gave me the energy I needed to birth my baby.

I totally understand that sometimes it can be incredibly disappointing when things don't work out the way we planned. But developing the ability to find a positive and empowering meaning when facing unexpected circumstances is not just going to help you if your birth plans have to change—it is a skill for life. And the more you practice it, the more resilient you will become. No matter what we face, God is always with us.

> *"God is our refuge and strength, a very present help in trouble. Therefore we will not fear though the earth gives way, though the mountains be moved into the heart of the sea, though its waters roar and foam, though the mountains tremble at its swelling."*
> – Psalm 46:1

Birth

"'Do I bring to the moment of birth and not give delivery?' says the Lord*."*
– Isaiah 66:9

IT'S ALMOST TIME

How you experience the onset of labor can be different for everyone. In the weeks before birth, your baby may engage (meaning they move deeper into the pelvis), and you may experience Braxton Hicks (or *practice*) contractions. These are all indications that your body is gently doing its work, preparing for labor. Prior to labor, you may experience loose bowel movements or feel cramps with a dull backache. Many women have the urge to nest and get a burst of energy to finish off last-minute projects they wanted to get done before the baby arrives.

During these weeks leading up to birth, it can be great to be aware of your posture and how you're sitting to help encourage babies into optimal positioning for birth. I really recommend taking a look at spinningbabies.com and the movement section in the Faith-

Filled Toolbox chapter. But generally speaking, doing your best to be in an upright and forward position can help the baby to settle into an LOA (left occiput anterior) position. The baby's back is the heaviest part of their body, so if you're spending a lot of time lying back on the couch, in a car seat, or in an armchair, the baby's back will tend to swing toward your back. So instead of lying back on the couch, try kneeling on the floor over cushions or a beanbag. You could also sit on a dining chair backward, leaning forward on the back of the chair, or sit on a birth ball (which is also great during labor). When driving, it's a good idea to sit on a wedge cushion in the car so your knees are lower than your pelvis.

Many women experience prodromal labor (also called *false labor*), where contractions come and go without settling into a regular pattern. A lot of moms tell me how frustrated they are when they think it's the real thing, but I think it's reassuring to know that your body is still doing important work and to do your best to relax and rest if you can. I had prodromal labor for days with our second son, and during those irregular surges that would come and go all through the night, I used to turn on the Christian Hypnobirthing tracks and do my best to rest, drifting in and out of sleep. I really recommend doing this if you can, as it meant that by the time real labor started, I was so well rested, and my body had already done a huge amount of the work.

Unfortunately, many mothers get so excited when they feel the gentlest hint of a contraction that they stay up all night or rush to the hospital only to get there and be told they're only 1cm dilated, which can be very disheartening. Not only that, but going to the hospital before 4cm dilation is associated with higher rates of intervention, neonatal resuscitation, admission to the special care nursery, and a longer hospital stay.[69]

If we think about this logically, when a mom hasn't slept because she thinks she's going into labor and rushes to the hospital before her body is anywhere near active labor, this means that by the time active labor actually starts, many women are exhausted and stressed. This is

Faith-Filled Childbirth

often when mothers get stuck in the fear-tension-pain cycle and are encouraged to get the epidural, which can begin the cascade of interventions.

So, for that reason, when you start having surges, as hard as it may be, try not to get excited. Obviously, check with your care provider if you have any concerns, but otherwise, just keep doing what you usually do. If it's nighttime, rest. Even if you can't sleep, just keep resting while listening to the Christian Hypnobirthing tracks. You might find you drift in and out of sleep throughout the night, and that's perfect. Even if you're not sleeping the whole time, your body is still resting while simultaneously doing its miraculous work to prepare you and the baby for birth. If you start having surges during the day, again, don't do anything differently. Stay relaxed and just keep going about your day as usual. Cook a meal. Go for a gentle walk. Putter around. Watch your favorite comedy movies or sitcoms to give your oxytocin a boost. Lie down on your left side for a nap while listening to worship music or the tracks, eating and drinking as you usually would. Carbs like bread, pasta, and rice are great for energy in early labor or easily digested foods as labor progresses. Just take it really easy. My aunty said her husband got her to go suit shopping with him during labor, and she was so focused on going from shop to shop and looking at different suits, that she hardly noticed she had to pause often for contractions. By the time they finally got to the hospital that evening, she was already eight centimeters dilated. So if you can, during early labor, just go about business as usual.

I know some people out there suggest hiking 1000 miles, eating all the curry, and having all the sex to try to get real labor started or increase contractions. And if that's what you genuinely feel like doing, go for it! But keep in mind that oxytocin is often referred to as a *shy hormone*. It's generated more when you feel relaxed. And a long hike doesn't sound relaxing to me, just exhausting. Not to mention, it's rare to hear anyone say those things have actually worked. So, before you set off, take a moment to tune into the wisdom of your body and what feels right for you and your baby. Also, try to think of prodromal labor and early labor as a gift. Your body is still doing really important work, but it's not that intense, and most of the time, you can continue to rest through it. Instead of rushing your body or feeling annoyed, do your best to embrace it and enjoy riding the gentle waves as you go about your day or drift in and out of sleep. And I know I sound like a broken record, but *rest, rest, rest*. Even after prodromal labor, sometimes early labor can still last a day or so for first-time moms, so as much as I don't want to quell your excitement, it's so much better to prepare for a marathon and then feel relieved if you only have to run 20 miles.

HOW WILL I KNOW IF IT'S THE REAL DEAL?

Generally, some signs that labor is fairly imminent or has begun are having a *show*, your water breaking and/or regular surges. A show refers to the release of mucus from your cervix that has a jelly-like sticky consistency and is normally pinkish (as it contains a small amount of blood). After a show, it can often still be anything from an hour to several days before the start of labor. So, if a show is the only sign of labor you've had, there's usually no need to go to the hospital or call your midwife yet unless you have any concerns. If you ever have any concerns like reduced movement from the baby, heavy bleeding, feeling unwell, or you're unsure for any reason, always call your medical care provider or go straight to emergency.

Another sign that labor is genuinely close to the beginning or has begun is your water breaking (which is when the amniotic sac around your baby breaks and amniotic fluid leaks from your vagina). Based on movies, we think that out of nowhere, our water breaks all over a restaurant floor, and we're automatically in the middle of active labor and need to rush to the hospital. The truth is, often, your waters won't release until later in labor, or sometimes they can break and then have no other signs of labor starting for hours or even days. In my case with our second son, they never broke at all! He was born in his amniotic sac, which is called "en caul" and pretty unusual. Even the midwives were surprised.

Faith-Filled Childbirth

If/when your waters do break, there are a couple of things to look out for. If they break before 37 weeks or the baby is breech, go straight to the hospital. The waters are normally clear, so if your waters are red, there may be bleeding, or if they're brown or green, then the baby may have passed meconium, which can be a sign of distress, so contact your care provider right away.

As sometimes it may not be a gush of water but more of a slow leak, it can be hard to tell if your waters have broken or you're leaking a little urine (it happens to the best of us). So, putting a maternity pad in your underwear for an hour and doing the *sniff test* can help to determine whether your waters have broken, as amniotic fluid is generally odorless. If it smells bad or offensive, it may mean there is a risk of infection, in which case you should also contact your care provider straight away.

Once your waters have broken, because of the increased risk of infection, many hospitals will want to induce labor. Policies on this change from hospital to hospital. The standard used to be 48-72 hours, then it went to 24 hours. And now, more and more hospitals seem to have a zero-hour policy. If your waters break and the hospital asks you to come in straight away, it's good to be aware that being in the hospital and having vaginal examinations also increases the risk of infection[71] and that you do not have to consent to vaginal examinations if you don't want to have them.

Most mothers will go into labor within 24 hours of their waters breaking, and almost all within 48 hours. So, if you're planning a hospital birth, it's great to relax in the comfort of your home for as long as you are able to. Talk to your care provider about their policies, and remember to use your B.R.A.I.N. to work out the benefits, risks, and alternatives, then tune into your intuition and ask what happens if you do nothing. It's worth knowing that before your waters break, the chance of infection is about one in 200. After they break within the first 24 hours, this goes to one in 100, then at 48 hours, two in 100, and at 72 hours, four in 100.[73] If you accept an induction, many hospitals will want to routinely give antibiotics to reduce the chance of infection, but according to a Cochrane review, there is not sufficient evidence to support this,[70] and it also increases the risk of developing oral thrush in the baby, nipple thrush[72] (which can impact breastfeeding), as well as the potential disruption to the baby's gut microbiota.

If you want to avoid an artificial induction, then it's possible that acupuncture, Bowen Therapy, or nipple stimulation may help to encourage contractions, but if the cervix is not ready, they will probably peter out. For the women who choose to wait for labor to begin, to reduce the chance of infection, it's important not to have sex or insert anything into your vagina. It's also important to be aware of how you and your baby are feeling. If you notice any changes, like a reduction in the baby's movements, changes to the color or smell of the amniotic fluid, or you have a fever or feel unwell, then contact your midwife or care provider. The same goes for after birth; be aware of signs of infection in both yourself (fever, feeling sick, smelly vaginal discharge, increased heart rate, or uterine pain) and your baby (fever, lethargy, noisy breathing, or looking pale), and contact your care provider if you're concerned. Most importantly, if you've made the decision to wait, remember that stress will reduce your likelihood of going into labor as the body will perceive it as a threat, so do your best to relax, do things to help you feel positive and happy, and get lots of rest.

WHEN ARE YOUR SURGES NO LONGER JUST WARM-UPS?

As I said earlier, sometimes it can feel frustrating when contractions are coming and going for hours or days, but I really recommend trying to get some rest through those if you can, so when they start becoming more consistent and powerful, you have the energy needed for labor. It can be reassuring to know that not one of these surges is wasted. Every single one is doing miraculous work to bring your baby to you. One of your biggest jobs is to surrender to the process and let go. Really, what we need to do is get out of our own way and let God's miraculous design do its amazing work. For people who love to achieve and control an outcome, this can be challenging, but you can do it! A really good affirmation for this is "I surrender" or "I let go." I also like to say the word *rapha* which immediately reminds me to be still, let go, and release.

One of the reasons we refer to contractions as surges or waves is because they usually feel gentle to start, then build in intensity to a peak, and then fade away. The muscles of the uterus are moving in a wavelike motion, drawing up to the top, ready to help push your baby down and out. To begin with, they may not be particularly intense, and you may still be able to talk through them. Then as they build in intensity, you may find you need to breathe through them really consciously, either using the breathing exercise in the Christian Hypnobirthing app or just counting your breath in for four, out for seven, or whatever feels good for you. Generally, a longer out breath will help you to come back into your parasympathetic nervous system, which is that rest and digest state, helping your blood and oxygen stay in the uterus and increasing oxytocin so surges are as efficient as possible.

During surges, as you're breathing, it can be helpful to think of the affirmation "I can do anything for 60 seconds" or "I am riding the waves." As they grow in intensity, the urge to get away may increase, so the affirmation "the surges cannot be stronger than me, because they *are* me" can help you to remember that you don't need to be afraid. The muscles of the uterus are working exactly as they should, and these sensations are *good*. These sensations also increase your release of beta-endorphins, which help you go deeper into labor land, allowing you to move instinctively, working with your baby to help them to move through the birth canal.

One visual image I like to think of is bison heading directly into a storm. When a storm is coming, instead of running away like other animals, bison turn and walk toward it because they know it will pass faster. The symbolism of this is so powerful as when we try to run from challenges in life, so often we make things so much harder for ourselves, and birth is the same. As soon as we tense up and try to get away from the surges, they become so much more painful, and we may be actively slowing labor down and prolonging the pain. Whereas, if we breathe deeply, surrender, and embrace the waves, not only do we feel more comfortable, but labor is usually able to progress faster. *Be like a bison*, turn, and face the storm—the sooner you do, the sooner it will pass.

Once a surge subsides, you then usually get this beautiful rest period afterward for a few minutes, where you can fully relax. It can be reassuring to think about that rest period and remember that if you were in active labor for 12 hours with surges lasting a minute and then having three minutes of rest, you would actually only be experiencing the surges for three hours, and the other nine hours you would be getting that complete break. Suddenly, 12 hours of active labor feels a lot more achievable when you realize you're only having to actively breathe and concentrate through three hours of surges during that time.

WHEN TO CALL YOUR MIDWIFE OR HEAD TO THE BIRTH CENTER OR HOSPITAL

This will differ depending on how far away your midwife lives or how far you are from the hospital or birth center. Also, labor times can vary significantly. As a general guide, though, many midwives and doulas recommend the 411 Rule, where you would call your midwife or head to the hospital when your contractions are coming regularly at four minutes apart, each one lasting for at least one minute, and they've been following this pattern for about an hour.

I would also take note of the intensity. If you're still able to talk or do anything else through contractions, then you're probably not in active labor yet. When you're no longer able to talk through them, and all you can do is focus on your breathing for the full minute duration (while possibly also swaying or instinctively moving to positions that feel good), then it's more likely that you are in active labor.

Have you ever lifted something really heavy? If not, just think of a world champion weightlifter for a minute. When they're in the middle of lifting the weight, would they be able to have a chat with someone? No. They are completely focused, and their muscles are working at their peak capacity. This is comparable to how you will be once you're in active labor. Your uterus muscles are contracting just like the weightlifter's arm muscles are contracting. So long as the weightlifter remains relaxed and focused, then lifting those weights shouldn't be characterized as painful, but it will be intense and it will be hard work, requiring all of their concentration. If this is the point you are at, where the contractions are lasting one minute every four minutes and have been that regular for an hour, plus they are so intense that your entire focus is on breathing through them, then it's a good indication that it's time to head to the hospital or call your midwife.

As mentioned earlier, going to the hospital in early labor is associated with an increase in intervention, so by waiting until you are in active labor before going, you increase the chance of having a physiological birth. As with everything, talk to your care provider about what's right for you, taking into consideration your unique circumstances.

You can use a contraction timing app if you'd like. There are lots on the App Store, but my only caution would be that being on your phone can activate the prefrontal cortex (or thinking part of the brain). It's really beneficial to switch off the thinking brain in labor to help you enter that labor land state. It might be beneficial for your birth partner to time contractions and also be in charge of the Christian Hypnobirthing tracks, so you don't need to look at your phone. If your birth partner notices your surges are getting more frequent and intense, it's probably a good idea for them to message your doula if you have one, but it might be best to avoid telling family and friends unless you want to spend your entire labor replying to texts that say, "*Any news?!*"

As the sensations increase, movement can really help, like rocking on a birth ball, swaying while on hands and knees, or slow dancing or swaying with your birth partner. You may feel like pushing on a wall or pulling down on something, so a birth support rope or sling can be really useful for that and can also help you to squat more easily, which can increase space in the pelvis.

THE THREE STAGES OF LABOR

As I mentioned at the beginning of the book, I'm not a huge fan of labeling labor with stages, as labor ebbs and flows differently for everyone, and there are no hard and fast rules about how long it will take to dilate or how intense surges will be at a certain number of centimeters. However, most care providers and pregnancy guides divide labor into three stages, and many women find it useful to know them, so I will share those guidelines again here. Stage 1 is dilation, where the cervix thins out and dilates to 10 centimeters. In hypnobirthing, we call this the *up stage* of labor, as that's when the uterus muscles are pulling up, thickening the fundus (the top of the uterus), which will help to push your baby out when your body is ready. Toward the end of Stage 1, between 8-10cm dilated, is normally when you enter a phase called *transition*.

During transition, your stress hormones that we wanted to keep at bay throughout early labor increase to meet your oxytocin levels. This important shift is to help give you the final burst of energy needed to push your baby out. Because of this quick increase in adrenaline, as well as surges that may feel like they're back-to-back, it's common for mothers to feel overwhelmed or nauseous during transition or to feel that they can't go on. If you experience that feeling, it's great to try to remember that it's normally a good indicator that you're very close to meeting your baby. One mamma told me that she found it incredibly helpful when her husband just said the words "you're safe" to her during transition. So maybe share that with your birth partner if you feel it could be helpful for you.

Stage 2 of labor is from when you are fully dilated to when your baby is born. In hypnobirthing, we call this the *down stage*, as this is where your uterus begins pushing your baby down and out and where you use your down breathing. As I mentioned in the Down

Breathing section of the Faith-Filled Toolbox, sometimes, when you reach full dilation, you may have a period where the surges disappear, which midwives often refer to as the "rest and be thankful phase." So long as the mom and baby are doing fine, there is no need to rush to start pushing, and Mom can just enjoy this brief rest. Then once surges begin again, they will start nudging the baby down. Moms will often get an uncontrollable urge to bear down, similar to the feeling of needing a really big bowel movement. I've also heard mothers describe it as a feeling of *throwing down* instead of *throwing up*. So, similar to when you get the urge to vomit, you lose all control, and your body completely takes over.

This is the time to use your down breathing, where you take a deep breath in, and as you breathe out, you send your breath purposefully down through your body. Some people prefer to make "mooing" or open "ooo" sounds here. Just be sure to keep the sounds low and open, as tight, high-pitched sounds can cause tension. You can also do horse lips where you blow out through your lips like a horse to help release any tension in your face or jaw. Coached or forced pushing can cause tension in the perineum, which can increase the likelihood of tearing. Whereas breathing your baby down with your surges allows your baby's head to gently stretch the vaginal tissue. It can feel a little like two steps forward—one step back, which is part of our beautiful design to give those tissues time to stretch.

If your labor has been relatively undisturbed, then there's a much higher chance you'll experience the Fetal Ejection Reflex (FER), where your uterus ejects the baby with no forced pushing on your part. Sometimes the strength of this experience of the body taking over can be a surprise, so doing the down breathing, horse lips, and mooing sounds can be helpful tools to stay focused if it feels very intense. Once the baby's head has emerged, it rotates so that the shoulders can come through the widest part of the pelvic outlet. Then finally, that final push, and the moment you've been dreaming of, your beautiful baby is in your arms.

Stage 3 begins after the baby is delivered and ends when the placenta is delivered. After your baby is born, they will continue to receive oxygen and nutrient-rich blood from the placenta through the cord. Up to 30 percent of your baby's blood is still in the placenta when they're first born, which is why we recommend delayed cord clamping, or *optimal cord clamping*, as it's now called. Some mothers have told me that despite requesting delayed cord clamping, their care provider clamped it after a minute, so it may even be worth saying that you "do not consent to clamping the cord until the cord has gone white and stopped pulsating." Allowing the cord to finish pulsating has been shown to have significant benefits for your baby.[74]

During the third stage, as discussed in the section on synthetic oxytocin, Active Management is standard practice in many hospitals, where synthetic oxytocin (or another uterotonic) is routinely injected into the mother's thigh to avoid postpartum hemorrhage, and this is normally combined with immediate cord clamping, controlled cord traction, and fundal massage. As an alternative to Active Management, some care providers practice Expectant Management, which is individualized care, as opposed to standardized care, and offers a more physiological approach to managing the third stage. This approach usually involves the baby being placed immediately on the mom's bare chest (which miraculously adjusts in temperature to help regulate the baby's temperature), with a towel or rug placed over them to keep them warm, and waiting for the placenta to separate from the uterus and be born naturally.

Oxytocin is responsible for the release of the placenta, as well as the contractions which clamp down on the blood vessels where the placenta has released (helping to prevent excess bleeding). Adrenaline is the antidote to oxytocin, meaning that if adrenaline spikes dramatically after birth, it may interfere with those important processes, increasing the risk of hemorrhage. To naturally boost oxytocin and help protect against the negative effects of adrenaline, it's important to make sure Mom is warm, the environment is calm, and she has immediate skin-to-skin contact with the baby. It can also be very helpful for her birth partner, doula, or midwife to gently massage her feet and legs or hands and arms while waiting for her to birth the placenta, as this will keep her feeling relaxed. Traditionally, more upright positions have also been used to allow gravity to help the placenta to fall out.

With Expectant Management, during this time, the care provider can observe the mom to make sure her bleeding levels are normal, only injecting a uterotonic if necessary. Be sure to talk to your provider about their approach to managing the third stage of labor and discuss the benefits and the risks.

THE GOLDEN HOUR

Research shows that what happens in the first hour of a baby's life (often referred to as the *golden hour*) can significantly impact bonding between the mother and baby.[102] This is a critically important time, so as long as the mom and baby are both doing well, then the baby should have immediate and uninterrupted skin-to-skin contact with their mom for at least that first hour. That means no routine weighing, no routine cleaning, or any other procedures, just straight onto mom's chest for uninterrupted skin-to-skin time. This is really pivotal for bonding and helps to keep oxytocin levels high, increasing the chance of successful breastfeeding and helping to reduce blood loss. It also helps regulate the baby's temperature and blood sugar levels, as well as decreasing stress levels in both the mom and baby.[75]

In rare cases where a baby needs extra support breathing after birth, it's still common practice in many hospitals to clamp the cord immediately so that the baby can be taken over to the resuscitation equipment. But instead, where possible, keeping the baby with Mom, bringing the resuscitation equipment over to them, and keeping the cord intact would mean that the baby could continue getting oxygen-rich blood from the placenta, helping support Baby as they transition into breathing air for the first time. If that's what you would want in the rare instance it was needed, then it's worth discussing with your care provider.

During the golden hour, when placed on Mom's bare chest, often babies will do something called the *breast crawl*, where if given that undisturbed time, they will work their way toward the breast, and latch within that first hour. This time can make such a difference toward successfully establishing breastfeeding and building that connection between mother and baby, so be sure to put it in your birth plan/preferences, if it's important to you.

8

Postpartum

*"I prayed for this child, and the L*ORD *has granted me what I asked of him."*
– 1 Samuel 1:27

Your beautiful baby is here! And you have witnessed an everyday miracle. No matter how many birth videos I watch, they still make me tear up. Whether it's a water birth, a maternal-assisted cesarean, or anything in between, there's just something about watching that beautiful baby breathe their first breath and cry their first cry that astounds me every time.

This baby grew inside of you for the best part of 10 months. All their intricate parts were created through no conscious effort of yours. You didn't have to wake up and say, "Okay, today's the day I grow my baby's eyes or feet or heart." They were perfectly formed according to our miraculous design as your body grew and nourished them. It brings to mind Psalm 139:13: "You made all the delicate, inner parts of my body and knit me together in my mother's womb. Thank you for making me so wonderfully complex! Your workmanship is marvelous—how well I know it."

Postpartum is a truly incredible time, but it can also be an incredibly challenging time. Often moms forget that practicing relaxation, mindfulness, and kindness toward yourself is just as important, if not more so, during postpartum than it was in the lead-up to birth. This is the time when all your mindset practice comes into its own, helping you overcome the voice in your head saying you're a bad mom because you're finding breastfeeding difficult, you didn't manage to get the baby out for a walk yesterday, and you haven't done the dishes in two days. Remembering that your breath is always available as a tool for relaxation and calming the nervous system, as well as filling your mind with positive affirmations and encouraging scriptures, will really help. When those thoughts come up, it is so important to observe them and question them. This will help to separate the thoughts from you. Remember, ask yourself, *Is that really true? Do those things make me a bad mom? Or do they make me a mom who is doing her absolute best in the circumstances of this moment?* When those thoughts come up, try to think of what you would say to your best friend. If your best friend was telling you that they felt like a bad mom, what would you say to them? I imagine you'd probably say something like, "You're doing an amazing job. You're adapting to a completely new way of living. Be kind to yourself. You're doing great."

The chapter on the power of words is even more relevant to postpartum. Looking at it again, Proverbs 18:21 "Death and life are in the power of the tongue." This is no small statement. The words that we say to ourselves postpartum matter. It's good to remember that what you speak over yourself impacts how you feel, which also impacts your oxytocin levels. Oxytocin is not only important for birth, but it's also responsible for bonding with your baby and your let-down reflex during breastfeeding.

Take a moment to picture two new moms a few days into their breastfeeding journey. Both are finding it challenging, but the words they're saying to themselves are different. One is telling herself, *I just can't do this, there's something wrong with me, my body just wasn't built for this.* Whereas the other is telling herself, *This might be challenging, but I can do this, I am getting there, my baby and I are learning together, and I trust that my body is designed to nourish my baby*. Which mother do you think is more likely to continue breastfeeding? Think of the amount of stress that first mom would be feeling as she's thinking those thoughts. Think of the adrenaline and cortisol that will be rushing through her body, impeding oxytocin production. The mind affects the body so much more than we realize. So do your best to speak words of *life* over yourself. If you're struggling to find those words, put on the "Postpartum Encouragement" or "Calm and Confident Breastfeeding" tracks in the Christian Hypnobirthing app.

The wonderful thing to remember is we can slow down a negative spiral simply by becoming aware of those thoughts. And once we are aware, taking a moment to choose more consciously what we want to say to ourselves, remembering how deeply loved we are by God, and allowing him to give us comfort, strength, and support when days feel challenging, can make such a difference. Once again, one of my favorite scriptures for parenting:

> *"As a mother comforts her child, so I will comfort you."*
> – Isaiah 66:13

When I look back at my first few days postpartum with our first son, I feel so sad to think of how much I rushed myself. At one stage, I was up at 5:30 a.m. doing the dishes. If I could speak to that new mom, I would say, "Slow down, be gentle with yourself, *give yourself grace*. All you have to do is to be here now. This is one season of your life. There will be plenty of days in the future where you can rush around cleaning the house, but your newborn will only be this little and need you this much for such a short time." Unsurprisingly, I struggled with getting my milk supply up initially because I didn't know how to just *be*.

The ability to just be still is such an incredible skill to practice for life, particularly for new parenting. All that rushing around not only impacted my milk supply and stress levels, but it also wasn't great for my pelvic floor. Many women have no idea of the negative impact physical activity can have on your pelvic floor if you rush into activity before your body has had time to heal. Your uterus has a wound roughly the size of a dinner plate. That is a pretty big wound. If it was on the outside of your body, I doubt anyone would let you lift a finger. Annoyingly, because it's on the inside and can't be seen, it's easy to underestimate just how much healing and recovery is needed.

THE 5-5-5 RULE

There's something called the 5-5-5 rule that is gaining popularity thanks to social media, and I really recommend you follow it if you can. This stands for five days *in* the bed, five days *on* the bed, and five days *near* the bed. Some people choose to do longer, and it basically means that you are spending those first five days *in* bed with your baby. You're not doing any housework; you're not doing any walking around other than just getting up to go to the bathroom or have a quick shower. Even if you had the most blissful, relaxed, easy birth without even a graze, your body still birthed a child. Your body is doing its best to heal the uterus and other tissues with any wounds or damage, and rest is the very best thing you can do to support it. So for those first five days, your only job is to be with your baby and rest. This helps your body to heal and lessens the chance of postpartum hemorrhage or infection. It can also help to lessen issues like urinary incontinence. I also really recommend seeing a pelvic floor physical therapist if you can in the lead-up to birth and postpartum, as they can be an enormous support and help you with physical exercises to minimize any physical trauma and help with recovery.

Then, for the next five days, you're *on* the bed. So, you're still mostly resting in the day with a little more activity here and there. You might start incorporating some stretching and a bit of walking around, sitting on top of the bed cuddling with your baby or other kids, or maybe moving to another comfortable, cozy place in the house during the day, but you are still predominantly taking it easy. And the final five days are *near* the bed. You are starting to resume a few more gentle activities, but not standing for longer than 30 minutes at a time. So that could look like holding your baby in a sling while you walk around a little or do a couple of gentle tasks around the house.

By the end of these 15 days, tune into your body and see how you feel. A pelvic floor therapist said to me that if bleeding increased after walking around, it was an indication that I might have pushed myself too hard. So, remember there are no hard and fast rules, much like the six-week birth check-up, where most doctors recommend waiting six weeks after giving birth to have sex again. That may still feel way too early for you, which is totally fine. You should never force yourself to have sex if you don't feel ready, and certainly not if it's painful. This is a time to be gentle with yourself.

I realize the 5-5-5 rule may not be realistic for some. I know that some fathers can get as little as two days of paternity leave, which I think is atrocious, and I cannot believe there is not more support for parents, but sadly, that is the case for many. If you are one of those families, then I really recommend doing what you can to line up some extra help where possible. Postpartum doulas can be amazing in supporting new mothers with help when it comes to feeding, healing, recovery, and soothing babies, and may also help with meal-making, some light cleaning, and looking after other siblings.

Alternatively, if someone asks you what you'd like for a baby shower gift, instead of more cute baby clothes, maybe they could put some money toward a cleaner or postpartum meal service. Often friends or relatives will want to come around to hold the baby, but actually, it would be far more helpful for them to do some cleaning or bring you a meal. I know that it can feel awkward to ask for help in that way because so many of us have been conditioned to manage things on our own, but if there was ever a time to ask for help, it's now. At our church, we do a meal train every time a member has a new baby, and if your church isn't doing that, I encourage you to suggest it. It makes such a difference.

The saying "it takes a village to raise a child" exists for a reason, but unfortunately, most of us no longer have access to a village, so we need to try to create our own. Going to new mom and baby groups and breastfeeding groups with our first son in that first year postpartum was truly such a blessing to me, and many of the moms are still great friends now. I didn't really realize it at the time, but it helped me feel connected to others and to know that I wasn't alone. I remember initially feeling like all the other moms seemed like they were finding it so easy, and then as we got to know each other more, they would share more of their challenges, and we were able to support and encourage each other.

If you haven't already, please feel free to join our private Christian Hypnobirthing Community Group on Facebook. I am always so touched when I see the moms in that group praying for each other, answering questions, and sharing their experiences. It truly is so special to feel the love and support of a group of women from all over the world, being there for one another. You can find the link for the group in the community section of the Christian Hypnobirthing app.

BREASTFEEDING

Breastfeeding is beneficial for both the mom and baby, with breast milk being the best source of nutrition for most babies. It is often referred to as liquid gold for good reason, in that it can even help protect babies against some illnesses and diseases,[77] lowering the risk of asthma, obesity, type 1 diabetes, and more. Breast milk also shares antibodies from the mother with her baby, helping the baby develop a strong immune system.[76] Not only is it beneficial for the baby, but breastfeeding is great for the mom too, reducing the mother's risk of breast and ovarian cancer, type 2 diabetes, and high blood pressure. Sometimes, establishing breastfeeding can be challenging as breast milk production is reliant on both physiological and psychological factors, which can be affected by stress, continuing to work, or other challenges personal to you.

During challenging moments, it can really help to motivate you to keep going if you remember the benefits and why you're doing this. While it's normal to experience a bit of discomfort in the first week or so, if you are experiencing a lot of pain or have any concerns, I always recommend contacting a lactation consultant to help support you.

Faith-Filled Childbirth

The Western Academy of Pediatrics recommends exclusive breastfeeding for about six months and then continuing breastfeeding while introducing complementary foods until a child is two years old or older.[78] One thing that can make breastfeeding particularly painful and also reduce the amount of milk your baby gets is a shallow latch. A deep, painless latch will help enormously in making breastfeeding more comfortable and effective. Feel free to take a look at the following YouTube playlist, which has some really useful videos on how to get a good latch. I also recommend listening to the breastfeeding track on the Christian Hypnobirthing app to help you feel relaxed and encouraged while you breastfeed.

Breastfeeding Playlist

SCAN THE QR CODE:

Colostrum is the first milk that your breasts produce during pregnancy, which then transitions to breast milk. Colostrum has double the protein and four times the zinc that breastmilk has. It's also easier to digest because it's lower in fat and sugar and is filled with immunoglobulins to boost the baby's immune system. This is another one of those things that I feel totally in awe of when I look at our miraculous design to grow, birth, and nourish our babies.

Much like I acknowledge that there are times when intervention is necessary in birth, I also acknowledge that there are times we can be grateful formula exists. But what I don't appreciate is how quickly mothers are encouraged to supplement with formula, often because of outdated hospital policies or hospitals being understaffed and no one having the time to help support a new mom in getting breastfeeding established. In many hospitals, sachets of formula are gifted to parents, which is a pretty fantastic marketing strategy by the formula companies. Formula is made with cow's milk or soybeans and doesn't have anywhere near the same nutritional benefits as colostrum and breastmilk. When your baby is first born, their stomach is about the size of a marble, and they only need about an ounce of colostrum per day. The amount of colostrum and, subsequently, milk that your baby needs steadily increases each day as their stomach expands. So as long as your baby is wetting diapers and seems happy and well in themselves, it's not normally necessary to supplement with formula.

If you're concerned that your baby is losing weight or you're experiencing pain when breastfeeding or having any other breastfeeding difficulties whatsoever, always, always get help as soon as possible, preferably from a lactation consultant. Don't delay. So often, issues can be resolved quickly with support. When the midwives came to my house three days after our first son was born, I told them I was finding breastfeeding really painful, and it turns out it was because my son was just latching onto the end of the nipple instead of the deep latch, which includes some of the areola. They showed me some small changes with how I was latching him and the impact was huge. I still felt some discomfort as my nipples toughened up over the next few days. It reminded me a bit of how you get calluses on the end of your fingers when you learn to play guitar. But after a week of breastfeeding, it felt like the most natural, normal thing in the world, and I feel so grateful for the time I had breastfeeding both my sons.

I'm not going to try to explain how to get a good latch because I think it's just so much easier to understand by watching videos, going to a breastfeeding group with other moms for learning and socializing, or seeing a lactation consultant. If you have our course, we also have a module on breastfeeding in there.

> *"The newborn has only three demands. They are warmth in the arms of its mother, food from her breasts, and security in the knowledge of her presence. Breastfeeding satisfies all three."*
> – Dr. Grantly Dick-Read

SLEEP

I'd like to start off this section by saying I'm not an infant sleep specialist, but I will share my journey with you and what helped us as a family. Please note that this is not advice. I do not recommend any particular type of sleeping arrangement, but recommend that parents do their own research into what safe sleep looks like, as only a parent can make the decision on what is right for their family.

When we got home from the hospital after our first son's birth, I was determined that our baby would never sleep in our bed. I had been told all about the risks and how dangerous it was and that the baby absolutely had to stay in his own cot on his back with no blankets or pillows, so I felt confident that would be what we would do. What I then found really confusing was that every time I put our son in his Moses basket, he would start crying. I'd manage to get him back to sleep by breastfeeding him or swaying him, and then the second he hit the mattress, his eyes would open, no matter how gently I put him down. I remember feeling so confused as to what I was doing wrong. I tried swaddling, I tried womb sounds, and white noise, but nothing seemed to help.

As the days went past, I became more and more exhausted, as at most, he'd sleep for an hour or two in a row. One night, because of pure exhaustion, I fell asleep while feeding him and then woke up in an absolute panic, thinking something awful must have happened. Thankfully, he was absolutely fine. But the really sad thing about this is that if I had been given information on how to co-sleep more safely, instead of just being told it was dangerous and not to do it, then I never would have fallen asleep out of exhaustion in a potentially dangerous position. I know so many people who have experienced similar things. One of my friends fell asleep while sitting in bed feeding her daughter and woke up when she felt her baby falling and caught her by the foot before she hit the floor.

A recent survey carried out by the Lullaby Trust has shown that nine in 10 parents co-sleep with their baby,[79] but only nine percent of parents who currently co-sleep with their baby had decided to do so before their baby was born. Over 50 percent of the parents surveyed had fallen asleep in bed with their baby by accident. Forty percent said they had fallen asleep on a sofa or armchair with their baby, which can increase the risk of SIDS by up to 50 times. It seems very clear that giving parents information on how to co-sleep safely, instead of just telling them not to, would save lives.

In some cultures, such as Japan, co-sleeping is the norm, and interestingly, they also have one of the lowest rates of SIDS in the world.[80] Their bedroom setup tends to be quite different from Western bedrooms in that they normally sleep on futons on the floor, which are firmer than regular mattresses, and remove the risk of falling off the bed. A little while after my scary experience falling asleep, I remember a friend telling me that when her baby was a newborn, she slept with him on a mattress on the floor in the spare room, and as she slept, her son would just help himself to breast milk throughout the night and that she'd wake up feeling refreshed. By this stage, our first son was sleeping a lot better in his cot, and I still had concerns about co-sleeping, so I didn't feel comfortable trying that. But when I got pregnant with our second son, when our first was just eight months old, I realized I would need any extra sleep I could get to look after a toddler and a newborn.

After doing some research, I found out about something called the "cuddle curl," which is essentially what my friend had been doing, where your baby sleeps on their back next to you, with their face next to your breast so they can quite easily feed if they want to. You are on your side with your arm above their head and knees curled underneath them. This creates a protected space for the baby, helping to prevent you from rolling toward them because your bent legs won't allow you to. I also learned about the La Leche League's Safe Sleep Seven, which is a set of criteria designed to minimize risks.

Safe Sleep 7 - La Leche League International[81]

- #1 **No smoking** in the home or outside.
- #2 **Sober adults**: no alcohol, no drowsy medications.
- #3 **Breastfeeding** day and night.
- #4 **Healthy baby** who is full-term.
- #5 **Baby on back** and face up.
- #6 **No sweat**: baby in light clothing, no swaddling.
- #7 **Safe surface**: no soft mattress, no extra pillows, no toys, no tight or heavy covers. Clear of strings and cords. Gaps firmly filled: use rolled towels or baby blankets.

For those first few months after our second son was born, my husband slept in the other room, which is what felt right for us. To me, it felt safer for our newborn and me to sleep in the middle of the double bed by ourselves, and it also allowed my husband to rest well and get up with our toddler if he woke up during the night. This worked really well for us for a few months, and then as Sammy slept longer, he moved into his cot and then eventually into the room with his brother. I couldn't believe how much easier this postpartum experience was compared to our first. Being able to do the cuddle curl through the night with Sammy meant that he could feed throughout the night without me having to get up, so I was so much more rested.

I think, as a society, we have such unrealistic ideas about baby sleep. We want them to fit in with our schedules. But babies are designed to wake up through the night, and we are designed to respond to them. With our first son, because I didn't know how to safely co-sleep, out of desperate exhaustion, I tried some different methods of sleep training, but I just couldn't get through it as it felt so unnatural to leave him crying. It's a controversial topic, and I understand that it may be upsetting to hear, but research has shown that babies who are left to cry it out don't stop waking up in the night. They do stop crying, but only because they know no one will come. When the director of the Child Development Laboratory at the University of Maryland, Nathan Fox, went to a Romanian orphanage, he was shocked by the silence. He said, "The most remarkable thing about the infant room was how quiet it was, probably because the infants had learned that their cries were not responded to."[82]

No doubt you'll get recommendations from different parents on the best books to read to sleep-train your child. And many of them will be effective at stopping your baby from waking you up at night. But it makes me wonder, did God get it wrong? Did he design us so that we can grow and birth our babies, and then, for no reason, they just cry all the time, which is really inconvenient for us? Or is it that our baby's cry affects us the way it does because it's supposed to, because we're meant to respond and be close to them? The only way they can communicate with us to tell us if they're hungry, wet, tired, sick, or they want to be held is by crying. So, if we ignore their cries, we cut off their only form of communication. There is so much noise out there that it can be really hard to know what to do when it comes to these issues. When family members or friends roll their eyes, saying, "You're spoiling them" or "You're letting that baby manipulate you," it can be difficult to feel confident in your choices as a parent. In these moments, I would suggest taking time to tune in to what feels right for you.

Consistently not responding to your baby's cries could potentially have long-term emotional consequences and impact their brain development.[83] So, when everything in your body is telling you to feed your baby to sleep and respond to their cries, but your mom says, "You're making a rod for your own back," try to remember this —your mom, the sleep training book everyone recommends, and your best friend who raves about the cry-it-out method aren't your baby's mother. You are. And I hope that by the time you're finished reading this book, you'll have the confidence to pick and choose what feels right for you and your baby. And that also includes all the contents of this book. There might be things that just don't resonate with you and that's okay. Take what does and leave the rest.

As I said earlier, because of the different factors involved in co-sleeping, I can only share my experience, and I can't recommend it to anyone else as there will be people for whom it is not a safe option.

There is, however, a fantastic book that I really recommend reading —if you're interested—called *Safe Infant Sleep* by Dr. James McKenna. I'd also recommend following @CoSleepy on Instagram. We also have a baby-led sleep module in our course led by sleep specialist Lauren Fucci from Holistic Mama Sleep.

MATERNAL MENTAL HEALTH

To close off this chapter, I'd love you to take a deep breath, wrap your arms around yourself, and give yourself a big hug. You are precious; you are loved.

Postpartum can bring with it some big hormonal shifts, and it's common to feel down a few days after birth. This is called *the baby blues* and usually goes away on its own. If, however, those feelings don't resolve or at any point postpartum, you start to regularly feel down, it's really important to talk to someone close to you about it and talk to your medical care provider. It's estimated that between 10 to 20 percent of new moms experience postpartum depression,[84] but it's good to know that there is help available, and mothers can usually be supported very quickly. It's also good to know that a lot of the time, PPD can be resolved with low intervention. Talking therapy and self-help strategies like CBT and mindfulness can really help lower rates of anxiety and postpartum depression, and where necessary, medication can also help. Many people don't realize that dads can also suffer from postpartum depression and may be less likely to talk about how they're feeling. It's important for them to know they're not alone and help is available. Always remember that it's okay to ask for help, and it's so important.

A few months into postpartum with our second son, with the combination of having two babies under two, a difficult situation with our extended family, financial and work pressures, living in a small two-bedroom flat, and then going onto hormonal birth control, my mood plummeted, and I started having intrusive thoughts like "the boys would be better off without me" which scared me. Growing up, there was a lot of stigma about therapy, but I'm so grateful that I got over that and asked for help. Thankfully, I was able to see a therapist really quickly, and it made such an incredible difference. I also got off hormonal birth control and have never used it again since. I track my cycle with Natural Cycles, which has been an amazing alternative for me personally, as my body and mental health do not respond well to hormonal contraceptives.

I share this because things often look fantastic from the outside. All the happy baby pictures posted on social media can make you think you're alone if you're struggling. But going through difficult times postpartum, especially in this modern world where mothers are often alone with their babies all day with no help or support, can be much more common than we realize. So, if you find yourself withdrawing from friends and family, crying a lot, having intrusive thoughts, feeling anxious or angry, having mood swings, or struggling to bond with your baby, tell someone. Do not suffer in silence. Postpartum depression can have negative impacts on your baby if left untreated. Talk to a professional.

To help support your mental and physical health postpartum, you can keep taking your prenatal vitamins and do your best to make sure you are eating enough nourishing foods and drinking enough water. It can be helpful to keep a water bottle next to where you're seated throughout the day, and if you haven't got a meal train going, there are some wonderful postpartum meal services out there that will deliver nutrient-dense foods to your door! Once you're physically recovered enough, going on walks with your baby in a stroller or carrier can help increase endorphin levels, which is great for helping boost your mood. You may also want to try dancing to music at home, doing some gentle yoga, or joining a stroller walking group or postpartum mom and baby fitness class.

As I mentioned earlier, doing our best to create a village can make such a massive difference. I believe we are designed to raise babies in the community. So, I really recommend getting out to mom and baby groups, catching up with friends, asking for help and support from loved ones, and hiring extra help like a postpartum doula or a cleaner if you can afford it. It can also help to lower your standards when it comes to the state of your house. The house will probably be a lot messier than it used to be for a while (maybe even many years!) Do your best to accept this and be kind to yourself. You are doing an amazing job.

PREPARING AS A COUPLE

Talk to your spouse before birth about expectations on who will do certain jobs. So many couples end up with a lot of resentment when a baby is born because of unrealistic expectations and the feeling that one person is doing more than the other. Have conversations before the baby arrives about who will be doing what and what jobs will be shared. It's good to keep in mind that for at least the first few weeks (if not months), you will probably feel like you're attached to your baby 24 hours a day, seven days a week, especially if you're breastfeeding. This sudden total lack of independence can come as a big shock for couples having their first baby.

When considering jobs like cooking and cleaning, it's vital to keep in mind that your uterus will have a wound the size of a dinner plate. You may also be healing from any damage to perineal tissues or a C-section wound if you had a cesarean. If you are breastfeeding, that is pretty much a full-time job (at least initially). This is why many cultures around the world have rituals supporting mothers during the early weeks postpartum. Countries like South Korea, India, China, Nigeria, Japan, and Brazil all have confinement periods of between 21 to 100 days, where the mother stays at home, is cared for by family members, and brought special nourishing foods and drinks that support healing and breastfeeding. Many of them also include daily massages for the mother! I mean, I just feel like we need to prioritize rolling this out worldwide... Sadly, with the way most of us live, this obviously isn't possible, but we can still find ways to honor this essential time of healing and forming a strong attachment with our baby. A mother should not be having to cook and clean in early postpartum. I would go as far as to say that it is dangerous for her physical and mental health. I was so grateful my husband stepped up to do virtually all of the cooking and cleaning during that time, but if that's not possible in your situation, then who else can help?

One thing that was an absolute game changer for us was baby wearing. It meant that on those days, I was exhausted from being up all through the night with our first son, my husband could put him in the baby wrap, and he would sleep so soundly, allowing me to get a bit of much-needed rest. Because baby wearing increases oxytocin in both the parent and the baby, this time was also really special for my husband and helped him feel more connected to our son. Research has also shown that wearing your baby reduces crying and can improve their sleep.[94] While initially learning how to wrap newborns safely can seem a little tricky, it is so worth it, and definitely one of my number one suggestions for both parents postpartum.

Another thing to consider is that some couples have very different views on parenting, discipline, and family dynamics, which they may not have realized, and often there may also be resentment about the over- or under-involvement of one spouse member's family. Having conversations about these expectations can really help to prepare you for a smoother transition into parenting together.

Here are a few subjects to discuss for a smoother transition into parenthood:

- **Division of labor**: Who will clean, make meals, do laundry, change diapers, feed the baby, and do night shifts? How will these jobs be split?
- **Childcare**: Will there be help from other family members? Who will go back to work? What maternity or paternity care is available? What childcare is available? Is one parent able or wanting to stay home?
- **Finances**: How will you manage a potential reduction in income while on leave, or if one parent isn't going back to work? Do you have life insurance to protect your family if the unexpected occurs? Do you have a budget you'd like to work toward to help you save or factor in new expenses for your baby?

- **Parenting style:** What kind of childhood did you and your partner have? How were they different? What were the good and bad things about how you were raised? How would you like to raise your child together? It's okay if you have different parenting styles, but it's important to talk about it so you can work to complement each other.
- **Having time for yourself:** Parental burnout is real, so designating times when you each get a break is important—even if it's just having a relaxing bath. Schedule time for both of you each week to go and do something by yourself (which isn't work). It can be as simple as going for a walk or getting a coffee with friends, but make sure to schedule it so it happens.
- **Adult time:** Making time for each other can feel hard postpartum, especially if breastfeeding all day has left you feeling "touched out." It's important to find ways to let each other know that you care for one another. Even if it's just a hug, a gentle touch, a loving text message, or snuggling together while watching a movie. Depending on how your healing and recovery has been, you may not feel ready physically or emotionally to have sex after the six-week checkup. It's important to have conversations about this and to know that there are lots of ways to be loving and intimate without intercourse.
- **Family and visitors:** Are you happy to have visitors when you have the baby? What involvement do you think your parents or in-laws will/should have? What are your expectations, and do you need to put any boundaries in place?

No matter how many books you read or courses you do, it's unlikely that anything could fully prepare you as a couple for the complete life change that having your first baby will be. Where you used to be able to walk out the door and not think about it, you now have a human being who is completely dependent on you for their survival. It's so important to do your best to be kind to one another and communicate in healthy ways. As I mentioned earlier in the book, assertive communication, which is neither passive nor aggressive, can go a long way. This is where you share your needs or feelings, do your best to understand the other person's perspective, and are willing to compromise. Try to talk about how you're feeling and remember that you're in this together. Praying together can also be a wonderful tool for forgiveness, understanding, and connection. Even though it can feel really challenging at times, and your relationship will not be the same as it was before the baby arrived, when you communicate well and do your best to swap your expectations for appreciation, having a baby can bond you even closer together.

> *"Love is patient, love is kind. It does not envy, it does not boast, it is not proud. It does not dishonor others, it is not self-seeking, it is not easily angered, it keeps no record of wrongs. Love does not delight in evil but rejoices with the truth. It always protects, always trusts, always hopes, always perseveres."*
> – 1 Corinthians 13:4

9

Conclusion

*"Peace I leave with you; my peace I give you.
I do not give to you as the world gives.
Do not let your hearts be troubled and do not be afraid."*
– John 14:27

As we've come to the end of the book, I want to address the biggest fear. The one that, deep down, most of us try to push away and ignore or avoid thinking about. But as I've already said, avoiding looking at our fears can often make them worse. So we're going to address it head on.

Sometimes no matter how many statistics we hear or books we read, the niggling worry that something bad will happen to our baby or to us just won't go away. And I can totally understand, as that was my biggest fear during my pregnancy with Charlie. At one stage, I tried to speak about this fear during the hospital birth class I took and felt the instructor brushed it off and tried to change the subject. Avoiding talking about it actually made me feel far worse. I wish she had just told me the truth, which is, yes, there is a very small chance that something tragic could happen.

Sadly in birth, much like in life, we can never eliminate all risk—as the saying goes, "Birth is as safe as life gets." Death may feel like a very taboo subject, but in some ways, that doesn't actually benefit us. As morbid as people may think it is to talk about, the reality is that all of us will die someday. Remembering this doesn't have to be a negative thing; it can actually be an opportunity to really deeply consider what life means, to think about what we want to do with the time that God has given us on this planet, what we want to contribute and to truly appreciate and nurture our relationships. I certainly don't recommend thinking about it all the time, but occasionally when I feel fed up with my husband or frustrated with my kids over silly little things, remembering that there's no guarantee they'll always be here, can help put my frustrations in perspective, and remind me of how incredibly precious they are.

When we're pregnant, we have a heightened awareness of death because babies seem so incredibly vulnerable, but the truth is, we're all vulnerable. It only takes a car accident or an unexpected diagnosis and, suddenly, we ourselves or someone we love can pass away, no matter how young or old. Instead of fearing this, we can use it to help us deeply value life. It can also help to deepen our faith when we remember that no matter what we face here on earth, Jesus has had the final victory.

> *"He will wipe every tear from their eyes. There will be no more death or mourning or crying or pain, for the old order of things has passed away."*
> – Revelation 21:4

No longer fearing talking about death, or the fact it's a reality for everyone, can also help us to far better support those who are grieving. Instead of turning away because we don't know what to say, we can turn toward. We can say the names of their loved ones and show them we remember, and that they aren't alone.

Shortly after we got married, my husband and I started trying for a baby. We were absolutely overjoyed when we saw a positive pregnancy test. We started reading all the books, planning the perfect nursery, and daydreaming about this beautiful new baby that we'd have the privilege of raising. When I began to miscarry only a few short weeks later, we were shocked and heartbroken. I remember both of us just lying on the bed crying for a long time. I kept asking, Why? *How could this have happened? Did our baby not know how loved they were?* Even now, almost ten years on, it still brings tears to our eyes when my husband and I talk about it. We then went on to have two more consecutive miscarriages, and it's hard to convey just how painful that time was. I had never even imagined once was a possibility, let alone three times... How could this be?

At the time, if someone had quoted Romans 5:3 to me, I don't think I would have appreciated it. But looking back, these words ring true. "We can rejoice, too, when we run into problems and trials, for we know that they help us develop endurance. And endurance develops strength of character, and character strengthens our confident hope of salvation. And this hope will not lead to disappointment. For we know how dearly God loves us because he has given us the Holy Spirit to fill our hearts with his love." When we go through trials, it's never for nothing, even though it might seem that way at the time.

When our son Charlie was conceived, I was so riddled with anxiety as a result of those losses that I searched desperately for tools to help me and was disappointed not to find any faith-based hypnobirthing materials. After the difficult birth experience I had with Charlie, I felt determined that Christian women deserved to have tools and resources that aligned with their faith, that would not only help them feel calm and confident, but also surrounded by and filled with God's love during their birth.

I find it so strange looking back and realizing that had we not gone through those losses, followed by a very difficult birth experience, I probably never would have created the Christian Hypnobirthing app. Not only that, but our son Charlie wouldn't be here, and likely neither would his brother Samuel, which is just unthinkable to me. I feel so grateful to God for our two beautiful boys and the work I get to do every day. It is truly the greatest honor and privilege to be a mother and to walk alongside women in their motherhood journeys. So many dreams that have come true, but that may not have been possible if it weren't also for the hardship we endured.

While we long for everything to be easy and perfect in our lives, the reality is that when we face difficulties, knowing that God is able to work in and through us and those circumstances for good will help give us the strength and courage to keep going. It allows us to rise to whatever challenges come our way, filled with a peace that surpasses all understanding. We can rest in trust, knowing that God has the ability to transform even our deepest pain into a profound purpose.

This isn't about being passive—there are certainly moments when we must take decisive action in the aspects of our lives we can influence. However, for those things that lie beyond our control, being able to trust in God's plans can free us from fear and anxiety. As the Serenity Prayer beautifully expresses, "God, grant me the serenity to accept the things I cannot change; courage to change the things I can; and wisdom to know the difference."

By educating yourself on birth, practicing the tools and relaxation techniques regularly, watching positive birth videos, putting together a supportive birth team, and creating a birth space that supports your physiology, you are doing your part to set yourself up for a positive, faith-filled birth experience—and beyond that, is *Grace*. I don't know what Grace looks like for you exactly. But I know that God knows what we need and that we can trust him.

> *"And we know that in all things God works for the good of those who love him, who have been called according to his purpose."*
> – Romans 8:28

When I look back at everything that's happened in my life, all of the joys and the challenges, the love and the heartbreak, I have one prayer—*thank you*. I know that God has given me exactly what I needed, and I'm so truly grateful.

My aim with this book is not that you will have an *Insta-perfect* birth, but that your birth will *deepen your faith* even further. That it will remind you that you don't need to do life on your own in your own strength, and that Jesus is inviting you to rest in his embrace. That you will know that you are loved—right now, exactly as you are. You don't need to do things perfectly; you don't have to try hard enough. God loves you just for being you. *That's Grace*.

I want to congratulate you for having the faith to read this book. It takes courage and vulnerability to believe that there's a different way. It's my belief that when we have happy and empowered mothers, we have happy and empowered children, and over time, we change the world. Please know that the work you are doing is *world changing*.

Thank you so much for coming on this journey with me. I can't tell you how much I appreciate it. Wherever you are, I'm sending you my love and prayers for a wonderful, blessed, and faith-filled birth.

May the Lord bless you and keep you. Amen.

10

Extra Resources

*"Put your outdoor work in order and get your fields ready;
after that, build your house."*
– Proverbs 24:27

I wanted to share a few extra resources that you can use for your birth if you wish. The first is a Birth Preferences Template. Some people prefer to say Birth Plan, but one reason I like calling it birth preferences is because sometimes things can happen in our birth that are unexpected. The word *plan* can feel quite rigid, meaning that if the plan has to change, we might feel disappointed or panicked. Whereas the word *preferences* helps to guide our birth partner and care provider in understanding our ideal birth, while also having the fluidity to still feel positive if things have to change for any reason.

Whether it's during pregnancy, birth, or motherhood, God is with us through the joys and the challenges. 1 Chronicles 16:11 says, "Look to the Lord and his strength, seek his face always." I heard a pastor speak about this recently, and he emphasized that it doesn't say "seek his *hand*" it says "seek his *face*." Of course, we can ask God for the things we want, and we know that God wants good things for us, but it's important to remember that *he* is the gift. Being in his presence is the gift. And by seeking his face and spending time with him, we can find a peace that doesn't depend on things going to plan; we can feel that peace no matter what happens.

> *"Though the storms may come and the winds may blow,*
> *I'll remain steadfast."*
> – Maverick City Music and Naomi Raine

So, as you think about the different aspects of your birth plan/preferences, you might also want to think about how you can continue to seek God's face, no matter what kind of birth you end up having. What will make that birth space and experience feel more spiritual and connected to you? What will invite the Holy Spirit in? Are there specific things that you want to have with you that will help you feel close to God? Maybe it's a scent like lavender or frankincense; maybe it's a cross that you wear, a photograph, your favorite scripture, or a special keepsake that has a special meaning for you. Feel free to jot anything down that comes to mind. And as you read over this next part, I encourage you to involve your birth partner so you can create your birth preferences document together. That way, you can discuss your choices and pray about them together if that's something you want to do. It also really helps them to fully understand your choices and be in a position to advocate for you during your birth if needed.

After the birth preferences template is a sample template filled in with what I would put if I were giving birth again. This is not a recommendation for anyone else; these are just my personal preferences.

Faith-Filled Childbirth

MY BIRTH PREFERENCES

NAME

CONTACT NUMBER:

ESTIMATED DUE DATE:

WHERE I PLAN TO GIVE BIRTH:

MY BIRTH PARTNER:

RELATIONSHIP TO ME:

CONTACT NUMBER:

HOW I'D LIKE TO BE MONITORED:

PAIN RELIEF:

THE ATMOSPHERE I'D LIKE:

IMPORTANT TO KNOW ABOUT ME:

POSITIONS FOR LABOR:

SECOND STAGE:

BIRTH POOL/BIRTHING EQUIPMENT:

TARA MENZIES

MY BIRTH PREFERENCES

IF BIRTHING IN HOSPITAL:

ASSISTED DELIVERY:

THIRD STAGE:

IN THE CASE AN UNPLANNED CESAREAN IS NECESSARY:

HOW I'D LIKE TO FEED MY BABY:

ROUTINE PROCEDURES FOR BABY

ANYTHING ELSE:

Faith-Filled Childbirth

MY BIRTH PREFERENCES
(SAMPLE - NOT A RECOMMENDATION)

NAME
Tara Menzies

CONTACT NUMBER:
XXXXXXXXX

ESTIMATED DUE DATE:
XX/XX/XX

WHERE I PLAN TO GIVE BIRTH:
At home

MY BIRTH PARTNER:
William Menzies

RELATIONSHIP TO ME:
Husband

CONTACT NUMBER:
XXXXXXXXXX

HOW I'D LIKE TO BE MONITORED:

If possible I'd rather my baby's heartbeat be listened to with a sonicaid, so I'm free to move about. There is no need to ask me, just feel free to listen in. I'd like to be asked as few questions as possible so I can stay relaxed.

PAIN RELIEF:

I don't want to use any medicated pain relief, so please do not offer it to me. To help me during surges I will be using relaxation exercises, light touch massage and warm water. I would appreciate it if you keep your words encouraging and positive.

THE ATMOSPHERE I'D LIKE:

I would like the room to be as calm and quiet as possible, with low lights. I plan to have my Christian Hypnobirthing tracks playing throughout, or may change to worship music, or silence depending on how I'm feeling. I also plan to use an essential oil vaporiser.

IMPORTANT TO KNOW ABOUT ME:

I don't have any allergies or medical conditions. I would prefer to be left alone with my birth partner whenever possible, and for all questions to be directed to him unless they're very important.

POSITIONS FOR LABOR:

I would like to birth in an upright position (eg all fours or squatting) and move instinctively to the birth position that is right for me.

I would like to remain active and mobile throughout labor. If I need a rest I plan to use my birthing ball, or lean on the side of the birthing pool or bed.

SECOND STAGE:

I do not want coached or forced pushing. I would like to breathe my baby down, and follow my body's birthing instincts.

I would like my baby to be placed on my chest immediately after delivery to have immediate skin to skin. I would like the environment to be kept calm and peaceful.

BIRTH POOL/BIRTHING EQUIPMENT:

I would like to use a birthing pool throughout labor and give birth in the pool.

MY BIRTH PREFERENCES
(SAMPLE - NOT A RECOMMENDATION)

IF BIRTHING IN HOSPITAL:

If I give birth in the hospital, I would like to have a private room with a birth pool.
I would like the lights to be kept low or off altogether, and plan to use LED candles for light.

I would like the room to be kept as quiet as possible with as few people as possible, so that I can labor undisturbed. I would prefer not to have any students, or any staff members who don't need to be there.

I would prefer to remain mobile and active throughout labor, so don't want to be cannulated unless absolutely necessary. I would prefer wireless monitoring if available so I can continue to move around.

ASSISTED DELIVERY:

I would rather not rush the process, however if baby is in distress then I will accept assistance.

HOW I'D LIKE TO FEED MY BABY:

I would like to breastfeed my baby, and plan to support my baby in finding their way to my breast during skin-to-skin contact, immediately after birth.

ROUTINE PROCEDURES FOR BABY

I would like to XXXXXXX the antibiotic eye ointment, and XXXXXXX the Vitamin K shot.

THIRD STAGE:

I would like baby to be placed on my chest immediately after birth and to have undisturbed skin to skin time for 'the golden hour' after birth.

I would like to wait until the cord has gone white and stopped pulsating before it is clamped and cut.

I would like to birth the placenta naturally without any drugs being introduced into my body. In the event of postpartum haemorrhage, I will accept the injection of synthetic oxytocin.

IN THE CASE AN UNPLANNED CESAREAN IS NECESSARY:

I would like to have a gentle/natural caesarean, and to be awake for this. I'd like the curtain to be lowered so I can see my baby being born. I'd like my baby to be placed on my chest immediately after delivery for skin to skin (before cleaning or weighing). I would like delayed cord clamping.
I'd like the lights near my head to be dimmed if possible, so the environment is more calm for my baby when they are put on my chest. I'd like my Christian Hypnobirthing tracks to be playing in the theatre throughout delivery.

ANYTHING ELSE:

Thank you so much for taking the time to read my birth preferences. We are believing for a positive, faith-filled birth experience and believe this is possible whatever path our birth journey takes. We really appreciate your support in helping us achieve this. Thank you for all you do.

God bless,
Tara

PACKING YOUR BIRTH BAG

Packing a birth bag is a wonderful way to feel prepared for birth. Whether you intend to give birth at home, in a birth center, or in the hospital, it's a great idea to have a bag packed. Even if you're giving birth at home, packing a bag can mean you know where everything is, and you don't need to hunt around the house. It also means that if you had to transfer to the hospital, then you have everything you need.

Packing a bag can also be a mindful activity that helps you find time and space to think about how you want your birth to feel (remember the power of visualization and how it can help you to feel more prepared and confident). As you're packing your bag, take the time to think about what's going to make you feel confident and relaxed during labor. For some people, that's super comfy clothes or fluffy slippers. For others, it might be a beautiful water birth outfit or bikini. It's great to keep in mind that what you're wearing affects how you feel. For instance, wearing a hospital gown can make you feel like a patient. Are you a patient? Is birth a medical event? Or is birth a totally normal physiological process, just like breathing, blinking, or going to the bathroom? Dress for the event you want it to be.

When putting together your birth bag, it can be helpful to imagine you're packing for a romantic weekend away. What helps you feel relaxed and loved up? What gets that oxytocin flowing? Massage oil? Candlelight? A lovely-smelling room? Some delightful treats? As well as creating your birth preferences together, packing your birth bag can also be a great activity to do with your birth partner so they know where things are, particularly if it's their job to set up the birth space and make sure you have everything you need. So, you may want to prepare a separate bag for them with all the things they'll need to set up, like speakers, chargers, LED candles, fairy lights, and massage oil. That way they can access the things they need quickly without having to rummage through your maternity pads. You may also want to pack a separate bag for the baby if that helps you feel organized and clear about where everything is. If you're planning a water birth at home, I'd recommend that your birth partner does a run-through of inflating and filling the birth pool so they know how long it will take and what to do. The following birth bag list is just a suggestion, so please change it as you want.

The Essentials:

- Your breath and the Holy Spirit (joking, but also not joking).
- Birth plan/preferences.
- Medical/hospital notes.
- Two or three comfortable bras, including nursing bras, if you're planning on breastfeeding. Remember, your breasts will be larger than usual.
- Loose comfortable clothes to wear during labor (perhaps about three changes of clothes). Swimwear if using a birth pool.
- Food to keep your energy up, like granola bars, banana or apple with nut butter, a sandwich, fruit and nut mix, a smoothie, coconut water, cartons of juice, and water.
- Towels and flannels.
- Five to six pairs of underwear, either comfortable old ones or disposables.
- Toiletries, including a toothbrush, hairbrush, hair bands, lip balm, soap, and deodorant.
- One to two packets of maternity pads, breast pads, clothing for going home, nightwear that's loose and front opening if you're planning on breastfeeding.
- Any medications you're taking.

Nice to have:

- LED candles and fairy lights.
- Positive affirmation cards.
- Dressing gown and slippers.
- Plastic bag for dirty clothing.
- Tablet or phone and headphones so you can listen to Christian Hypnobirthing or worship music, etc.
- Books or magazines.
- Your favorite pillow.
- Blue light blocking glasses if you have to be under fluorescent lighting.
- Water spray and massage oil.
- Birth ball or peanut balls.
- Aromatherapy oils and a vaporizer.
- Birth comb.
- A TENS machine if you intend to use one.
- Some kind of special treat because you deserve it! Chocolate is always my go-to.

What to pack for your newborn:

- 12 to 15 diapers.
- Diaper bag.
- Fold up changing mat or towel.
- Small pack of sensitive baby wipes.
- Cotton wool balls.
- Bodysuits, vests, and sleepsuits.
- An outfit for going home.
- Hat, scratch mittens, and socks or booties.
- Muslin squares.
- Blanket for trip home.
- A pram suit if it is cold.
- Car seat ready for the trip home from the hospital.

Birth partner:

- Snacks and drinks.
- Change of clothes.
- Blanket.
- Magazines and books.
- Toiletries, such as deodorant, toothbrush, and toothpaste.
- Money, including change for vending machines and the hospital car park.
- Camera, mobile phone, and chargers.
- List of phone numbers.

THE CHRISTIAN HYPNOBIRTHING APP

If you haven't already, please download the Christian Hypnobirthing App and give it a try. You can listen to all the tracks for free for one week when you subscribe monthly, so if it's not for you, all you need to do is cancel your subscription in that first week, and you won't be charged. You can find the app by searching for *Christian Hypnobirthing* on the App Store or Google Play or visit this QR code:

Get the Christian Hypnobirthing App

SCAN THE QR CODE:

You can start listening at any point throughout pregnancy, but we really recommend listening more regularly from 30 weeks and as often as every day if you can from 36 weeks. It's great to listen while napping, taking a bath, or going to sleep at night to help the tracks become an anchor for deep relaxation. This will help bring you back

Faith-Filled Childbirth

into that beautiful relaxed, faith-filled state when you turn them on during labor. If you want to include the other senses while you practice, you could light some candles, diffuse lavender oil (or another oil that's safe to smell in pregnancy), or your birth partner could practice light touch massage with you while you listen. It also doesn't have to be complex, personally, my favorite was just drifting off to sleep while I listened. I'd try to start with a different track each night. Also, it's okay to have favorites that you listen to more regularly, and if there's one you enjoy less, don't force yourself to listen to it. Give that track a break, and maybe try it again at a later point.

You can use the playlist option to put together the tracks in the order you want, and there's a sleep timer that can be accessed by pressing the *ZZZ* button when you click on a track. During labor some mothers listen to all the tracks over and over, others listen to just one track on repeat, and some also change between having silence, a worship music playlist and the Christian Hypnobirthing tracks. There's no right or wrong way to listen in labor, so trust what feels good to you at the time.

POSITIVE BIRTH STORIES AND VIDEOS

We have lots of positive birth stories on our blog and share many positive birth videos on Instagram and Facebook (links are available in the app). Reading positive birth stories and watching positive birth videos is such a powerful way to change the way we think about birth and to open our mind to what's possible. So even if you're not really sure if you want to watch positive birth videos, I really recommend giving it a go because that initial awkwardness quickly fades away, and you start to get a sense of how miraculous birth really is.

OUR COURSE

The information in this book is very similar to that in our Faith-Filled Childbirth course; however, if you're a more visual person, or you feel it would be easier for you or your birth partner to watch videos than read this book, you may be interested in doing our course also. It has over four hours of childbirth educational video content led by me, which can be watched online from any device, as well as our printable birth affirmation cards, a birth partner relaxation script, and one-month free access to the Christian Hypnobirthing app. It also includes modules: Setting Yourself Up for a Great Postpartum led by nurse midwife Nancy Pohl, Infant Sleep led by baby-led sleep specialist Lauren Fucci, Pelvic Floor Health and Recovery led by physical therapist Dr. Laura Gordey, Feeding Your Baby led by lactation consultant Christina Deleon, and Maternal Mental Health led by nurse practitioner Stacia Scott.

Enroll in the Faith-Filled Childbirth Course

SCAN THE QR CODE:

BIRTH AFFIRMATION CARDS

Christian Hypnobirthing subscribers get 50 percent off our printable birth affirmation cards; in the app click "more" and then "affirmation cards" for the discount code.

A PLAN OF ACTION

I recommend going over any notes you've taken while you've been reading this book or taking a look at the tools in the faith-filled toolbox chapter and writing down three to five things you can begin to implement immediately. Knowledge is not power—*taking action* on the things you've learned is! It is practicing these tools every day that will make the difference to your pregnancy, birth, and postpartum, so be sure to write down those three to five things now, see if there are any daily habits you can stack them with, schedule them in your calendar, and start practicing them today.

Extra Recommended Reading and Resources:

- *Ina May's Guide to Childbirth* by Ina May Gaskin.
- *Mindful Breastfeeding* by Tracy Donegan
- *Real Food for Pregnancy* by Lily Nichols
- *Gentle Birth, Gentle Mothering* by Dr. Sarah Buckley
- *Reclaiming Childbirth as a Rite of Passage* by Rachel Reed
- *Childbirth Without Fear* by Dr. Grantly Dick-Read
- *Birthing from Within* by Pam England
- *Bringing Forth Life* by Jodie McIver
- *The Birthing Instincts Podcast*
- *The Down to Birth Podcast*
- www.evidencebasedbirth.com
- NICE guidelines www.nice.org.uk
- www.birthrights.org.uk
- www.sarawickham.com

For anyone who is new to Christianity and would like to learn more, I'd personally suggest starting with the Gospels in the *New Testament* (Matthew, Mark, Luke, and John) and attending an Alpha Course if you can, as it's a wonderful introduction to the basics of Christianity. You can learn more here: www.alpha.org

Thank You

I appreciate your interest in my book, and value your feedback as it helps me improve future versions. I would be so grateful if you could leave your invaluable review on Amazon.com. Thank you!

If you have any questions about this book, would like to request prayer or get in touch for any reason, please reach out anytime at info@christianhypnobirthing.com. I'd love to hear from you.

Acknowledgments

It's challenging to know where to begin with my acknowledgments, as so many incredible individuals have significantly influenced me and contributed to the writing of this book through their important work and research. I am deeply grateful to the pioneers and thought leaders in childbirth and maternity care. In particular, I'd like to extend my thanks to Ina May Gaskin, Dr. Grantly Dick-Read, Marie Mongan, Katherine Graves, Dr. Sara Wickham, Professor Hannah Dahlen, Dr. Rachel Reed, Dr. Sarah Buckley, Carla Hartley, Lily Nichols, Dr. Rebecca Dekker, Pam England, Blyss Young, Dr. Stuart Fischbein, Robin Lim, and Tracy Donegan. Your dedication to improving the resources and support for expecting mothers is truly inspiring.

My deepest gratitude to the thousands of remarkable mothers I've had the privilege to support and learn from; it has been an immense honor. To the team at Game Changer Publishing, thank you for your expertise, encouragement, and motivation. A heartfelt thank you to my friend and extraordinary midwife, Lindsey Meehleis. Your profound reverence for birth, life, and death has deeply impacted my life and work.

To my dedicated doula prayer team—Kezia, Charlotte, and Helena—your incredible support, feedback, and advice have been invaluable. Members of our church, especially Kim, Emma, Scott, Eilidh, Emily, Kate, Mark, Pete, and Steph, thank you for enduring my endless theological questions and providing wise and gentle counsel.

Thank you to Vanessa; your faith and hope amidst grief have both inspired and humbled me, profoundly influencing my journey in writing this book. Thank you Suzannah, my dear friend of over twenty years, for being a source of strength and support through every phase of life. Many thanks to Kirsty for your steadfast advice and friendship, and to Alice, Naomi, Kate, Katherine, and Dusty, for the many wonderful and thought-provoking conversations over the years.

To my parents, Kelly and William, thank you for giving me life and fostering an expansive mindset of lifelong learning, self-improvement and limitless possibilities. To my brother Vincent and sister Grace, thank you for instilling in me a love of birth and babies and for a lifetime of friendship.

Thank you to Sara, Victoria, and Ticia for your encouragement. To my grandmother Jennifer for your unconditional love, my grandmother Marie Louise for your unwavering support, and to my late grandfathers Terence and David and late grandfather-in-law Bernard for the many deep, insightful, and encouraging conversations. Thank you to Mary, Laura, Mike, Jessica, James, Andy, Chrissie, and Marcia for being such wonderful in-laws. To all my extended family and friends, notably Laura and Rob, and to everyone not mentioned by name who has helped and encouraged me on this journey, thank you so much.

To my incredible husband, Will, your boundless support has made all of this possible. Thank you for your love, kindness, amazing sense of humor, and for being my best friend. I feel truly blessed to be your wife. To our beautiful children, Charlie and Sam, you are the inspiration behind this book. You have taught me so much, and being your mom is the greatest gift.

Finally, to our Heavenly Father, Lord Jesus, and Holy Spirit. Thank you for the blessing of life in all its fullness—the joy, the sorrow, the love, and the laughter—and for being with us throughout it all and beyond.

References

1. Dick-Read, G. (1959). *Childbirth without Fear: The Principles and Practice of Natural Childbirth*. Harper & Brothers Publishers.
2. Facebook. n.d. "Carla Hartley Post." . https://www.facebook.com/carla.hartley/posts/pfbid0KuCBZ18BNA51EXbELgBRcUBk3B24GrSmrkWkwJMas5g51VXRej1jfHLKzZi7k4GEl.
3. Steele, C. M. (1988). The psychology of self-affirmation: Sustaining the integrity of the self. In L. Berkowitz (Ed.), *Advances in experimental social psychology, Vol. 21. Social psychological studies of the self: Perspectives and programs* (pp. 261–302). Academic Press.
4. Simon Constable Equine Vets. (2019, August 7). *Foaling*. Equine Vets. https://equine-vets.com/health/f/foaling/
5. Gaskin, I. M. (2011). *Birth Matters: A Midwife's Manifesta*. Pinter & Martin Publishers.
6. Provan, I., & Boda, M. J. (2012). Let us go up to Zion. In *BRILL eBooks*. https://doi.org/10.1163/9789004226586
7. BibleProject. (2023, April 18). *Does God Punish Women with Pain in Childbirth?* [Video]. YouTube. https://www.youtube.com/watch?v=h_zIJtoKpes
8. Davies-Tuck, M., Wallace, E., Davey, M., Veitch, V., & Oats, J. (2018). Planned private home birth in Victoria 2000–2015: a retrospective cohort study of Victorian perinatal data. *BMC Pregnancy and Childbirth*, *18*(1). https://doi.org/10.1186/s12884-018-1996-6
9. De Jonge, A., Geerts, C. C., Goes, V. D., Mol, B. W., Buitendijk, S., & Nijhuis, J. (2014). Perinatal mortality and morbidity up to 28 days after birth among 743 070 low-risk planned home and hospital births: a cohort study based on three merged national perinatal databases. *BJOG: An International Journal of Obstetrics and Gynaecology*, *122*(5), 720–728. https://doi.org/10.1111/1471-0528.13084
10. *The Birthplace cohort study: key findings | SHEER | NPEU > Birthplace*. (n.d.). https://www.npeu.ox.ac.uk/birthplace/results
11. Hutton E. K., Cappelletti A., Reitsma A. H., Simioni J., Horne J., McGregor C., & Ahmed R. (2016). Outcomes associated with planned place of birth among women with low-risk pregnancies. *CMAJ*, 188, E80–E90. https://www.ncbi.nlm.nih.gov/pmc/articles/PMC4786402/

References

12. *Odds of Dying - Injury Facts*. (2023, March 1). Injury Facts. https://injuryfacts.nsc.org/all-injuries/preventable-death-overview/odds-of-dying/
13. Mikolajczyk, R., Zhang, J., Grewal, J., Chan, L., Petersen, A., & Gross, M. M. (2016). Early versus Late Admission to Labor Affects Labor Progression and Risk of Cesarean Section in Nulliparous Women. *Frontiers in Medicine*, *3*. https://doi.org/10.3389/fmed.2016.00026
14. Khorshid, R., Almadani, S. H., Shehri, A. M. A., Abduljawad, L. M., & Alsaleh, A. (2021). The effect of fluorescent light on anxiety patients. *Cureus*. https://doi.org/10.7759/cureus.13436
15. Burns, E., Zobbi, V. F., Panzeri, D., Oskrochi, G., & Regalia, A. (2007). Aromatherapy in childbirth: a pilot randomized controlled trial. *BJOG: An International Journal of Obstetrics and Gynaecology*, *114*(7), 838–844. https://doi.org/10.1111/j.1471-0528.2007.01381.x
16. Dekker, R. (2024, March 6). *Evidence on: Eating and drinking during labor - Evidence Based Birth®*. Evidence Based Birth®. https://evidencebasedbirth.com/evidence-eating-drinking-labor/
17. Roth, L. M. (2023). Defensive versus evidence-based medical technology: Liability risk and electronic fetal monitoring in low-risk births. *Social Science & Medicine*, *317*, 115565. https://doi.org/10.1016/j.socscimed.2022.115565
18. Yu, S., Fiebig, D. G., Viney, R., Scarf, V., & Homer, C. (2022). Private provider incentives in health care: The case of cesarean births. *Social Science & Medicine*, *294*, 114729. https://doi.org/10.1016/j.socscimed.2022.114729
19. Olsen, O., & Clausen, J. A. (2023). Planned hospital birth compared with planned home birth for pregnant women at low risk of complications. *Cochrane Library*, *2023*(3). https://doi.org/10.1002/14651858.cd000352.pub3
20. World Health Organization: WHO. (2021, May 5). New report sounds the alarm on global shortage of 900 000 midwives. *https://www.who.int/news/item/05-05-2021-new-report-sounds-the-alarm-on-global-shortage-of-900-000-midwives*
21. Maternal mortality and maternity care in the United States compared to 10 other developed countries. (2020). *www.commonwealthfund.org*. https://doi.org/10.26099/411v-9255
22. Kozhimannil, K. B., Hardeman, R. R., Alarid-Escudero, F., Vogelsang, C. A., Blauer-Peterson, C., & Howell, E. A. (2016). Modeling the Cost-Effectiveness of Doula Care Associated with Reductions in Preterm Birth and Cesarean Delivery. *Birth*, *43*(1), 20–27. https://doi.org/10.1111/birt.12218

References

23. *Experimental inhibition of labor through environmental disturbance.* (1966, March 1). PubMed. https://pubmed.ncbi.nlm.nih.gov/5909557/
24. Demirel, G., & Guler, H. (2015). The effect of uterine and nipple stimulation on induction with oxytocin and the labor process. *Worldviews on Evidence-based Nursing, 12*(5), 273–280. https://doi.org/10.1111/wvn.12116
25. Mph, M. R. V. (2024, May 21). *Is prayer good for your health?* EverydayHealth.com. https://www.everydayhealth.com/emotional-health/power-of-prayer.aspx
26. *Stress during pregnancy may change brain development in babies.* (2024, March 19). The University of Edinburgh. https://cardiovascular-science.ed.ac.uk/news-events/news/stress-pregnancy-baby-brain-development#:~:text=Stress%20in%20pregnant%20mothers%20%E2%80%93%20measured,children's%20social%20and%20emotional%20development.
27. Attanasio, L. B., McPherson, M. E., & Kozhimannil, K. B. (2013). Positive Childbirth experiences in U.S. hospitals: A Mixed methods analysis. *Maternal and Child Health Journal, 18*(5), 1280–1290. https://doi.org/10.1007/s10995-013-1363-1
28. CNP, A. L. A. (2024, March 19). *Can expressing gratitude improve your mental, physical health?* Mayo Clinic Health System. https://www.mayoclinichealthsystem.org/hometown-health/speaking-of-health/can-expressing-gratitude-improve-health#:~:text=Studies%20have%20shown%20that%20feeling,problem%2D-solve%20rather%20than%20appreciate.
29. DiFranco, J. T., & Curl, M. (2014). Healthy birth practice #5: Avoid giving birth on your back and follow your body's urge to push. *The Journal of Perinatal Education, 23*(4), 207–210. https://doi.org/10.1891/1058-1243.23.4.207
30. Hawk, R. (2022, February 11). *The bannister effect.* The Learning Leader Show. https://learningleader.com/bannister/
31. Blascovich, J., Mendes, W. B., & Forgas, J. (2000). Feeling and thinking: The role of affect in social cognition. *Studies in Emotion and Social Interaction*, 59-82.
32. Bush, B., & Welsh, H. (2018, August 2). Hidden hunger: America's growing malnutrition epidemic. *The Guardian.* https://www.theguardian.com/lifeandstyle/2015/feb/10/nutrition-hunger-food-children-vitamins-us
33. *Healthy diet before and during pregnancy linked to lower risk of.* (2021, June 2). National Institutes of Health (NIH). https://www.nih.gov/news-events/news-releases/healthy-diet-before-during-pregnancy-linked-lower-risk-complications-nih-study-suggests

References

34. Higuera, V. (2019, November 27). *Is eating dates during pregnancy safe — and can it help labor?* Healthline. https://www.healthline.com/health/pregnancy/dates-during-pregnancy#easier-labor

35. Clapp, J. F. (1999). *Exercising through your pregnancy.* https://ci.nii.ac.jp/ncid/BB14741949

36. Koenig, R. (2023, August 9). *Should you give birth while squatting?* Parents. https://www.parents.com/pregnancy/giving-birth/preparing-for-labor/squatting-birth/#citation-2

37. Dundes, L. (1987). The evolution of maternal birthing position. *American Journal of Public Health*, *77*(5), 636–641. https://doi.org/10.2105/ajph.77.5.636

38. Dekker, R. (2023, September 7). *Evidence on: Birthing Positions - Evidence Based Birth®*. Evidence Based Birth®. https://evidencebasedbirth.com/evidence-birthing-positions/

39. Burns, E., Feeley, C., Hall, P. J., & Vanderlaan, J. (2022). Systematic review and meta-analysis to examine intrapartum interventions, and maternal and neonatal outcomes following immersion in water during labour and waterbirth. *BMJ Open*, *12*(7), e056517. https://doi.org/10.1136/bmjopen-2021-056517

40. Field, T. (2010). Touch for socioemotional and physical well-being: A review. *Developmental Review*, *30*(4), 367–383. https://doi.org/10.1016/j.dr.2011.01.001

41. Dresden, D. (2020, November 4). *What to know about the health benefits of sunlight.* https://www.medicalnewstoday.com/articles/benefits-of-sunlight

42. *Social media use increases depression and loneliness | Penn Today.* (2018, November 9). Penn Today. https://penntoday.upenn.edu/news/social-media-use-increases-depression-and-loneliness

43. *What happens when you use your phone around your kids.* (n.d.). Greater Good. https://greatergood.berkeley.edu/article/item/what_happens_when_you_use_your_phone_around_your_kids

44. *Multitasking and how it affects your brain health | Lifespan.* (n.d.). Lifespan. https://www.lifespan.org/lifespan-living/multitasking-and-how-it-affects-your-brain-health#:~:text=What%20our%20brains%20are%20doing,when%20we%20are%20not%20multitasking.

45. Beck, C. T., Watson, S., & Gable, R. K. (2018). Traumatic childbirth and its aftermath: Is there anything positive? *The Journal of Perinatal Education*, *27*(3), 175–184. https://doi.org/10.1891/1058-1243.27.3.175

46. Gonzalez, B., Gonzalez, S. R., Rojo, M., & Mhyre, J. (2021). Neuraxial analgesia in pregnant Hispanic women: an assessment of their beliefs and expectations. *International Journal of Women S Health*, *Volume 13*, 87–94. https://doi.org/10.2147/ijwh.s270711

References

47. Buckley, S. (2009). *Gentle Birth, Gentle Mothering: A Doctor's Guide to Natural childbirth and early parenting choices*. Celestial Arts.
48. Oxytocin deficiency at delivery with epidural analgesia. (1983). In *British Journal of Obstetrics and Gynaecology*. https://pure.knaw.nl/ws/files/489235/19171_286_buijs.pdf
49. Kearns, R. J., Shaw, M., Gromski, P. S., Iliodromiti, S., Lawlor, D. A., & Nelson, S. M. (2021). Association of epidural analgesia in women in labor with neonatal and childhood outcomes in a population cohort. *JAMA Network Open*, 4(10), e2131683. https://doi.org/10.1001/jamanetworkopen.2021.31683
50. *Two-step shoulder delivery method reduces the incidence of shoulder dystocia*. (2017). PubMed. https://pubmed.ncbi.nlm.nih.gov/29949271/
51. *Group B streptococcus - UK National Screening Committee (UK NSC) - GOV.UK*. (n.d.). https://view-health-screening-recommendations.service.gov.uk/group-b-streptococcus/
52. *Medications for pain relief during labor and delivery*. (n.d.). ACOG. https://www.acog.org/womens-health/faqs/medications-for-pain-relief-during-labor-and-delivery
53. Declercq, E., Belanoff, C., & Iverson, R. (2020). Maternal perceptions of the experience of attempted labor induction and medically elective inductions: analysis of survey results from listening to mothers in California. *BMC Pregnancy and Childbirth*, 20(1). https://doi.org/10.1186/s12884-020-03137-x
54. Dahlen, H. G., Thornton, C., Downe, S., De Jonge, A., Seijmonsbergen-Schermers, A. E., Tracy, S., Tracy, M., Bisits, A., & Peters, L. L. (2021). Intrapartum interventions and outcomes for women and children following induction of labour at term in uncomplicated pregnancies: a 16-year population-based linked data study. *BMJ Open*, 11(6), e047040. https://doi.org/10.1136/bmjopen-2020-047040
55. Wickham, S. (2024, February 29). *Routine induction in healthy women not supported by evidence*. Dr Sara Wickham. https://www.sarawickham.com/research-updates/routine-induction-in-healthy-women-not-supported-by-evidence/
56. Seijmonsbergen-Schermers, A., Peters, L. L., Downe, S., Dahlen, H., & De Jonge, A. (2022). Induction of labour and emergency caesarean section in English maternity services: Examining outcomes is needed before recommending changes in practice. *BJOG an International Journal of Obstetrics & Gynaecology*, 130(5), 542–543. https://doi.org/10.1111/1471-0528.17359

References

57. Rosenstein, M. G., Cheng, Y. W., Snowden, J. M., Nicholson, J. M., & Caughey, A. B. (2012). Risk of stillbirth and infant death stratified by gestational age. *Obstetrics and Gynecology*, *120*(1), 76–82. https://doi.org/10.1097/aog.0b013e31825bd286
58. Lothian, J. A. (2006). Saying "No" to induction. *The Journal of Perinatal Education*, *15*(2), 43–45. https://doi.org/10.1624/105812406x107816
59. Buckley, S., Uvnäs-Moberg, K., Pajalic, Z., Luegmair, K., Ekström-Bergström, A., Dencker, A., Massarotti, C., Kotlowska, A., Callaway, L., Morano, S., Olza, I., & Magistretti, C. M. (2023). Maternal and newborn plasma oxytocin levels in response to maternal synthetic oxytocin administration during labour, birth and postpartum – a systematic review with implications for the function of the oxytocinergic system. *BMC Pregnancy and Childbirth*, *23*(1). https://doi.org/10.1186/s12884-022-05221-w
60. Dekker, R. (2024, April 21). *What is the Evidence for Induction or C-section for a Big Baby?* Evidence Based Birth®. https://evidencebasedbirth.com/evidence-for-induction-or-c-section-for-big-baby/
61. Sadeh-Mestechkin, D., Walfisch, A., Shachar, R., Shoham-Vardi, I., Vardi, H., & Hallak, M. (2008). Suspected macrosomia? Better not tell. *Archives of Gynecology and Obstetrics*, *278*(3), 225–230. https://doi.org/10.1007/s00404-008-0566-y
62. Chauhan, S. P., Grobman, W. A., Gherman, R. A., Chauhan, V. B., Chang, G., Magann, E. F., & Hendrix, N. W. (2005). Suspicion and treatment of the macrosomic fetus: A review. *American Journal of Obstetrics and Gynecology*, *193*(2), 332–346. https://doi.org/10.1016/j.ajog.2004.12.020
63. Landon, M. B., Spong, C. Y., Thom, E., Carpenter, M. W., Ramin, S. M., Casey, B., Wapner, R. J., Varner, M. W., Rouse, D. J., Thorp, J. M., Sciscione, A., Catalano, P., Harper, M., Saade, G., Lain, K. Y., Sorokin, Y., Peaceman, A. M., Tolosa, J. E., & Anderson, G. B. (2009). A multicenter, randomized trial of treatment for mild gestational diabetes. *New England Journal of Medicine*, *361*(14), 1339–1348. https://doi.org/10.1056/nejmoa0902430
64. Hannah, M. E. (2004). Planned elective cesarean section: A reasonable choice for some women? *Canadian Medical Association Journal*, *170*(5), 813–814. https://doi.org/10.1503/cmaj.1032002
65. Website, N. (2023, January 6). *Risks*. nhs.uk. https://www.nhs.uk/conditions/caesarean-section/risks/
66. Blustein, J., & Liu, J. (2015). Time to consider the risks of caesarean delivery for long term child health. *BMJ*, *350*(jun09 3), h2410. https://doi.org/10.1136/bmj.h2410

References

67. Hummadi, S. (2024, February 17). Premature gorilla born at Fort Worth Zoo in emergency C-section. *NBC 5 Dallas-Fort Worth*. https://www.nbcdfw.com/news/local/premature-gorilla-born-at-fort-worth-zoo-in-emergency-c-section/3462312/
68. Dominguez-Bello, M. G., De Jesus-Laboy, K. M., Shen, N., Cox, L. M., Amir, A., Gonzalez, A., Bokulich, N. A., Song, S. J., Hoashi, M., Rivera-Vinas, J. I., Mendez, K., Knight, R., & Clemente, J. C. (2016). Partial restoration of the microbiota of cesarean-born infants via vaginal microbial transfer. *Nature Medicine*, 22(3), 250–253. https://doi.org/10.1038/nm.4039
69. Miller, Y. D., Armanasco, A. A., McCosker, L., & Thompson, R. (2020). Variations in outcomes for women admitted to hospital in early versus active labour: an observational study. *BMC Pregnancy and Childbirth*, 20(1). https://doi.org/10.1186/s12884-020-03149-7
70. Wojcieszek, A. M., Stock, O. M., & Flenady, V. (2014). Antibiotics for prelabour rupture of membranes at or near term. *Cochrane Library*, 2014(10). https://doi.org/10.1002/14651858.cd001807.pub2
71. Gluck, O., Mizrachi, Y., Herman, H. G., Bar, J., Kovo, M., & Weiner, E. (2020). The correlation between the number of vaginal examinations during active labor and febrile morbidity, a retrospective cohort study. *BMC Pregnancy and Childbirth*, 20(1). https://doi.org/10.1186/s12884-020-02925-9
72. Dinsmoor, M. J., Viloria, R., Lief, L., & Elder, S. (2005). Use of intrapartum antibiotics and the incidence of postnatal maternal and neonatal yeast infections. *Obstetrics and Gynecology*, 106(1), 19–22. https://doi.org/10.1097/01.aog.0000164049.12159.bd
73. *Your waters have released (waters have broken) – what are your options?* (n.d.). Chelsea and Westminster Hospital NHS Foundation Trust. https://www.chelwest.nhs.uk/your-visit/patient-leaflets/womens-services/your-waters-have-released-waters-have-broken-2013-what-are-your-options
74. World Health Organization. (2014). *Background*. Guideline: Delayed Umbilical Cord Clamping for Improved Maternal and Infant Health and Nutrition Outcomes - NCBI Bookshelf. https://www.ncbi.nlm.nih.gov/books/NBK310514/#:~:text=Waiting%20to%20clamp%20the%20umbilical,which%20occurs%20within%203%20min.
75. Neczypor, J. L., & Holley, S. L. (2017). Providing Evidence-Based care during the golden hour. *Nursing for Women S Health*, 21(6), 462–472. https://doi.org/10.1016/j.nwh.2017.10.011
76. Gopalakrishna, K. P., Macadangdang, B. R., Rogers, M. B., Tometich, J. T., Firek, B. A., Baker, R., Ji, J., Burr, A. H. P., Ma, C., Good, M., Morowitz, M.

J., & Hand, T. W. (2019). Maternal IgA protects against the development of necrotizing enterocolitis in preterm infants. *Nature Medicine*, *25*(7), 1110–1115. https://doi.org/10.1038/s41591-019-0480-9

77. *Recommendations and benefits*. (2022, August 17). Centers for Disease Control and Prevention. https://www.cdc.gov/nutrition/infantandtoddler-nutrition/breastfeeding/recommendations-benefits.html#:~:text=Breast-feeding%20is%20good%20for%20both,long%2Dterm%20illnesses%20and%20diseases.

78. Meek, J. Y., & Noble, L. (2022). Policy Statement: Breastfeeding and the Use of Human Milk. *PEDIATRICS*, *150*(1). https://doi.org/10.1542/peds.2022-057988

79. Barker, L. (2023, March 10). *New survey shows 9 in 10 parents co-sleep but less than half know how to reduce the risk of SIDS*. The Lullaby Trust. https://www.lullabytrust.org.uk/9-in-10-parents-co-sleep-but-less-than-half-know-how-to-reduce-the-risk-of-sids/

80. *Cosleeping Around the World - The Natural Child Project*. (n.d.). https://www.naturalchild.org/articles/james_mckenna/cosleeping_world.html

81. La Leche League International. (2023, April 17). *Safe Sleep 7 Infographic - La Leche League International*. https://llli.org/breastfeeding-info/safe-sleep-7-infographic/

82. Weir, K. (n.d.). *The lasting impact of neglect*. https://www.apa.org. https://www.apa.org/monitor/2014/06/neglect

83. Boseley, S. (2017, November 27). Leaving baby to cry could damage brain development, parenting guru claims. *The Guardian*. https://www.the-guardian.com/society/2010/apr/21/leaving-baby-to-cry-brain-development-damage#:~:text=Using%20sali-va%20swab%20tests%2C%20scientists,tox-ic%22%20to%20the%20developing%20brain.

84. Saharoy, R., Potdukhe, A., Wanjari, M., & Taksande, A. B. (2023). Postpartum Depression and Maternal Care: Exploring the complex effects on mothers and infants. *Cureus*. https://doi.org/10.7759/cureus.41381

85. Dekker, R. (2023a, July 11). *Evidence on: The Vitamin K shot in newborns - Evidence Based Birth®*. Evidence Based Birth®. https://evidencebasedbirth.com/evidence-for-the-vitamin-k-shot-in-newborns/

86. Thurber, C., Dugas, L. R., Ocobock, C., Carlson, B., Speakman, J. R., & Pontzer, H. (2019). Extreme events reveal an alimentary limit on sustained maximal human energy expenditure. *Science Advances*, *5*(6). https://doi.org/10.1126/sciadv.aaw0341

87. Condon, J. C., Jeyasuria, P., Faust, J. M., & Mendelson, C. R. (2004). Surfactant protein secreted by the maturing mouse fetal lung acts as a

hormone that signals the initiation of parturition. *Proceedings of the National Academy of Sciences*, *101*(14), 4978–4983. https://doi.org/10.1073/pnas.0401124101

88. Hutton, E. K., Reitsma, A., Simioni, J., Brunton, G., & Kaufman, K. (2019). Perinatal or neonatal mortality among women who intend at the onset of labour to give birth at home compared to women of low obstetrical risk who intend to give birth in hospital: A systematic review and meta-analyses. *EClinicalMedicine*, *14*, 59–70. https://doi.org/10.1016/j.eclinm.2019.07.005

89. Dekker, R. (2024a, March 6). *Evidence on: Eating and drinking during labor - Evidence Based Birth®*. Evidence Based Birth®. https://evidencebasedbirth.com/evidence-eating-drinking-labor/

90. *Planned home birth*. (n.d.-b). ACOG. https://www.acog.org/clinical/clinical-guidance/committee-opinion/articles/2017/04/planned-home-birth

91. *Male circumcision: 1 in 3 globally but almost universal in Muslim and Jewish countries*. (2016, March 8). The University of Sydney. https://www.sydney.edu.au/news-opinion/news/2016/03/08/male-circumcision--1-in-3-globally-but-almost-universal-in-musli.html#:~:text=The%20prevalence%20of%20circumcision%20varies,Ireland%20(1%20per%20cent).

92. Moldenhauer, J. S. (2024, March 6). *Management of normal labor*. MSD Manual Professional Edition. https://www.msdmanuals.com/professional/gynecology-and-obstetrics/labor-and-delivery/management-of-normal-labor

93. *Sand more dangerous than sharks, docs say*. (2007, June 21). CBS News. https://www.cbsnews.com/news/sand-more-dangerous-than-sharks-docs-say/#:~:text=People%20naturally%20worry%20about%20splashier,to%20University%20of%20Florida%20statistics.

94. Fourth Trimester Postnatal Retreat. (2024, March 11). *10 Science-Backed Benefits of Babywearing*. https://fourthretreat.com/10-science-backed-benefits-of-babywearing/#:~:text=Babywearing%20has%20been%20found%20to,baby%20means%20a%20happier%20household.

95. *Instagram*. (n.d.). https://www.instagram.com/p/DBG8qaexdcj/?utm_source=ig_web_copy_link&igsh=MzRlODBiNWFlZA==

96. Harvard Health. (2023, June 13). *Oxytocin: The love hormone*. https://www.health.harvard.edu/mind-and-mood/oxytocin-the-love-hormone

97. Professional, C. C. M. (2024, May 1). *Endorphins*. Cleveland Clinic. https://my.clevelandclinic.org/health/body/23040-endorphins

98. Roberts, J. R., Karr, C. J., Paulson, J. A., Brock-Utne, A. C., Brumberg, H. L., Campbell, C. C., Lanphear, B. P., Osterhoudt, K. C., Sandel, M. T.,

References

Trasande, L., & Wright, R. O. (2012). Pesticide exposure in children. *PEDIATRICS*, *130*(6), e1757–e1763. https://doi.org/10.1542/peds.2012-2757

99. Professional, C. C. M. (2024b, May 1). *Midwife*. Cleveland Clinic. https://my.clevelandclinic.org/health/articles/22648-midwife
100. Dekker, R. (2024c, September 4). *Evidence on: Due dates - Evidence based birth®*. Evidence Based Birth®. https://evidencebasedbirth.com/evidence-on-due-dates/#:~:text=The%20researchers%20-found%20that%2050,gave%20birth%20by%2041%20weeks.
101. Walsh, S. (1968). MATERNAL EFFECTS OF EARLY AND LATE CLAMPING OF THE UMBILICAL CORD. *The Lancet*, *291*(7550), 996–997. https://doi.org/10.1016/s0140-6736(68)91107-0
102. Widström, A., Brimdyr, K., Svensson, K., Cadwell, K., & Nissen, E. (2019). Skin-to-skin contact the first hour after birth, underlying implications and clinical practice. *Acta Paediatrica*, *108*(7), 1192–1204. https://doi.org/10.1111/apa.14754

www.ingramcontent.com/pod-product-compliance
Lightning Source LLC
Chambersburg PA
CBHW072004060526
44107CB00159B/1411/J